# *Applied*
# COMPUTER
# KEYBOARDING

*Use with MicroType™ Software*

**Jack P. Hoggatt, Ed.D.**

*Professor of Business Communication*
*University of Wisconsin — Eau Claire*
*Eau Claire, Wisconsin*

◆

**Jon A. Shank, Ed.D.**

*Professor of Education*
*Robert Morris University*
*Moon Township, Pennsylvania*

**6e**

SOUTH-WESTERN
CENGAGE Learning™

Australia • Brazil • Canada • Mexico • Singapore • Spain • United Kingdom • United States

Printed in the United States of America
1 2 3 4 5 6 7 12 11 10 09 08

# Build Students' Keyboarding Skills
## with Software from South-Western Cengage Learning

### The Lost Keys: A Keyboarding Skill-Building Game

**The Ultimate Keyboarding Adventure**

Designed for students who have already taken beginning keyboarding, *The Lost Keys* is a skill-building game focused on improving keying speed and accuracy. Students are recruited as agents of a secret organization called The Lost Keys (TLK) and sent to locations around the world in search of lost objects.

- Students' skills are assessed at the beginning of the program and then reassessed at regular intervals.

- Teachers can generate a variety of reports to monitor student progress.

- *The Lost Keys* is based on South-Western's proven, time-tested pedagogy for building typing skills.

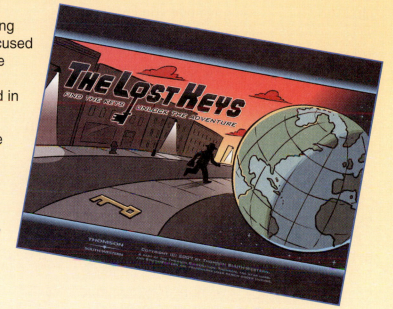

**Network license (Win/Mac)**    0-538-44448-7
**Individual license (Win/Mac)**    0-538-44449-5
**Demo CD-ROM (Win/Mac)**    0-538-44450-9

### MicroPace 3 with Skill-Building Lessons

**Help Build Students' Keying Skills…The MicroPace Way!**

*MicroPace 3 with Skill-Building Lessons* continues the longstanding success of the *MicroPace* program for improving keyboarding skills. The latest version offers several enhancements for an even more successful—and fun—classroom experience.

- Timed writings measure progress in keying under different conditions, such as speed or accuracy for a fixed- or variable-length period of time.

- Error diagnostics report accuracy problems and provide intensive practice for improvement.

- 60 new lessons offer exercises for building speed and accuracy, as well as assessing student skill.

- *MicroPace* templates are available for a variety of South-Western textbooks.

**Network/site license (Windows)**    0-538-72989-9
**Demo CD-ROM (Windows)**    0-538-73023-4

**SOUTH-WESTERN**
CENGAGE Learning™

school.cengage.com/keyboarding

# Contents

# Preface

## About the Authors

**Dr. Jon A. Shank** is a Professor of Education at Robert Morris University in Moon Township, Pennsylvania. For more than 20 years, he served as Dean of the School of Applied Sciences and Education at Robert Morris. Dr. Shank retired as Dean in 1998 to return to full-time teaching. He currently teaches methods courses to students who are studying to become business educators. Dr. Shank holds memberships in regional, state, and national business education organizations. He has received many honors, including Outstanding Post-Secondary Business Educator in Pennsylvania.

**Dr. Jack P. Hoggatt** is Assistant Dean and Department Chair for the Department of Business Communications at the University of Wisconsin-Eau Claire. He has taught courses in Business Writing and Advanced Business Communications. Dr. Hoggatt has held offices in several professional organizations, including President of the Wisconsin Business Education Association. He has served as an advisor to local and state student business organizations. He is the recipient of Wisconsin's Outstanding Post-Secondary Business Educator Award and was recently named as his university's nominee for the UW system Regent's Teaching Excellence Award.

## To the Student

*Applied Computer Keyboarding 6th Edition* is designed to teach you touch keyboarding and word processing skills. Knowing how to key properly by touch will help you use computers effectively for school and personal activities. After you have learned to key by touch, you will learn to create reports, letters, and other documents. You will apply the features of your word processing software as you create these documents.

This textbook is divided into two parts. Part 1 contains lessons that will teach you the alphabetic, number, and symbol keys. This part also contains lessons covering the numeric keypad. Basic word processing features are presented in Part 1. Part 2 covers documents and additional word processing features. Part 2 also contains lessons to help you build your keying skills. Both parts include enrichment activities to build your math and communication skills, provide practice in doing research on the Internet, and help you learn about the world around you.

*Applied Computer Keyboarding 6th Edition* correlates with the lessons in South-Western's *MicroType 4* software program. The software lessons reinforce the alphabetic, number, and symbol key reaches presented in the textbook. Using this textbook, you can master basic keyboarding, word processing, and document production skills.

# Know Your Computer

The numbered parts are found on most computers. The location of some parts will vary.

1. **CPU (Central Processing Unit):** Internal operating unit or "brain" of computer.

2. **CD-ROM drive:** Reads data from and writes data to a CD.

3. **Monitor:** Displays text and graphics on a screen.

4. **Mouse:** Used to input commands.

5. **Keyboard:** An arrangement of letter, figure, symbol, control, function, and editing keys and a numeric keypad.

© FRANKSITEMAN.COM 2007

## KEYBOARD ARRANGEMENT

© FRANKSITEMAN.COM 2007

1. **Alphanumeric keys:** Letters, numbers, and symbols.

2. **Numeric keypad:** Keys at the right side of the keyboard used to enter numeric copy and perform calculations.

3. **Function (F) keys:** Used to execute commands, sometimes with other keys. Commands vary with software.

4. **Arrow keys:** Move insertion point up, down, left, or right.

5. **ESC (Escape):** Closes a software menu or dialog box.

6. **TAB:** Moves the insertion point to a preset position.

7. **CAPS LOCK:** Used to make all capital letters.

8. **SHIFT:** Makes capital letters and symbols shown at tops of number keys.

9. **CTRL (Control):** With other key(s), executes commands. Commands may vary with software.

10. **ALT (Alternate):** With other key(s), executes commands. Commands may vary with software.

11. **Space Bar:** Inserts a space in text.

12. **ENTER (RETURN):** Moves insertion point to margin and down to next line. Also used to execute commands.

13. **DELETE:** Removes text to the right of insertion point.

14. **NUM LOCK:** Activates/deactivates numeric keypad.

15. **INSERT:** Activates insert or typeover.

16. **BACKSPACE:** Deletes text to the left of insertion point.

# Getting Started

With the *MicroType 4* software, you can use the power of your computer to learn alphabetic and numeric keyboarding and the numeric keypad. The lessons in the *Applied Computer Keyboarding, 6th Edition* textbook correlate with and reinforce the software lessons. Follow your teacher's instructions regarding when to complete the software and textbook lessons.

You can use the Word Processor option of the *MicroType 4* software or another word processing program to complete the word processing activities. Instructions are given in this section for using a mouse and for starting *MicroType 4*. Follow your teacher's instructions for starting the software if you are using a different word processing program.

## Using the Mouse

A **mouse** is a tool for giving commands, choosing options, and moving around in a program. The same mouse actions are used in any software program. The results, however, will vary with the program. The basic ways to use a mouse are described below.

- **Point.** Move the mouse (roll it on the work surface) so that the **pointer** points to an item. (The pointer is the arrow that shows the mouse's position on the screen. The pointer is also called the cursor.) The arrow pointer may change to a pointing hand when the mouse is placed near an option.
- **Click.** Press the left mouse button once and let go.
- **Double-click.** Press the left mouse button twice quickly and let go.
- **Drag.** Press and hold down the left mouse button and move the pointer to another location. Then release the mouse button.

In the first illustration, the mouse is being used to select the Open command from the File menu. In the second illustration, the mouse is being used to select the Word Processor option in *MicroType 4*.

Most of the exercises in the *Applied Computer Keyboarding* textbook require students to key textbook copy in a word processor. *MicroType 4* software provides two options: Word Processor and Textbook Keying.

1. The *Word Processor* is a full-featured word processor that includes numerous formatting options, a spell checker, and a built-in timer. The Word Processor can be used as your word processing program for learning, for drill work, and for ungraded practice. Students can **practice their keyboarding** skills, key letters and reports, and take speed timed writings. Upon completion of an activity, the GWAM will be reported; there are no accuracy checks. The Word Processor is ideal for completing any exercises that focus on formatting or that require students to continually save and edit their work.

2. The *Textbook Keying* feature makes **keying and checking** exercises easy. Simply follow the steps in the Textbook Keying feature and, upon completion of the exercise, the program will automatically compute the speed and highlight any errors. Timed writings, language skills, and application measurements are good activities to use in this mode. (Exercises that deal only with formatting or that contain headers and footers should not be completed in Textbook Keying.)

## Special Notes for MicroType Software

Mouse pointer displayed as an arrow

Mouse pointer displayed as a pointing hand

It is important to remember that not all classroom activities should be graded. For the best skill development, a student must have time for learning and practice in an ungraded environment. Although the Textbook Keying section contains an extensive list of activities that can be graded, the full list is provided for classroom flexibility rather than as a suggestion for grading.

(**Note:** The teacher CD includes a complete list of the drills, timed writings, and documents that can be completed in Textbook Keying.)

## Starting MicroType 4 Software

To start the *MicroType 4* software, your computer should be turned on with the operating system window (the desktop) displayed.

1. *Windows:* Click the *Start* button. Point to the *Programs* or *All Programs* menu. A submenu displays listing programs and program groups. Click *South-Western Keyboarding* and then click *MicroType 4*.

2. Click anywhere on the splash screen to remove it and bring up the Log In dialog box.

3. Select the appropriate name from the list that appears in the Log In dialog box and click *OK*. Then, enter the correct password and click *OK* to continue. (Students using the program for the first time must click the New User button and complete the New Student dialog box.)

# Maintaining and Using Your Computer and Media

Follow these guidelines when using your computer hardware and software to avoid a variety of problems and prevent harm to you, others, or the hardware, software, disks, and data.

## Operating Electrical Equipment

Follow these rules to operate all electrical equipment safely.

1. Do not unplug equipment by pulling on the cord. Instead, grasp the plug near the outlet.

2. Do not stretch an electrical cord across an aisle where someone might trip over it.

3. Do not touch frayed electrical cords. Instead, immediately report them to your teacher.

4. Do not drop books or other objects on or near the equipment.

5. Do not take food and liquids (including aerosol sprays or cleaners) near the equipment. If your computer does get wet, turn it off immediately and report the situation to your teacher.

6. Do not move equipment without permission and proper assistance.

## Using Your Computer Safely

Follow these guidelines for using a computer, monitor, and keyboard safely.

1. Keep the area around the equipment's air vents open and unblocked to prevent overheating.

2. Place your keyboard where it will not be bumped off the desk.

3. Adjust the angle, brightness, and focus of the monitor for comfortable viewing and to reduce glare.

4. Do not remove or insert computer cables or attach any device to your computer without your teacher's permission and without first turning off the equipment.

5. Keep the screen free of dust and fingerprints by dusting it often with a soft, lint-free cloth.

6. Do not put fingers, pencils, pens, paper clips, etc. into disk drives.

7. Do not attempt to clear paper jams in a printer unless you have been trained to do so and have your teacher's permission.

8. Use correct keying techniques and posture to prevent repetitive stress injury.

## Working with Printers

Your documents will look better if you take good care of the printer and learn to operate it properly. One of the most common tasks related to using a printer is loading paper. Follow these guidelines to get good print quality and avoid paper jams.

1. Use the type of paper recommended for the printer or an all-purpose paper.

2. Store paper in a cool, dry place to keep it in good condition before use.

3. Fan the paper to separate any pages that may be stuck together before placing the paper in the printer.

4. Place only the recommended amount of paper in the paper feed tray. Overloading the feed tray can cause paper jams.

5. Do not use paper smaller or larger than the size recommended for the printer by the manufacturer. You may need to feed envelopes and paper cut in small sizes (such as note cards) manually into the printer.

6. Follow the manufacturer's or your teacher's instructions for clearing paper jams. (Be sure you have your teacher's permission before attempting to clear a paper jam. In some schools, students should report paper jams to the teacher or computer lab attendant and not attempt to clear the jam.) Many printers have a Help program to provide operating and troubleshooting information.

### Typical Procedure for Clearing a Paper Jam

- Open the operator panel and remove any paper from the document path.

- If paper is still jammed in the printer, open the cartridge access door and remove any paper from the printer paper path.

- Close the cartridge access door. Then close the operator panel firmly until it snaps into place.

- Press Stop/Clear.

## Protecting Software and Data

Follow these precautions to avoid damage to programs, drives, data files, and storage media.

1. Do not press down on a CD-ROM or DVD drive when opening or closing it. Keep the tray closed when you are not using it.

2. Handle disks by their labels or edges. CDs and DVDs are easily scratched.

3. Do not insert or remove a disk while the drive's in-use light is on.

4. Keep disks away from extreme heat or cold, direct sunlight, static electricity, and magnetic fields.

5. To prevent data loss, exit any application program and save/close files you have open before you shut down your computer.

6. Do not change a filename extension (the last three characters after the period). Doing so may make the file unusable.

7. Do not delete or move files that are part of an installed program. Doing so may make the program unusable.

8. Do not disable virus-scanning software unless you have your teacher's permission to do so. (Disabling virus-scanning software may be necessary when installing some commercial software programs.)

9. Computers can be damaged by magnets or magnetic fields. Do not place magnets on or near computer equipment. Do not place your monitor or computer near equipment that has a magnetic field. Examples of equipment that may produce a magnetic field include telephones, radios, and speakers not designed for use with computers.

9. Static electricity can cause damage to your computer equipment. Static electricity may build up in your body from walking across some types of carpeting or in very dry room conditions. To prevent a static discharge that can damage equipment, ground yourself by touching a metal object such as a desk or table before touching the computer.

**Cleaning a Printer.** An important part of maintaining a printer is keeping it clean—both inside and out. If you are instructed to clean a printer, follow these suggestions. Before cleaning the printer, turn it off and unplug the power cable. Wipe the outside of the printer with a slightly damp cloth. If the printer came with a cleaning brush, use it according to the manufacturer's directions. You can clean some parts of the inside of the printer with a dry, lint-free cloth. For hard-to-reach areas, use a can of compressed air to remove paper dust or toner. (Do not to touch the drum inside a laser printer. The oils from your skin can cause problems with print quality. Do not touch the contact on the ink cartridge for an inkjet printer.) Be sure to plug in the printer when you are finished cleaning it.

**Changing cartridges or toner.** Periodically, someone will need to change the ink cartridge or ribbon or add toner to the printer. Many printers will give a low toner or low ink warning on the computer monitor or the printer display before all the ink or toner is used. Notify your teacher or the computer lab attendant if you see such a warning. If you have your teacher's permission, follow the manufacturer's instructions to remove and replace ink cartridges or ribbons or place toner in the printer. You may need to print a test page after changing cartridges in an inkjet printer. The test page allows you to see the print quality and make alignment adjustments if needed.

**Cost-effective printing.** To use a printer in a cost-effective way, view documents onscreen before printing. Use color only when needed because printing in black is less expensive than printing in color. Some printers offer you a choice of print qualities. You may be able to print documents for proofreading purposes in a "draft" or "quick" mode, which uses less ink than the normal print mode. Some printers allow you to print on both sides of a page. This option is helpful for saving paper or for creating booklets. Become familiar with the options available for your printer.

**Sharing a Printer.** Be considerate of others with whom you share a printer. When you pick up your documents from the printer, make sure you have only your documents. Place other documents in a tray or basket provided for that use. Respect the privacy of the people with whom you share a printer. Do not read documents printed by others. Print very long documents when others are least likely to need the printer, if possible. You may be responsible for helping to maintain a shared printer. If you have been instructed to do so, add paper to the printer, if needed, when you retrieve your printed documents. Check for printer warning lights and report problems to the appropriate person.

## Understanding What You Have Learned

Write a short paragraph describing each of the following:

1. The action you will take if your computer becomes wet.

2. The action you will take if your printer becomes jammed.

3. How you should remove dust and fingerprints from your monitor.

4. How you will arrange the monitor, keyboard, and speakers (if any) within your work area.

5. How you will hand a CD-ROM to a classmate.

6. What may happen if you change the filename extension of a file.

7. Steps you can take to help avoid paper jams in a printer.

## Computer and Media Use Check Sheet

Your teacher may use a check sheet similar to the one shown on the following page to rate your ability to use and care for your computer equipment and media properly.

# Computer and Media Use Check Sheet

**Rating and Grades**

| | | | |
|---|---|---|---|
| Excellent | 4 points | (3.5–4.0) | A 93–100 |
| Good | 3 points | (2.6–3.5) | B 85–92 |
| Average | 2 points | (1.6–2.5) | C 78–84 |
| Poor | 1 point | (0.6–1.5) | D 70–77 |

| | Rating Periods | | | | | | | | | | | |
|---|---|---|---|---|---|---|---|---|---|---|---|---|
| | 1 | 2 | 3 | 4 | 5 | 6 | 7 | 8 | 9 | 10 | 11 | 12 |
| **Operating electrical equipment** · · · · · · · Rating | | | | | | | | | | | | |
| 1. Unplugs equipment properly | | | | | | | | | | | | |
| 2. Does not place electrical cords across aisles | | | | | | | | | | | | |
| 3. Reports frayed or damaged cords as needed | | | | | | | | | | | | |
| 4. Keeps food and liquids away from equipment | | | | | | | | | | | | |
| 5. Does not drop books or other objects on or near equipment | | | | | | | | | | | | |
| 6. Does not move equipment without permission | | | | | | | | | | | | |
| **Using computers safely** · · · · · · · · Rating | | | | | | | | | | | | |
| 1. Keeps equipment air vents open and unblocked | | | | | | | | | | | | |
| 2. Places keyboard and monitor properly | | | | | | | | | | | | |
| 3. Does not remove or add cables and devices without permission | | | | | | | | | | | | |
| 4. Keeps screen free of dust and fingerprints | | | | | | | | | | | | |
| 5. Does not place fingers, pencils, etc. in disk drives | | | | | | | | | | | | |
| 6. Uses correct keying techniques and posture | | | | | | | | | | | | |
| 7. Discharges static electricity before touching computer | | | | | | | | | | | | |
| **Protecting software and data** · · · · · · · Rating | | | | | | | | | | | | |
| 1. Does not press down on a CD-ROM or DVD drive | | | | | | | | | | | | |
| 2. Handles disks by their labels or edges | | | | | | | | | | | | |
| 3. Does not insert or remove a disk while the drive's in-use light is on | | | | | | | | | | | | |
| 4. Keeps disks away from extreme heat or cold, direct sunlight, static electricity, and magnetic fields | | | | | | | | | | | | |
| 5. Exits programs and saves/closes files before shutting down computer | | | | | | | | | | | | |
| 6. Does not change filename extensions | | | | | | | | | | | | |
| 7. Does not disable virus-scanning software | | | | | | | | | | | | |
| 8. Does not place computer near magnetic fields | | | | | | | | | | | | |
| **Working with printers** · · · · · · · · Rating | | | | | | | | | | | | |
| 1. Uses the proper types and sizes of paper | | | | | | | | | | | | |
| 2. Loads the paper tray correctly with an appropriate amount of paper (if instructed to do so) | | | | | | | | | | | | |
| 3. Reports paper jams or clears jams with teacher's permission | | | | | | | | | | | | |
| 4. Cleans outside and inside of printer correctly (if instructed to do so) | | | | | | | | | | | | |
| 5. Installs ink cartridges, toner, or ribbons correctly (if instructed to do so) | | | | | | | | | | | | |
| 6. Uses the printer in a cost-effective way | | | | | | | | | | | | |
| 7. Is considerate of others with whom a printer is shared | | | | | | | | | | | | |
| 8. Respects the privacy of others with whom a printer is shared | | | | | | | | | | | | |
| 9. Helps maintain a shared printer | | | | | | | | | | | | |
| **Total** | | | | | | | | | | | | |

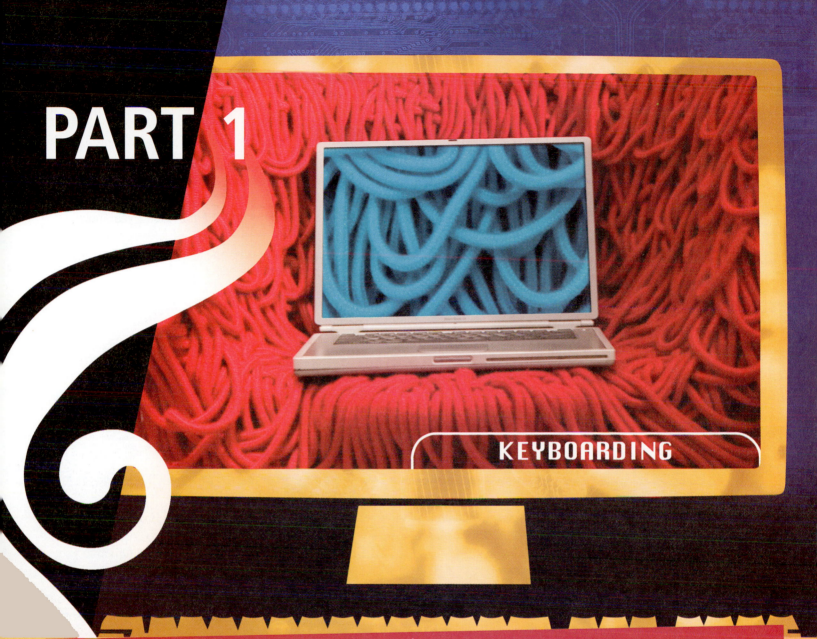

# PART 1

**KEYBOARDING**

## Preparation for Word Processing

Computers have become a central part of our lives. They are everywhere. Nearly everyone has access to a computer at work, at school, or at home. The computer is rapidly becoming as common in the home as the television.

To take full advantage of the speed of a computer, a person must be skilled at using a keyboard. Most computers are instructed to do things through the keyboard. Therefore, being able to input through the keyboard can be viewed as a basic literacy skill.

Your input or keying speed determines how much you will be able to accomplish with the computer. For example, if you key 40 words a minute, you will be able to do twice as much in the same amount of time as the person who keys 20 words a minute.

By completing the lessons in Part 1 you will:
- Learn to key alphabetic keys by touch
- Be introduced to numbers and symbols
- Learn to operate the numeric keypad
- Be introduced to word processing software

Once you learn the alphabetic keys, you will apply your new skill in these activities designed to develop your communication skills:
- Writing
- Speaking
- Listening
- Reading
- Internet
- Our World

**2C ▪ Math Challenge 15**

## APPLY MATH SKILLS BY USING MENTAL MATH

1. Work with a classmate to determine the answers to the following questions mentally—without using a pencil or calculator. Key the answers in a new document. If your answers don't agree, explain to each other how your answer was calculated. Check your answers with those provided by your instructor.

    1a. If there are 400 students in my class and 60% of them participate in school activities, how many students participate?

    1b. If my previous test score was 80 and my latest score was 88, what was the percent of increase?

    1c. If Tom borrows $500 at 6% for ½ year, how much interest will he pay?

    1d. If I can buy a $300 suit for $240, what is my percent of discount?

2. Save as *U18L2Math*.

---

### Careers

### 2D ▪ Career Exploration Portfolio – Activity 15

▪ You must complete Career Activities 1-3 before completing this activity.

1. Retrieve your Career folder and review the information that relates to the career cluster that is now your top choice.

2. Reflect on everything you have learned about this career cluster and then create a plan that you will follow to become prepared for a career in this cluster. Include items such as courses you will take until you are graduated, where you plan to further your education, the cost of furthering your education, where you will get the money, etc.

3. Write a report of at least one page that describes the items in your plan. Exchange papers with a classmate and have the classmate offer suggestions for improving the content and correcting any errors he or she finds in your paragraph(s). Make the changes that you agree with and print a copy to turn in to your instructor. Save the report as *U18L2Career15*.

4. Return your folder to the storage area. When your instructor returns your paper, file it in your Career folder.

# Unit 1
## Learn Letter-Key Technique

### Lessons 1–20

## OBJECTIVES

1. *To learn control of home keys (**asdf jkl;**).*
2. *To learn control of the **Space Bar** and **ENTER (RETURN)** key.*

## HOME KEYS (asdf jkl;)

### 1A | Work Area Arrangement

Arrange your work area as shown.

- Keyboard directly in front of chair
- Front edge of keyboard even with edge of desk
- Monitor placed for easy viewing
- Disk drives placed for easy access
- Book at right of keyboard

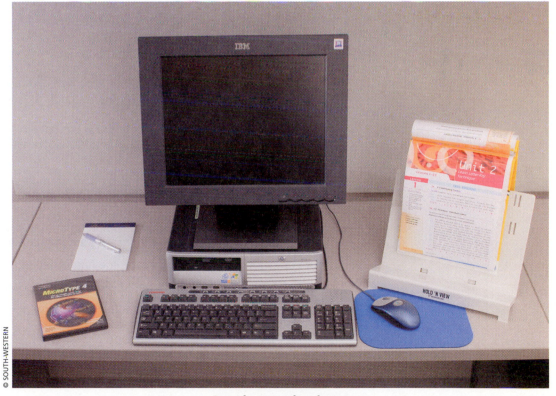

© SOUTH-WESTERN

**Properly arranged work area**

Physical Activity

The road to better health starts with good eating and physical activity habits. Being active means moving more every day. You can choose activities that are fun and do them on your own or with your friends.

Being more active will make you feel better and give you more energy. Being active can also help you think and concentrate better, which will help you in school or at work.

> Activity can help you feel less bored or depressed and can help you handle stress.

Get Moving

Don't wait--start today! Begin slowly and make small changes in your daily routine.

1. Spend less time in front of the TV.
2. Walk the stairs instead of riding the elevator.
3. Ride your bike, skateboard, rollerblade, or play basketball.
4. Walk with a friend or family member; make it "quality time."
5. Join a school sports team or club.
6. Walk the family dog. If you don't have a dog, find a neighbor who does.
7. Go dancing, go for a hike, wash the car, clean the house, or mow the lawn.

What you choose to do is up to you. Simply choose something that you like to do and keep it up. Have fun while being active each day to stay healthy and fit. Remember, you don't have to give up the video games--just make sure that you also fit activity into your day.

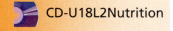 CD-U18L2Nutrition

2. Open the file *CD-U18L2Nutrition*. Select and copy the entire document. Open the file *U18L2Health*, if it is not already open. Paste the *CD-U18L2Nutrition* text at the end of the document.

3. Use 1" top, side, and bottom margins.

4. Format the title in a 24-point, bold font and the date in a 20-point, bold font. Use one or two fonts and font colors of your choice in this document. Center-align the title and the date across all columns.

5. Format the text as a three-column document in landscape orientation.

6. Use a 14-point font for the text.

7. Use single spacing. Set 0.25" first-line paragraph indentations for the paragraphs in the body. (Do not set the indentation for the paragraphs with a border or the headings.)

8. Format all the paragraphs (including the headings) for 6 points of space after paragraphs.

9. Format the numbered items for a 0.25" left indentation and a 0.25" hanging indentation.

10. Format the text within the borders with shading or a border. Use a bold, 14-point font for the text. Center-align the text in these paragraphs.

11. Center-align the side headings in a 16-point, bold font. Add bold to the three paragraph headings that are in an italicized font.

12. Balance the columns appropriately. Save as *U18L2Health2*.

# MicroType

## Word Processing

### Word Processing Program

A word processing program allows you to key and format text to create documents.

## MicroType
### TIP

The insertion point is where the letters and spaces you key appear on the screen.

## MicroType

## Word Processing

### Program Commands

Program commands and options can be selected by using menus and/or the toolbar. The Save command is highlighted on the File pull-down menu shown at the right.

---

## 1B | Access the Word Processor

### Learn to Access Your Word Processor

To access the *MicroType 4* word processor:

1. Start the *MicroType 4* program.

2. Complete the Log In procedure.

3. When the *MicroType 4* main screen appears, click the Word Processor button.

   The Word Processor screen appears (see screen illustration below).

### Practice What You Have Learned

1. Start your software program.

2. Access the word processor. Notice the blinking line. The line is called the insertion point. The insertion point is where the letters and spaces you key appear on the screen.

## 1C | Program Commands

### Learn to Use Program Commands

1. Click the menu name on the menu bar to display a pull-down menu of commands, features, and options.

2. Click the button on the toolbar to execute a command.

3. Click the Maximize button to change the screen size.

4. Click the Close button to close the word processor.

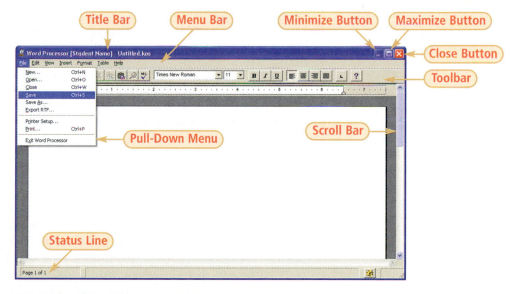

### Practice What You Have Learned

1. Click each item on the menu bar to see the commands available for each menu. If a menu command is not currently available, it appears in light gray type.

2. Click the Close button.

3. Access the word processor again.

---

## Wall Art Contest

Each month, five Jones School teachers select three pictures to post on the school's website. People who visit the website may vote for their favorite picture. If you are a winner, your picture is posted on the website for one month where everyone can see it. After that, your picture is hung on the "Wall of Fame" for one year. Have fun and good luck!

Please read all the rules carefully before entering the contest.
Submit Entries To: Mrs. Beatrice Veres, Art Teacher Room 303

### Contest Entry Rules

1. You must be a student at Jones School to enter the contest.
2. All entries must be on a flat medium no larger than 8.5" x 11".
3. Entries must be submitted by the third Friday of each month.
4. The back of the picture must include:
   Contestant's First and Last Name
   Grade and Homeroom
   Parent/Guardian's First and Last Name
   Home Phone Number
   Date Submitted
5. Include a title for your art, an explanation of what it is, and what it means to you (100 words or less).
6. Include an approval form that is signed by your parent or guardian. The form is available in the principal's office.
7. Pictures will not be returned unless specifically requested in writing.

### Document 2

1. Using default settings and a 0.5" indentation for the first line of each paragraph, key the following document. Save as *U18L2Health*.

Take Charge of Your Health

November 20--

What's Happening?

Are you going through a lot of changes? Is your body changing and growing? Have you noticed that every year, you can't seem to fit into your old shoes anymore? Are your favorite jeans tighter or too short?

| Your body is on its way to becoming its adult size. |
| --- |

Along with your physical changes, you are also becoming more independent. You are starting to make more choices about your life. You are relying less on your parents and more on yourself and your friends when making decisions. Some of the biggest choices that you face are those about your health.

Why should you care about your health? Your health affects how you feel, look, and grow. Doing well in school, work, or other activities (like sports) can all be affected by your health!

Now is the time to take charge of your health by eating better and being more physically active. Even small changes will help you look and feel your best!

*(continued)*

## 1D | Keying Position

The features of proper keying position are shown and listed below.

- Fingers curved and upright (not slanted) over home keys

- Wrists low, but not touching keyboard

- Forearms parallel to slant of keyboard

- Body erect, sitting back in chair

- Feet on floor for balance

- Eyes on copy

**Proper keying position**

## 1E | Home-Key Position

The keys where you place your fingers to begin keying are called the home keys. The home keys are **a s d f** for the left hand and **j k l ;** for the right hand.

1. Find the home keys on the keyboard illustration shown below.

2. Locate and place your fingers on the home keys on your keyboard with your fingers well curved and upright (not slanting).

3. Remove your fingers from the keyboard; then place them in home-key position again, curving and holding them *lightly* on the keys.

**Home-key position**

## 1F | Keystroking and Space Bar

To key, tap each key with the tip of the finger. Keep your fingers curved as shown below. The Space Bar is used to place a space between words. Tap the Space Bar with the right thumb. Use a quick down-and-in motion (toward the palm). Avoid pauses before or after spacing.

**Curve fingers and tap the keys**     **Tap the Space Bar with a quick down-and-in motion**

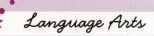

## 1E Writing: Number Expression

Read the following number usage rule. Key the Learn line, noting number choices. Key the Apply lines, making the necessary corrections. Save as *U18L1Writing*.

***Rule 10:*** Spell indefinite numbers.

Learn 1 About thirty players will be cut from the team before Friday.

Apply 2 Approximately 90 applicants applied for the job.

Apply 3 Almost 60 students were delayed by the storm.

CD-U18L1Reading

## 1F | Barriers to Effective Listening

Open the file *CD-U18L1Reading*. Read the document carefully; then close the file. Let your instructor know when you are ready to answer questions covering the content of the report. Save your answers as *U18L1Reading*.

## LESSON

# 2

### OBJECTIVE

*To assess your ability to prepare column documents.*

# COLUMN DOCUMENT FORMATTING SKILLS

## 2A | Conditioning Practice

Key each line twice SS; then key a 1' writing on line 3. Determine *gwam*.

Alphabet 1 Jay Zuvella had two questions to complete before taking the exam.

Figures 2 Call Harris at 422-6890 this morning or at 537-1895 this evening.

Speed 3 Di saw the hand signal to go right when she got by the cornfield.

GWAM 1' | 1 | 2 | 3 | 4 | 5 | 6 | 7 | 8 | 9 | 10 | 11 | 12 | 13 |

## 2B | Column Documents

### Document 1

1. Key the information on the following page as a one-column poster to fit on one 8.5" by 11" page.

2. Include an appropriate picture if available.

3. Use borders and/or shading. Use two different fonts and vary the font sizes, color, and effects. You decide all other formatting features.

4. Save as *U18L2Poster*.

## 1G | Home-Key Position

1. Place your fingers in home-key position as directed in **1E**.

2. Key the line below. Tap the Space Bar once at the point of each arrow.

a s d f j k l ; aa jj ss kk dd ll ff ; ;

## 1H | Hard Return at Line Endings

1. Read the information below and study the illustration.

2. Practice the ENTER (Return) key reach several times.

3. Review proper position at the keyboard (**1D**).

4. Key the line in **1G** above again.

**ENTER** Right little finger

### Hard Return

To return the insertion point to the left margin and move it down to the next line, tap ENTER.

This is called a hard return. Use a hard return at the end of all drill lines. Use two hard returns when directed to double-space.

### Hard Return Technique

Reach the little finger of the right hand to the ENTER key, tap the key, and return the finger quickly to home-key position.

## 1I | Home-Key, Space Bar, and ENTER-Key Practice

1. Place your hands in home-key position (left-hand fingers on **a s d f** and right-hand fingers on **j k l ;**).

2. Key the lines once single-spaced (SS), with a double space (DS) between 2-line groups. Do not key line numbers.

```
1  a  aa  s  ss  d  dd  f  ff
2  a  aa  s  ss  d  dd  f  ff
                             DS
3  j  jj  k  kk  l  ll  ;  ;;
4  j  jj  k  kk  l  ll  ;  ;;
                             DS
5  aj  lf  d;  ks  ja  fl  ;d  aja
6  aj  lf  d;  ks  ja  fl  ;d  aja
                             DS
7  djd  kak  s;s  flf  jal  d;k;
8  djd  kak  s;s  flf  jal  d;k;
                             QS
```

## 1C | Prepare for Assessment

Key each line. If your goal is to improve control, try to complete each sentence within the 15", 12", or 10" time with one or no errors. If your goal is to increase speed, try to key more on each timing.

**Emphasis: high-frequency balanced-hand words**

| | GWAM | 15" | 12" | 10" |
|---|---|---|---|---|
| 1 The haughty men did the work on the bus for Henry. | | 40 | 50 | 60 |
| 2 The big social for the man may be held in the city. | | 40 | 50 | 60 |
| 3 Diane paid the girls for the eight big bushels of corn. | | 44 | 55 | 66 |
| 4 Orlando may keep the food for the fish by the big bowl. | | 44 | 55 | 66 |
| 5 Their sign by the soggy field by the dog kennel was visible. | | 48 | 60 | 72 |
| 6 He owns the antique keys and the enamel whale on the mantle. | | 48 | 60 | 72 |

## 1D | Assess Speed and Control

Key two 3' timings on paragraphs 1–2 combined; find *gwam*.

**MicroType**

*Timed Writing*

**A**

**All letters used**

| | GWAM | 3' | 5' |
|---|---|---|---|
| As you move through the grades in your school, you are apt to | | 4 | 2 | 42 |
| need to maintain a calendar to keep track of your major | | 8 | 5 | 44 |
| activities. The calendar system you choose might be recording your | | 12 | 7 | 47 |
| activities on pages in a pocket organizer, on a monthly calendar | | 17 | 10 | 50 |
| posted at home, or in a personal digital organizer. Regardless of | | 21 | 13 | 52 |
| the method you choose, you usually need to record such things as | | 25 | 15 | 55 |
| the date, time, place, length, and purpose of each activity. Also, | | 30 | 18 | 58 |
| you need to remember who is involved in the activity. | | 33 | 20 | 60 |
| Using a calendar will lessen the chance that you will forget | | 38 | 23 | 62 |
| or be late to a practice or club meeting in school. People have | | 42 | 25 | 65 |
| the right to expect you to be where you are required to be and | | 46 | 28 | 67 |
| arrive and depart appointments at the appropriate time. You will | | 50 | 30 | 70 |
| be much more successful if you do not gain the reputation of being | | 55 | 33 | 73 |
| forgetful and tardy. The habits you develop while attending school | | 59 | 36 | 75 |
| will carry over into your professional and personal affairs after | | 64 | 38 | 78 |
| you are graduated from school. | | 66 | 40 | 79 |

GWAM 3' | 1 | 2 | 3 | 4
5' | 1 | 2 | 3

## 1J | Technique: ENTER-Key Practice

Key the lines once SS, with a DS between 2-line groups. Do not key line numbers.

1  jj ss ll
2  jj ss ll
            DS
3  aa kk dd ;; ff
4  aa jj dd ;; ff
               DS
5  ll ff jj dd kk ss ;;
6  ll ff jj dd kk ss ;;
                  DS
7  aa as fd l; kj j; lk af ds
8  aa as fd l; kj j; lk af ds
                     DS
9  ;f; ;f; ala ala djd djd ksk ksk;
10 ;f; ;f; ala ala djd djd ksk ksk;
                        DS
11 kkff kkff jjss jjss aall aall dd;s dd;
12 kkff kkff jjss jjss aall aall dd;s dd;
                           QS

## 1K | Home-Key Mastery

Key each line twice SS; DS between 2-line groups.

1  j j jk jk l l l; l; a a as as d d df df af kl dsj;
                                                    DS
2  jj kjk kjk ll ;l; ;l; ja ja dk dk ls ls ;f ;f kjd;
                                                    DS
3  sad sad lad lad all all ask ask jak jak fall fall;
                                                    DS
4  a sad lass; ask all dads; a lad ask; a salad; as a
                                                    QS

### Keying Cue

Reach the little finger to the ENTER key, quickly tap the key, and return the finger to the home-key position.

### Keying Cue

Keep fingers curved and upright over home keys, right thumb curved in and just barely touching the Space Bar.

Space once after ; (semicolon) used as punctuation.

Correct Finger Alignment

UNIT 1   LESSON 1      Home Keys (asdf jkl;)      6

# Unit 18

## Assess Straight-Copy Skill and Column Documents

### Lessons 1–2

## LESSON 1

### OBJECTIVES

1. *To improve keying techniques.*
2. *To improve keying speed and control.*

**Technique Goals**

**Word-level keying.**

*Lines 1–3:* Key each word three times (slowly, faster, top speed).

*Lines 4–6:* Key each phrase three times (slowly, faster, top speed).

*Lines 7–9:* Key each sentence three times (slowly, faster, top speed).

## ASSESS STRAIGHT-COPY SKILL

### 1A | Conditioning Practice

Key each line twice SS; then key a 1' writing on line 3. Determine *gwam*.

Alphabet 1 Jack Gomez will be the equipment manager for the next seven days.
Figures/ 2 I wanted 47026*#* or 58139(#) in my password for my bank account.
Symbols
Speed 3 A field hand kept the lame fox in the big pen to keep it in sight.

**GWAM** 1' | 1 | 2 | 3 | 4 | 5 | 6 | 7 | 8 | 9 | 10 | 11 | 12 | 13 |

### 1B | Technique: Reading/Keying Response Patterns

**Emphasize quick finger reaches, wrists low and relaxed.**

Balanced-hand words
1 us if he an by is jam fur hen row pay map man sit the and big may
2 dusk dock corn busy both keys firms land rock sign owns mend sick
3 docks bucks eight goals right they shame social towns vivid turns

**Emphasize high-speed phrase response.**

Balanced-hand phrases
4 he owns it | make the signs | paid the man | go to work | if they fix the
5 go to the | they may make | to the problem | with the sign | and the maps
6 with the city | the eighth neighbor | social problem | the big ornament

**Emphasize high-speed, word-level response; quick spacing.**

Balanced-hand sentences
7 Jaynel paid the man by the city dock for the six bushels of corn.
8 Keith may keep the food for the fish by the big antique fishbowl.
9 The haughty girls paid for their own gowns for the island social.

**GWAM** 1' | 1 | 2 | 3 | 4 | 5 | 6 | 7 | 8 | 9 | 10 | 11 | 12 | 13 |

## MicroType
**Word Processing**
Save Command

The Save command allows you to exit the program without losing the text you have keyed.

## MicroType
**TIP**

Click the Save button on the toolbar to access the Save As dialog box quickly.

---

## 1L | Save a Document

### Learn to Save a Document

To save a document:

1. Click File on the menu bar.

2. Click Save. The Save As dialog box appears.

3. Key the filename in the File name text box and click Save.

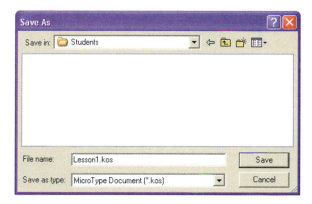

### Practice What You Have Learned

1. Save the document containing the text you have keyed in the practice session.

2. Use *Lesson1* for the filename.

## 1M | End-of-Lesson Routine

Follow this routine at the end of each practice session.

1. Save the document if you have not already done so. Use the word *Lesson* and the lesson number (*Lesson1*) for the filename unless directed to use another filename.

2. Exit the word processing software.

3. Remove the disk from the disk drive.

4. Turn off the equipment if directed to do so.

5. Clean up your work area and push in your chair.

For additional practice **MicroType** + **Alphabetic Keyboarding** + **Lesson 1**

**Job 11**

Key this personal-business letter in block format with mixed punctuation. Place a letterhead that includes your name and the return address shown at the top of the page. The letter will be sent with your completed newsletter. Save as *U17Letter*.

775 Manassas Court
Fort Myers, FL 33905-0452
May 5, 20--


Mrs. Loretta Debbons
Publications Director
Ford School District
3929 Braddock Road
Fort Myers, FL 33912-8357

Dear Mrs. Debbons:

The Ford School District newsletter that I prepared as part of the contest you are conducting for students in our district is enclosed.

Thank you for the opportunity to participate in this realistic activity. It has enabled me to apply many of the skills I have learned in my English, keyboarding, and word processing classes.

I hope you find my newsletter attractive and easy to read. I followed the document design principles I learned.

Sincerely,


*(Student Name)*

Enclosure

OBJECTIVES

1. *To improve control of home keys (**asdf  jkl;**).*
2. *To improve control of **Space Bar** and **ENTER** key.*

**Tip**

Keep your eyes on the copy as you key.

# REVIEW HOME KEYS (asdf jkl;)

### 2A | Keying Readiness

1. Arrange your work area as shown on page 2.
2. Position yourself at the keyboard as shown below.
   - Fingers curved and upright over home keys
   - Wrists low, but not touching keyboard
   - Forearms parallel to slant of keyboard
   - Body erect, sitting back in chair
   - Feet on floor

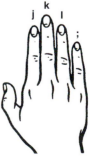

**Proper keying position**

### 2B | Home-Key Position

1. Find the home keys on the chart: **a s d f** for left hand and **j k l ;** for right hand.

2. Locate and place your fingers on the home keys on your keyboard with your fingers well curved and upright (not slanting).

3. Remove your fingers from the keyboard; then place them in home-key position again, curving and holding them *lightly* on the keys.

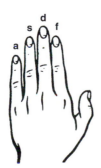

**Home-key position**

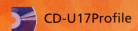CD-U17Profile

**Job 8**

1. Open the file *CD-U17Profile*.

2. Copy this article into your newsletter.

3. Make the following changes to the article:

   • In paragraph 1, change *IT* to **Information Technology**.

   • In paragraph 1, change the first occurrence of *MCAS* to **Microsoft Certified Application Specialist (MCAS)**.

   • Change all occurrences of *cert* to **certification** and *certs* to **certifications**.

   • Change all occurrences of *UTC* to **Upton Technical Center**.

**Job 9**

Key this directory as the final item in your newsletter.

Ford School District Directory

School Board:  Janice Allegre, Amanda Neff, Stephanie Balavage, Andrew Strutt, Richard Humenik, Joseph Szalanwiecz, Sarah Manula, Kevin Wright, and Jessica Gwaley, President

Administrative Staff:  Kathleen Morgan, Superintendent; Steven Ball, Assistant Superintendent; Bill Hoffman, Business Manager; Thomas Repine, Technology Director; and Mary Lee Kite, Publications Director

**Job 10**

Make final design and formatting changes to the newsletter.  Check for these items:

• Only three colors (or shades of each color) were used.

• The newsletter title was included on page 1.

• Two or more columns are used for the articles.

• Text is formatted appropriately and consistently.  Columns are balanced.

• Pictures, shading, borders, and headers (or footers) are added as required and desired.

• All errors have been found and corrected.

• The design and format are attractive and easy to read.

### Keystroke

Curve fingers over home keys. Tap each key lightly with the tip of the finger.

### Space

Tap the Space Bar with a quick down-and-in motion of the right thumb. Do not pause before or after spacing.

### Hard Return

Reach the right little finger to the ENTER key; quickly tap the key and return the finger to home key.

## 2D | Home-Key and Space Bar Review

Key the lines once (without the numbers), single-spaced (SS) with a double space (DS) between 2-line groups.

**Fingers curved and upright**

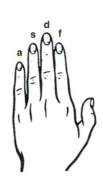

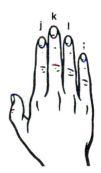

```
1  asdf jkl; s ss f ff a aa d dd k kk ; ;; j jj l ll;
2  asdf jkl; s ss f ff a aa d dd k kk ; ;; j jj l ll;
```

*Tap the ENTER key twice to double-space (DS).*

```
3  jj dd ;; aa ss kk ff ll aka lfl s;s jdj kfk dfd ;;
4  jj dd ;; aa ss kk ff ll aka lfl s;s jdj kfk dfd ;;
```

**DS**

```
5  ak ls fj ;d jsj d;d kfk ada s;s l;l fkf sflj kadl;
6  ak ls fj ;d jsj d;d kfk ada s;s l;l fkf sflj kadl;
```

**QS**

**Job 6**

Key these three announcements in your newsletter. Place them in a shaded box or one with a border. The announcements can be inserted separately or grouped as desired.

The musical *Barnum* will be presented at Ford High School on May 26, 27, and 29 at 7:30 p.m. Tickets are $5 for students and senior citizens and $7.50 for adults. Call (239) 555-0133 to order tickets or make reservations.

Registration for Beginners and Advanced Beginners swim classes will be held on June 9 from 7 to 7:30 p.m. at the High School Pool Office. Please contact the Athletic Office if you have any questions.

Gwen Minoza, a fourth grader at Fairlane Elementary School, won first place in the Compu-Solve Math competition at Newton Community College on April 4. She and six other Ford District students competed with about one hundred students from area school districts. They were given seven individual problems to solve.

**Job 7**

Key this article as part of your newsletter.

Middle School Students Celebrate the Century

10 teams of Seventh Grade students studied each decade from 1900 to 1990 in the thematic unit, "Celebrate the 20th Century". Each team studied the life style and major events of the decade. The teams shared what they learned at a school-wide fair on April 15th. Each team had a display to show the events of the century in a timeline. Many of the teams dressed in costumes popular during the decade. A panel of Ford Township Historical Society members spoke to all the students before the fair and then judged each teams display.

## 2E | Home-Key Reinforcement

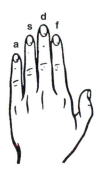

**Goal**

To improve keying and spacing techniques.

Key the lines once SS, with a DS between 2-line groups. Do not key the line numbers.

LEFT FINGERS   4 \ 3 \ 2 \ 1   1 \ 2 \ 3 \ 4   RIGHT FINGERS

**Home-key position**

1  d dd l ll a aa k kk f ff j jj s ss ; ;; jsl fka d;

2  d dd l ll a aa k kk f ff j jj s ss ; ;; jsl fka d;

Tap the ENTER key twice to DS.

3  kk ff jj dd aa ll ;; ss ff kk dd jj ll aa ss ;; dd

4  kk ff jj dd aa ll ;; ss ff kk dd jj ll aa ss ;; dd

DS

5  jaj fkf ;d; s;s aja kfk d;d lsl jaj fkf jsl akd s;

6  jaj fkf ;d; s;s aja kfk d;d lsl jaj fkf jsl akd s;

QS

## 2F | Technique: Hard Return at Line Endings

**Keying Cue**

At the end of each line, reach out with the little finger; quickly tap the ENTER key; return finger to home key (;).

Key each line twice SS; DS between 2-line groups.

1  ask a lass

2  all dads; add a

3  a fad; as dad; a jak

4  all lads; a sad lass; ask

5  ask dad; all fall; a sad lass;

6  a sad lass; a flask; a salad; a jak

QS

**Job 4**

Key this article as part of your newsletter.

*Ford High's College in High School Program*

*For the past six years, Ford High has partnered with Victoria College to offer Calculus and Computer Technology as college in high school courses. This year Ford's partnership with local colleges has expanded to include Harvey University, which is now offering for college credit European History, U.S. History, Spanish V, Information Systems Technology, Computer Aided Drafting, and Biology.*

*These college partnerships allow students to complete college-level courses as part of their regular high school schedule. The professors at each institution have approved both the courses and the credentials of the high school teachers who teach the courses.*

*Once students have the courses recorded on a college transcript, they may transfer the courses to other colleges. If accepted, students will be waived from the course and will not have to pay tuition for the credits they earned in Ford's College in High School Program.*

*A grant that Ford High received from the Noble Foundation pays for the tuition and books charged by Victoria College and Harvey University for these three-credit courses.*

**Job 5**

Key this article about Ford alumni as part of your newsletter.

## Alumni News

The Ford Alumni and Friends Association is inviting the FSD community to log on to their website at fordalumni.org. This website provides some new and exciting Ford alumni news. A reunion link lets you find out what your class is planning. The e-mail directory can help you keep in touch with classmates and friends. You will enjoy the pictures from the past and present in the Photo Tour section. The website is funded by donations from the alumni. You can download a donation form from the website. Other activities of the organization include providing mini grants to teachers, holding an annual Hall of Fame Induction banquet, and making gifts to the school district.

## 2G | Home-Key and Space-Bar Mastery

### Technique Goals

- curved, upright fingers
- quick-snap keystrokes
- down-and-in spacing
- quick return without spacing at line ending
- eyes on copy

Do not attempt to key line numbers or the vertical lines ( | ) separating word groups.

Key the lines once SS, with a DS between 2-line groups. Do not key line numbers.

```
1  jsj jsj|dkd dkd|ala ala|f;f f;f|ajf ajf|kdl kdl|s;
2  jsj jsj|dkd dkd|ala ala|f;f f;f|ajf ajf|kdl kdl|s;
                                                      DS
3  ask ask|all all|jak jak|lad lad|dad dad|lass lass;
4  ask ask|all all|jak jak|lad lad|dad dad|lass lass;
                                                      DS
5  fall fall;|jaks jaks;|salad salad;|flasks; flasks;
6  fall fall;|jaks jaks;|salad salad;|flasks; flasks;
```

Tap the ENTER key 4 times to quadruple-space (QS).

## 2H | End-of-Lesson Routine

Follow this routine at the end of each practice session.

1. Save the document. (Refer to **1L** on page 7 if needed.) Use *Lesson2* for the filename.
2. Exit the word processing software.
3. Remove the disk from the drive.
4. Turn off the equipment if directed to do so.
5. Clean up your work area and push in your chair.

## MicroType
### TIP

Click the Save button on the toolbar to access the Save As dialog box quickly.

For additional practice ▶ MicroType ✦ Alphabetic Keyboarding ✦ Lesson 2

### MicroType
#### TIP

Footers are inserted in the same way as headers but will appear at the bottom of the page. To insert a footer, select Footer from the Format menu.

**Job 2**

Key this article as part of your newsletter.

NEW ID PROGRAM

*Replace all*

The Ford School District began [started] a district-wide photo ID *[sp identification]* badge program this year. The middle school students, teachers, and staff were asked to be the first group to wear the badges. The ID program is proceeding very well. Next year, the badges will be used at the high school. The three elementary schools will join the program the following year. The photo ID badge serves as a way to prove right ful access to the school building. This helps ensure safety and security. The badge also serves as the students' library card and can be used to pay for food *[in the cafeteria]*. Students will no longer need to carry cash on a regular basis.

Parents of middle school students have received information about the ID badge program. Instructions for depositing [putting] money into the students' meal accounts were included. Over 300 students now use the badge instead of cash!

Please call the building principals [principles] or the Director of Community Relations if you have any questions.

**Job 3**

Key this as part of your newsletter.

### Congratulations

These teachers will retire at the end of the school year. Please join us in the Ford High School cafeteria on June 2 at 7 p.m. to recognize them for their many years of outstanding service to Ford School District.

Brad Arico—36 years
Karen Cappie—32 years
Raena Darr—40 years
Ashley Konjas—25 years
April Schimmel—27 years
Kristina Streit—39 years
David Weibl—34 years

# 3

**OBJECTIVE**

*To learn reach technique for **h** and **e**.*

## NEW KEYS: h AND e

### 3A | Get Ready to Key

Before starting each lesson, follow the *Standard Plan for Getting Ready to Key* below.

**Standard Plan for Getting Ready to Key**

1. Arrange work area as shown on page 2.
2. Start your word processing software.
3. Align the front of the keyboard with the front edge of the desk.
4. Position the monitor and the textbook for easy reading.

### 3B | Plan for Learning New Keys

All remaining keys that you will learn require the fingers to reach from the home keys. Follow the *Standard Plan for Learning New Keys* shown below to learn the proper reach for each new key.

**Standard Plan for Learning New Keys**

1. Find the new key on the keyboard chart shown on the page where the new key is introduced.
2. Look at your keyboard and find the new key on it.
3. Study the reach-technique picture near the practice lines for the new key. Read the statement below the illustration.
4. Identify the finger to be used to tap the new key.
5. Curve your fingers; place them in home-key position (over **asdf jkl;**).
6. Watch your finger as you reach to the new key and back to home position a few times (keep it curved).
7. Refer to the set of drill lines near the reach-technique illustration. Key each line twice SS—once slowly to learn the new reach and then again at a faster rate. DS between 2-line groups.

### 3C | Home-Key Review

1. Key each line twice SS; once slowly, then again, at a faster pace. DS between 2-line groups.
2. After keying the lines, save the document using *Lesson3* for the filename.

**All keystrokes learned**

```
1 ss jj ff ;; dd ll aa kk jj ff kk ss dd ll ;; aa kk
2 fk ja ld s; aj d; fl sk ka jf ls d; jd kf sl ;a dj
3 js sl sl lk lk ka ka ad ad d; d; ;f ;f fa fa al al
4 d; d; fa fa jk jk sl sl ad ad sf sf ;j ;j lk lk a;
5 ajk lsf d;s jda flk sla ksd fjl sa; ljk dfs lj; ds
6 a sad lass; all ads; ask a lad; all fall; a flask;
7 a lad ask; a salad; a fall ad; ask a dad; all fall
```

Tap ENTER 4 times to QS between lesson parts.

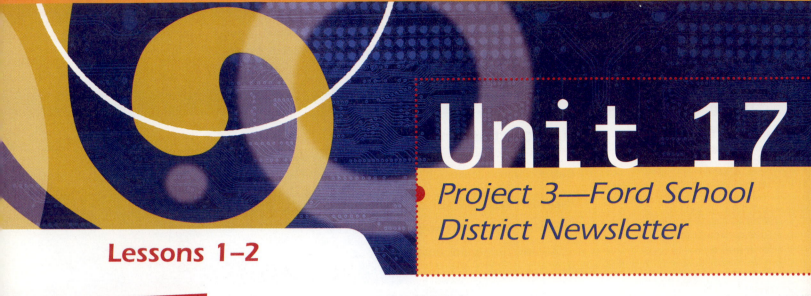

# Unit 17

## Project 3—Ford School District Newsletter

### Lessons 1–2

## LESSONS

# 1–2

### OBJECTIVES

1. *To format a newsletter.*
2. *To make appropriate formatting decisions and follow directions.*
3. *To use previously learned word processing commands, particularly those used to format column documents.*

### 1-2A | Conditioning Practice

Complete this drill each day you work on Project 3. Key each line twice SS; then key a 1' writing on line 3. Determine *gwam*.

| | |
|---|---|
| Alphabet 1 | Sixty glazed rolls with jam were quickly baked and provided free. |
| Figures 2 | The listing on May 19, 2008, had 87 cars, 45 vans, and 36 trucks. |
| Speed 3 | The six sorority girls in the dormitory may go to the big social. |

**GWAM** 1' | 1 | 2 | 3 | 4 | 5 | 6 | 7 | 8 | 9 | 10 | 11 | 12 | 13 |

### 1-2B | Project 3

**Project Assignment**

Assume that your school district, Ford School District, is revising its newsletter. This newsletter is sent to all households within the district. To involve the students in this revision, the publications director has announced a newsletter design contest. You decide to enter it. Prizes will be awarded to the top three designs, as selected by a panel of teachers.

All contestants will use the same articles in the newsletters. The colors must be limited to black, white, and another color that you choose. Shades of each color can be used. The newsletter articles must be formatted in two or more columns.

Your teacher will give you a series of articles to include in the newsletter during the next two class periods. You decide the order in which the articles will appear in your newsletter. Also, you are to decide all design elements and formatting features that are not specified. You should, of course, use what you have learned in this class as the basis for your decisions. Name the newsletter file *U17Newsletter*. Remember to save the file again after each item is added to the newsletter.

**Job 1**

Design a newsletter title using the following guidelines.

1. The name (title) of the newsletter is *Ford Forum*.

2. The title should be center-aligned and span all columns. Include the date *May 20--* in the title.

## 3D | Close Command

### Learn to Close a Document

To close a document:

1. On the menu bar, click File. Click Close. If the document has been saved and additional changes have been made, or if the document has not been saved, a Caution dialog box appears.

2. Click Yes to save the document and close it. Click No to close the document without saving it.

MicroType

TIP

Click the New button to close the current document and open a new blank document.

### Practice What You Have Learned

1. Close *Lesson3*.

2. Save changes if prompted to do so.

MicroType

Word Processing

Open Command

The Open command is an option on the File menu. Use it to open a document you saved earlier.

## 3E | Open Command

### Learn to Open a Document

To open a document:

1. On the menu bar, click File. Click Open. The Open dialog box appears.

2. Click the filename (*Lesson3*). It will appear in the File name box. (The filename extension, such as *kos*, will vary depending on the word processing program you use.)

3. Click Open.

MicroType

Click the Open button on the toolbar to access the Open dialog box quickly.

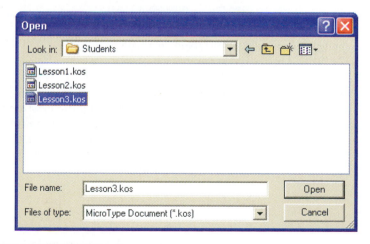

### Practice What You Have Learned

1. Open *Lesson2*. Close the document.

2. Open *Lesson3* and leave the document open, and continue the lesson.

## Math Activities

**4F** ▪ **Math Challenge 14**

### FIND THE TIME ON A SIMPLE INTEREST LOAN

1. Key a sentence to explain how you find the time on a simple interest loan problem like this: *What is the time of the $500 loan if the interest is $15 and the interest rate is 6%?*

2. Find the time for the following loans and key your answers in sentence form. For example, an appropriate sentence for the answer to the problem stated above is: *The time of a $500 loan that charges $15 interest at the rate of 6% is ½ year.*

   2a. Loan amount is $4,000; interest is $240; interest rate is 6%.

   2b. Loan amount is $5,000; interest is $500; interest rate is 5%.

   2c. Loan amount is $600; interest is $40.50; interest rate is 4.5%.

   2d. If Dom borrowed $10,000 and the bank charged him 5.5% interest, which was $412.50, what was the time of Dom's loan?

3. Save as *U16L4Math*.

## Careers ⋯⋯⋯⋯⋯⋯

### 4G ▪ Career Exploration Portfolio – Activity 14

▪ You must complete Career Activities 1-3 before completing this activity.

1. Retrieve your Career folder and the information in it that relates to the three career clusters you have chosen.

2. Identify the career cluster that is now your second choice.

3. Use the Internet to search for schools that you could attend after you are graduated from high school to pursue an occupation in this cluster. Then write a paragraph or two describing what kind of school it is, where it is, the cost to enroll, whether it has resident students and/or commuter students, and other information that interests you. Print your file, save it as *U16L4Career14*, and keep it open.

4. Exchange papers with a classmate and have the classmate offer suggestions for improving the content and correcting any errors he or she finds in your paragraph(s). Make the changes you agree with and print a copy to turn in to your instructor. Save your file as *U16L4Career14* and close it.

5. Return your folder to the storage area. When your instructor returns your paper, file it in your Career folder.

**h** Right index finger

**e** Left middle finger

Do not attempt to key line numbers, the vertical lines ( | ) separating word groups, or the labels (**Learn h**).

## 3F | New Keys:  h and e

1. Use the *Standard Plan for Learning New Keys* (page 12) for each key to be learned. Study the plan now.

2. Relate each step of the plan to the illustrations and copy below.  Then key each line twice SS; leave a DS between 2-line groups.

### Learn h

1  j h jh jh|hj hj|ha ha|has has|dash dash|hall hall;

2  jh jh|had had|ash ash|has has|half half|lash lash;

3  ha ha; a half; a dash; has had; a flash; had half;

DS

### Learn e

4  d e de de|ed ed|elk elk|elf elf|see see|leak leak;

5  fake fake|deal deal|leaf leaf|fade fade|lake lake;

6  jade desk; see a lake; feel safe; see a safe deal;

DS

### Combine h and e

7  he he|she she|shelf shelf|shake shake|shade shade;

8  he has; half ashes; he fed; held a shelf; she has;

9  held a sale; he has a shed; he has a desk; she has

QS

Toxics from Cars Reduced

Toxic fumes from gasoline will decrease significantly to further reduce health risks under new standards adopted by EPA. By 2030, the new and existing standards will lower toxic emissions from cars to 80 percent below 1999 emissions.

These new standards will permit Americans to continue driving the cars they love and pave the road toward healthier drivers and a cleaner environment.

Once the new standards are fully implemented in 2030, they are expected to reduce emissions of mobile-source air toxics annually by 330,000 tons. EPA estimates annual health benefits from the particulate matter reductions of the vehicle standards to total $6 billion in 2030. The estimated annual cost for the entire rule is about $400 million in 2030.

The new standards will take effect in 2011 for gasoline, 2010 for cars, and 2009 for fuel containers.

---

★ *Language Arts*

## 4D Writing: Word Choice

Study the spelling and definitions of the following words. Key the Learn line, noting the word choices. Key the Apply lines, selecting the correct words. Save as *U16L4Writing*.

**stationary** (adjective) fixed in position, course, or mode; unchanging in condition

**stationery** (noun) paper or envelopes used for processing personal and business documents

Learn 1   We stock company **stationery** on **stationary** shelves in the closet.

Apply 2   Desks will remain (stationary, stationery), but the files will move.

Apply 3   We were able to get a big discount on the (stationary, stationery).

---

*Our World*

### 4E ▪ Great Leaders

Use the Internet to research traits and characteristics that great leaders possess. Identify a person in your community whom you consider an effective leader. Write a paragraph explaining why you believe this person is a leader. Include some of the traits and characteristics you found from your research.

Save as *U16L4Leader*.

*Social Studies*

1. Key the lines once SS with a DS between 2-line groups.

2. Key the lines again with quick, sharp strokes at a faster pace.

3. Save the document again using *Lesson3* for the filename.

**Fingers curved**

**Fingers upright**

Home row
1  add add│dad dad│jak jak│ask ask│lad lad│fall falls
2  all fall; as a jak; a sad lad falls; all salad ads

DS

h/e
3  he he│had had│see see│she she│held held│shed shed;
4  half a shelf; a jade sale; she has a jak; he deals

DS

All keys learned
5  jell jell│half half│sale sale│lake lake│held held;
6  a lake; she has half; he held a flask; a jade sale

DS

All keys learned
7  she held a deed; a flash; a jade keel; has a shed;
8  a jak; half a flask; he has a desk; he held a sale

For additional practice **MicroType** ♦ **Alphabetic Keyboarding** ♦ **Lesson 3**

## 4C | Multiple-Column Document

1. Key the following information using default settings. Place a border around the text that appears below in italic.

2. Format the document as a multiple-column document in either portrait or landscape orientation.

3. You decide all formatting features and balance the columns. Save as *U16L4Update*.

Environmental Update

Volume 12, November 20--

Where Can I Get Help?

Have you ever wondered where to turn for answers to environmental problems? If so, you are not alone. One good place to start is the U.S. Environmental Protection Agency's (EPA) website. The website, www.epa.gov, contains links to helpful information. You can link to sections for concerned citizens, small businesses, and industry. You can even get the EPA agency telephone numbers and addresses.

Protecting our environment is a big job. Federal, state, and local agencies are involved. Every city, county, and state agency shares information with the EPA.

Therefore, you can get help at any level. If the first person you contact can't answer a question, he or she will know who can.

*No longer can we say, "I'm too busy to be concerned with the environment. Someone else can take care of it."*

Funding for Reducing Risks from Toxics

EPA recently announced that $2.7 million is available to support communities that wish to reduce risks from toxics. Two types of cooperative agreements are available.

Level I cooperative agreements will help establish community-based partnerships and set priorities for reducing risks from toxics in a community. Examples of past projects include addressing water quality in Puget Sound and helping to rebuild St. Bernard Parish in Louisiana. EPA expects to award up to ten cooperative agreements in Level I, ranging from $75,000 to $100,000.

Level II cooperative agreements are for communities that already have undertaken a process to assess risks and are ready to implement risk reduction strategies. EPA expects to award up to eight cooperative agreements in Level II, ranging from $150,000 to $300,000.

A range of community groups may apply for funding, including county and local governments, tribes, nonprofit organizations, and universities. Applications for funding are due by April 9.

*(continued)*

# LESSON

# 4

## OBJECTIVES

To learn reach technique for *i* and *r*.

### Tips

- Key the line at a slow, steady pace, tapping and releasing each key quickly.
- Key the line again at a faster pace; move from key to key quickly.

### Keying Cue

Keep up your pace to the end of each line, tap the ENTER key quickly, and start the new line without a pause.

## 4A | Get Ready to Key

Follow the steps in the *Standard Plan for Getting Ready to Key* on page 12.

## 4B | Conditioning Practice

Key each line twice SS; DS between 2-line groups.

Home keys 1   ll aa ff jj ss kk dd ;;   jd f; ls ak sj ;a df kl ak
                                          DS

h/e 2   he he|she she|held held|heed heed|shed shed|ahead;
                                          DS

All keys learned 3   as he fled; she had a sale; a jade desk; she ask a
                                          QS

## 4C | Technique: ENTER Key

Key each line twice SS; DS between 2-line groups.

1 ask a
2 as he fell
3 a desk; a sale;
4 he had a sled; a lad
5 ask a lass; a sled; a jak
6 a lake sale; a shelf; he led a
7 had a lash; he feels safe; half see

## 4B | One-Column Document

1. Format the following text as a one-column document. You decide all formatting features, but you must do the following:

   - Use one font with various sizes, styles, effects, and colors.
   - Insert an appropriate picture related to sports if available.
   - Use borders or shading.

2. Save as *U16L4Fitness*.

Total Fitness™

Since 1985

Special Offer 50% Off Joining Fee!

Joining Fee
Single $552
Couple $804
Family $936

Print this page and bring it with you to Total Fitness™

4623 W. Bancroft Street
Toledo, OH
(419) 555-0162

Aerobics, Stepping, Free Weights, Power Pacing,
Yoga, Body Pump, Kick Boxing, and more.
After your workout enjoy a beverage at our Energy Bar.

On-site day care is available.

Not valid with other offers.

**i** Right middle finger

**r** Left index finger

Follow the *Plan for Learning New Keys* outlined on page 12.

### 4D | New Keys: *i and r*

Key each line twice SS (slowly, then faster); DS between 2-line groups. If time permits, key lines 7–9 again.

**Learn i**

1  k i|ki|ki|ik; ik;|is; is;|lid lid|kid kid|aid aid;

2  ill; ill;|said said|like like|jail jail|file file;

3  if likes; file a lease; a slide; if he is; his kid

**Learn r**

4  f r|fr fr|far far|red red|are are|ark ark|jar jar;

5  dark dark|real real|rake rake|hear hear|rear rear;

6  a red jar; hear her; dark red; a real rake; read a

**Combine i and r**

7  ride ride|fire fire|hair hair|hire hire|liar liar;

8  air air|risk risk|fair fair|dire dire|rifle rifle;

9  fire risk; hire a; her side; like air; a fire; sir

QS between lesson parts.

## 3E Writing: Number Expression

Read the following number usage rule. Key the Learn lines, noting the number choices. Key the Apply lines, making the necessary corrections. Save as *U16L3Writing*.

**Rule 9:** Use figures for a series of fractions, but spell isolated fractions.

Learn 1   What do you get when you add **1/3**, **1/4**, and **1/2**?

Learn 2   Only **one half** of the students attended the ceremony.

Apply 3   You will need 1/3 cup nuts, one half cup water, and 3/4 cup flour.

Apply 4   Exactly 3/4 of the delegates voted for Senator Smythe.

*Language Arts*

## 3F | Preparing to Speak

You are competing in a public speaking contest in your school. You have chosen to speak about your family for two minutes. Save as *U16L3Speaking*.

1. Key an outline of the points you want to include. Suggestions follow:

   • State the names of your family members and identify where they work or go to school.

   • Describe the things you admire most in your family members.

   • Describe some of the activities you do as a family.

   • Describe a project you completed with family members.

   • Describe some of the rules the family members are expected to honor.

2. If time and resources permit, record your speech in a sound file.

3. Submit your outline (and sound file, if made) to your instructor.

## LESSON

# 4

### OBJECTIVE

*To format column documents.*

# COLUMN DOCUMENTS

## 4A | Conditioning Practice

Key each line twice SS; then key a 1' writing on line 3. Determine *gwam*.

Alphabet 1   Pamela was sure Jaxon would get his sizeable refund very quickly.

Figures/ Symbols 2   I paid the $746.89 bill with 10% off on 5/23/08 with check #205.

Speed 3   Jen sat by the right aisle for the ritual at the downtown chapel.

**GWAM** 1' | 1 | 2 | 3 | 4 | 5 | 6 | 7 | 8 | 9 | 10 | 11 | 12 | 13 |

- fingers deeply curved
- wrists low, but not resting on desk
- hands/arms steady
- eyes on copy as you key

## 4E | New-Key Mastery

1. Key the lines once SS with a DS between 2-line groups.
2. Key the lines again at a faster pace.

Reach review
1 de ki jh fr ed ik rf ik ki rf jh ed ik fr jh de ki
2 are are|hair hair|hear hear|risk risk|shear shear;

DS

h/e
3 she she|her her|seeks seeks|shed sheds|shelf shelf
4 her shelf; he had; he held a jar; he heard; he has

DS

i/r
5 ir ir|air air|hair hair|hired hired|riddle riddle;
6 hire a kid; ride like; her hair; like her; a fire;

DS

All keys learned
7 jar jar|half half|fire fire|liked liked|lake lake;
8 fire fire|jail jail|hire hire|sake sake|deal deal;

DS

All keys learned
9 hire a kid; he has her shelf; free jar; dark hair;
10 has a jar; he ask her; had a fire; she has a deal;

## 4F | Technique: ENTER

Key each line twice SS; DS between 2-line groups.

1 had a deal
2 see if she did;
3 ask if she has read;
4 her dad did ask her if he
5 a sled ride; half a jar; he is
6 ask dad if she has had a real sale;
7 her aide asked if he has real dark hair;
8 she has a shed; half a flask; she has a desk;

For additional practice **MicroType** + **Alphabetic Keyboarding** + **Lesson 4**

2. Make these formatting changes:

   - Set the top, bottom, and side margins at 1". Set the page orientation to Portrait.

   - Format all text in a 12-point Times New Roman font.

   - Format the headings in a 14-point, bold Times New Roman font. (Use the Copy Style and Apply Style commands.) Center-align the headings.

   - Format each paragraph in the body for a 0.25" first-line indent.

   - Insert 9 points of space after each paragraph.

3. Key **Strategies for Success** as the title. Center-align it in a 28-point Times New Roman font. You decide if it should span all columns.

4. Format the document for three columns.

5. Insert a new line between the first and second paragraph and key this text center-aligned. Format the text in a 12-point, Arial font. Place a black border around the text.

A bad reputation can result from one mistake.

6. Insert a new line after the last line of the Reputation and Choice section and key this text:

Choices you make destroy or enhance your reputation.

7. Insert a new line after the last line of the first paragraph of the *Learning About People* section and key this text:

Relating well to others is a major challenge.

8. Insert a new line after the last paragraph of the *Business Ethics* section and key this text:

Learn from experienced workers.

9. Use the Copy/Apply Ruler and Copy/Apply Style commands to format all text inserted in steps 6–8 like the text in the first box.

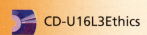

CD-U16L3Ethics

10. Insert a new line after the first paragraph of the *Business Ethics* section. Insert the picture file *CD-U16L3Ethics* at this location.

11. Balance the columns. (The picture may move down.) Save as *U16L3Success*.

## 3D | Three-Column Document

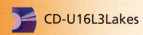

CD-U16L3Lakes

1. Open the file *CD-U16L3Lakes* and make these formatting changes:

   - Format the text as a three-column document with 0.75" side, top, and bottom margins. Use landscape orientation.

   - Format the text in a 12-point Times New Roman font.

   - Use single spacing and 6 points of space after paragraphs including the headings. Use 0.25" first-line indents for the paragraphs in the body of the report.

   - Format the long quotation (the second paragraph) using a 10-point font and a 0.25" indentation from the left margin.

   - Format the references using a 10-point font and a 0.25" hanging indent.

   - Format the titles (*The Great Lakes and References*) in an 18-point, bold font and center-align them. You decide if *The Great Lakes* is to span all columns.

   - Center-align the side headings and format them in a 14-point, bold font.

   - Balance the columns appropriately.

2. Save as *U16L3Lakes*.

# LESSON 5

## OBJECTIVES

1. *To improve reachstroke control and keying speed.*
2. *To improve technique on Space Bar and ENTER.*

### Technique Goals

- fingers curved and upright
- wrists low, but not touching keyboard
- forearms parallel to slant of keyboard
- body erect, sitting back in chair
- feet on floor

**SPACE** with the right thumb using a down-and-in motion.

## 5A | Get Ready to Key

1. Review the steps for arranging your work area on page 2.
2. Review proper keying position on page 4.

## 5B | Conditioning Practice

Key each line twice SS (slowly, then faster); DS between 2-line groups. If time permits, practice each line again.

```
1  jh ki de fr hj ik ed rf ak sj fl d; ka js lf ;d ki
2  his; see; ask jar his sad fall head read jade lake
3  ask desk jail risk file hill rash dear lake drier;
```

## 5C | Technique:  Space Bar

Key each line twice SS (slowly, then faster); DS between 2-line groups. If time permits, practice each line again.

### Short, easy words

```
1  if has his far kid jar her ask elk lead fair idea;
2  iris leaf jeer half read lake jade like heir dial;
3  here ease deal sled jail leek dire seek fade hail;
```

### Short-word phrases

```
4  ask her|had a|his jar|see his|as if he|is her half
5  has a|if she did|red hair|a sled ride|if she feels
6  he likes|as he said|ask her if|she read a|as if he
```

## 3C | Three-Column Document

1. Using default settings, key the following three articles; then complete the directions in steps 2 to 11 after the last article.

### Reputation and Choice

Reputation is the image or view in which a person is commonly held. It reflects your ethical and moral principles. Most people think that a good reputation is needed for success in any job. Therefore, it is one of the most important personal assets you can acquire.

A good reputation is a valuable asset. It takes time, effort, and discipline to develop and protect. A bad reputation can develop in a very short time and can last a long time. It can result from just one mistake and can be a heavy burden to carry.

Realize that you have an opportunity to develop and protect the reputation you want. You have many choices to make that will destroy or enhance the image you want to project. The choices are hard, but honesty, loyalty, and dedication are most often involved.

### Learning About People

Many aspects of a job present challenges to those who strive to do their best. One of the biggest challenges most workers face is being able to relate well with others. Workers commonly have daily dealings with bosses, peers, and subordinates. Also, workers interact with telephone callers and visitors from outside and inside the company daily.

Learning all they can about their company is important for workers. Learning about the people with whom they work is often just as important. Often, new workers can depend upon experienced workers for information that will help them learn about the company. What they learn may help workers determine what is expected of them and will help them adjust.

### Business Ethics

Ethics is a popular topic today. Many businesses that had written codes for ethical practice years ago had set them aside. These businesses are now going back to these codes.

The main purpose of a code of ethics is to convey a company's values and standards. A business is ethical to the extent that each person in it subscribes to and applies the values and standards. Ethics involve how workers treat each other as well as how customers, suppliers, and the general public are treated. Ethics should be more than a list of do's and don'ts.

When an individual's values are in line with the employer's, the situation is good for both. If either of them is inclined to "take shortcuts" or "look the other way," an unethical practice is likely to result.

**Keying Cue**

Keep up your pace to the end of the line; return immediately; start the new line without pausing.

## 5D | Technique: Hard Return

Key each line twice SS (slowly, then faster); DS between 2-line groups. If time permits, practice each line again.

1  if she is;
2  ask her if she;
3  see if she did read;
4  her dad is as safe as he;
5  if her dad has had a sled ride
6  her dad asks if she had a real rake
7  her dad has had a sales lead as he said;
8  she said she had half a deal if her aide asks

## 5E | Speed Building: Words & Phrases

Key each line twice SS (slowly, then faster); DS between 2-line groups. If time permits, practice each line again.

**Space with the right thumb using a down-and-in motion.**

**Goal: to speed up the combining of letters**

1  elk elk|her her|ask ask|jar jar|did did|like like;
2  risk risk|safe safe|jade jade|half half|lake lake;
3  said said|ride ride|safe safe|hike hike|desk desk;

**Goal: to speed up spacing between words**

4  a kid|a kid|if he|if he|she is|she is|as he|as he;
5  ask her|ask her|like a|like a|red dress|red dress;
6  is he|is he|ask a kid|ask a kid|half jar|half jar;
7  a jail|a jail|did she|did she|fresh air|fresh air;

**Keying Cue**

Key each word at an easy speed; key it again at a faster speed. Think and say each word.

Speed up the second keying of each phrase; space quickly between words and phrases.

## OBJECTIVES

1. *To learn and practice the copy and apply style word processing features.*

2. *To format three-column documents.*

### MicroType
**TIP**

You can apply the same style settings more than once provided you have not copied different style settings to the Clipboard.

# THREE-COLUMN DOCUMENTS

## 3A | Conditioning Practice

Key each line twice SS; then key a 1' writing on line 3. Determine *gwam*.

Alphabet 1  Marylou, a clerk, showed Giji the exquisite topaz before leaving.

Figures 2  Our indoor soccer league had 459 players in 1987 and 632 in 2008.

Speed 3  The girls are to dismantle the cycle when they visit us downtown.

**GWAM** | 1' | 1 | 2 | 3 | 4 | 5 | 6 | 7 | 8 | 9 | 10 | 11 | 12 | 13 |

## 3B | Copy/Apply Style

Use the Copy Style and Apply Style commands to copy style settings (font name, size, style, and color) to save time when formatting text and to ensure consistency in a document.

To copy and apply a style:

1. Select the text with the style you want to copy. From the Format menu, select Copy Style.

2. Select the text you want to format. From the Format menu, select Apply Style.

### Practice What You Have Learned

1. Key the following lines:
   Tim Harris, Janet Yee, Kyle Tepper, and Maria Everett are going to the movies.

   Career Opportunities in Sports Medicine

   Career Opportunities in Sports Management

   Career Opportunities in Health Management

   Career Opportunities in Physical Therapy

2. Make these formatting changes:
   - Format *Tim Harris* in Arial 16-point, bold, underlined, red font.
   - Use the Copy Style and Apply Style commands to format the other names in line 1 with the same settings.
   - Format *Career Opportunities in Sport Medicine* in Verdana 16-point, bold, italic, blue font.
   - Use the Copy Style and Apply Style commands to format the remaining three lines with the same settings.

3. Save as *U16L3Style*.

The Print command allows you to print an open document.

## MicroType
### TIP

Click the Print button on the toolbar to access the Print dialog box quickly.

## 5F | Print a Document

1. Click File on the menu bar. Click Print. The Print dialog box appears.

2. Click the down arrow for the Printer Name drop-down list to choose a printer if yours is not displayed. Click OK.

3. Practice what you have learned. Print Lesson 5.

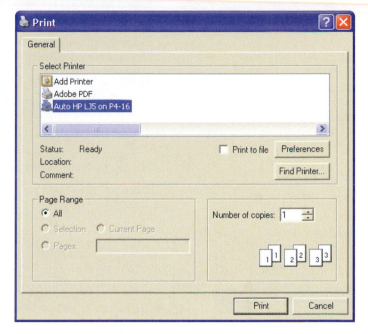

## 5G | Keyboard Mastery

1. Key the drill once SS at an easy pace to gain control of all your reachstroke motions. DS between 2-line groups.

2. Key the drill again to speed up your motions and build continuity (keeping the insertion point moving steadily across the screen).

Reach Review
```
1  ki ki|fr fr|de de|er er|jh jh|ed ed|rf rf|kid kid;
2  is is|air air|red red|his his|hark hark|fire fire;
```

h/e
```
3  held held|hear hear|half half|here here|dash dash;
4  he held|hear her|a red shelf|red ashes|she did ask
```

l/r
```
5  if she likes|if he hires her|ask her if|real hike;
6  free rides|a real risk|a riddle|a red rail|a hair;
```

All keys learned
```
7  he has a red|like a fish|half jars;|ask if she is;
8  if she likes red; a jade fish; is she; a red shed;
```

**For additional practice** ▶ **MicroType** ✦ **Alphabetic Keyboarding** ✦ **Lesson 5**

## 2E Writing: Word Choice

Study the spelling and definitions of the following words. Key the Learn line, noting the word choices. Key the Apply lines, selecting the correct words. Save as *U16L2Writing*.

**farther** (adverb) at or to a greater distance

**further** (adverb) in greater depth, extent, or importance; additional

Learn 1 The **farther** I hike, the **further** my mind wanders.

Apply 2 With (farther, further) effort, I ran (farther, further) ahead of Tim in this race.

Apply 3 Jill could see (farther, further) into the distance than Mary.

*Our World*

## 2F ▪ Research an Interesting Person

Select a person you would like to research. You might choose a famous explorer, a world leader, an inventor, a champion of human rights, a sports figure, or some other person. Focus your research by writing one or two main points you want to learn about this person. For example, "What did Thomas Jefferson do before he was president?" Or "Why did Susan B. Anthony become the first woman to be shown on U.S. currency?" Then, go to sites such as the following to find the information you're looking for.

http://www.biography.com
http://www.freeality.com/biograph.htm
http://www.biography-center.com/

Key the answer to your question(s) and a few sentences describing other things you learned about this person. Save as *U16L2Internet*.

*Social Studies*

© IMAGE100

# LESSON
# 6

## OBJECTIVE

*To learn reach technique for* **o** *and* **t**.

**Technique Goal**
**fingers curved and upright**

**O** Right ring finger

**T** Left index finger

## 6A | Conditioning Practice

Key each line twice SS (slowly, then faster); DS between 2-line groups.

h/e 1  her head; has had a; see here; feed her; hire her;

i/r 2  hire a; fire her; his risk; fresh air; a red hair;

All keys learned 3  a lake; ask a lad; a risk; here she is; a red jar;

## 6B | New Keys: o and t

1. Key each line twice SS (slowly, then faster); DS between 2-line groups. If time permits, key lines 7–9 again.

2. Save the document as *Lesson6*.

Follow the *Plan for Learning New Keys* outlined on page 12.

**Learn o**

1  l o lo lo olo olo|fold fold|sold sold|holds holds;

2  of of|do do|oak oak|soil soil|does does|roof roof;

3  load of soil; order food; old oil; solid oak door;

**Learn t**

4  f t ft ft tf tf|the the|tea tea|eat eat|talk talk;

5  at at|fit fit|set set|hit hit|talk talk|test tests

6  flat feet|eat the treat; the first set|take a hike

**Combine o and t**

7  total total|tooth tooth|toast toast|otters otters;

8  the total look; other tooth; took a toll; too old;

9  those hooks; the oath; old tree fort; took a tool;

supports the new IT curriculum that has been identified as a model that other schools should follow.

Open house is scheduled on November 7–11 from 2:35 p.m. to 5:30 p.m. Just come to Room 305. IT students will greet you. They will explain how they use hardware and software in their studies.

You will learn how the new program develops the student's IT skills to high levels. See the up-to-date word processing, spreadsheet, database, and presentation software packages that are used in the many courses. Students will show what each software package does. You too will be given a chance to use them!

To help us plan, please return this form to:

Mr. Kerry Session
Elliott School 2413
Big Knob Road
Etna, PA 15233-2467

✂✂✂✂✂✂✂✂✂✂✂✂✂✂✂✂✂✂✂✂✂✂✂✂✂✂✂✂✂✂✂✂✂

| Elliott School | |
|---|---|
| Name | |
| Street Address | |
| City | State and ZIP |
| Phone | E-mail |
| Visit Plans | |
| Day | Time |

2. Make these formatting changes:

- Use 1" side margins; 1.5" top and bottom margins. Use 0.5" first-line indentations for the paragraphs and 12 points of space after each paragraph except the name and address.

- Format the document title in a 16-point, bold Verdana font.

- Use 14-point Verdana for body text. Use 11-point Verdana for text in the table.

- Format as a two-column, vertically centered document in landscape orientation. The title should span all columns.

- Balance the columns appropriately.

3. Save as *U16L2Elliott*.

- curved, upright fingers
- wrists low, but not resting
- down-and-in spacing
- eyes on copy as you key

## 6C | New-Key Mastery

Key each line twice; DS between 2-line groups.

**Tip**

In lines of repeated words (lines 3, 5, and 7), speed up the second keying of each word.

Reach review
1 ki lo de ft jh fr ei or th olo ere hjh iki edr iro
2 here is; the fort; their old trail; first look at;

h/e
3 the the|hear hear|here here|heat heat|sheet sheet;
4 the sheets; hear her heart; their health; heat the

i/t
5 sit sit|fit fit|silt silt|kites kites|tried tried;
6 a little tire; he tried to tilt it; he tied a tie;

o/r
7 tort tort|tore tore|fort fort|road road|roof roof;
8 a road|a door|a rose|or a rod|a roar|for her offer

Space Bar
9 to do it he as are hit dot eat air the ask jar let
10 if he|do it|to see|had it|is the|for her|all of it

All keys learned
11 ask jet art oil old fit hit the sad did soil risk;
12 oil the; the jail; oak door; he said; their forts;

What Must You Do

All students are urged to attend and speak to as many of the participants as possible. To ensure your participation, you will need to get the signature of the career representatives you speak with. You are to give the signatures to the Career Fair Coordinators when you leave the gym. If you have 20 or more signatures, you will receive a $5 gift certificate from Pizza Works. This certificate is valid for the next four weeks.

How Should You Dress and Act

Please dress and act appropriately during the career fair. Standard or casual business dress is suggested. You should have a list of questions that you can ask. Bring paper and a pen to take notes about what you learn. Use correct grammar and speak clearly without using slang to improve your chances of making a favorable first impression.

2. Make these formatting changes:
   - Set the side margins at .75", the top and bottom margins at 2".
   - Set the page orientation to Portrait.
   - Format the title in an 18-point, bold font and center it across the line of writing. See the MicroType Tip at the left.
   - Format text into two columns.
   - Insert 9 points of vertical space after the paragraphs.
   - Use 0.25" first-line indentations for the paragraphs in the body (not the headings).
   - Format the text in a 12-point Times New Roman font.
   - Format the side headings in a 14-point, bold font.
   - Insert columns breaks and adjust spacing to balance the columns appropriately.
3. Save as *U16L2Fair*.

### Two-Column Document with Table

1. Using default settings, key the following document. Use 2" column widths in the table. Merge cells as needed to create the table as shown. Insert a line of scissors between the text and the table. (See the MicroType Tip.)

### YOU ARE INVITED TO ELLIOTT!

Have you visited a school in your community lately? If not, you should visit Elliott School this coming month. Come see the information technology (IT) classroom. It has state-of-the art computing hardware and software. It

*(continued)*

The Save As command is an option on the File menu. Use it to save a document under a new name—the original file remains unchanged. The file created using this command contains the original document with the changes made to it.

## 6D | Save As Command

### Learn to Save a Document Using a New Name

To save a document using a new name:

1. Click File on the Menu bar. Click Save As. The Save As dialog box appears.

2. Key the new filename in the File name box.

3. Click Save.

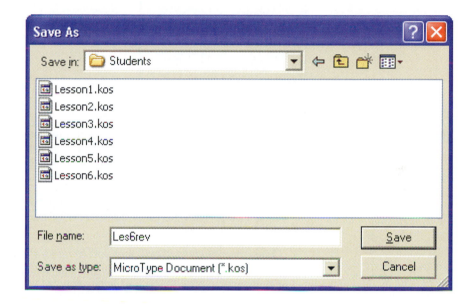

### Practice What You Have Learned

1. Save the current document (*Lesson6*) using a new name.

2. Use *Les6rev* for the new filename.

## 6E | Technique: ENTER Key

Key each line twice; DS between 2-line groups.

```
1  it is
2  the jet is
3  he had the rose
4  ask to hear the joke
5  she took the old shirt to
6  she told her to take the tests
7  at the fort; the lake road; did she
```

## 2C | Column Breaks

The Column break feature is used to set where a column of text will end. A column break takes all text to the right of the insertion point and places it in a new column or page. Column breaks should be inserted to balance the length of the columns and ensure columns end and begin correctly.

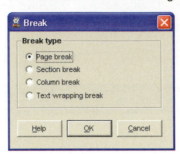

To insert a column break:

1. Place the insertion point at the place you want to end a column. From the Insert menu, select Break.

2. Select Column break. Click OK to close the Break dialog box. If the column break is not at the correct place, click Undo and set a new column break.

### Practice What You Have Learned

1. Open the file *U16L2Text1* that you created earlier. Insert a column break so column 1 and column 2 are equal (or nearly equal) in length and end and begin correctly. Set the page orientation for Portrait before printing. Save as *U16L2Columns1*.

2. Open the file *U16L2Text2* that you created earlier. Insert column breaks so columns 1–3 are equal (or nearly equal) in length and end and begin correctly. Center the text vertically on the page. Set the page orientation for Landscape before printing. Save as *U16L2Columns2*.

3. Open the file *U16L2Text3* that you created earlier. Insert column breaks so columns 1–4 are equal (or nearly equal) in length and end and begin correctly. Center the text vertically. Set the page orientation for Landscape before printing. Save as *U16L2Columns3*.

## 2D | Column Documents

### Two-Column Document

1. Using default settings, key the following document.

### ANNUAL CAREER FAIR

The Annual Career Fair will be held May 15 from 9 a.m. to 12:30 p.m. in Gym A. The Student Council and the Parent Teacher Organization are sponsoring this year's fair.

Who Will Be There

Over forty people from more than 30 different careers will attend. Many kinds of careers will be represented. You can meet people who have jobs that require a high school diploma plus additional training. You can talk with people who have completed college and work in their chosen fields. We have people from the building trades coming. Men and women who own businesses will be there. People from public service occupations such as police, firefighters, and paramedics will be represented. In short, a wide variety of career opportunities will be available for you to explore.

*(continued)*

---

### MicroType

Columns should end and begin in the same way as pages. That is, headings should be kept with at least two lines of text following them. At least two lines of a paragraph should be at the bottom of one column and at the top of the next column. A three-line paragraph cannot be divided between pages or columns.

**Tip**

In lines of repeated words (lines 3–8), speed up the second keying of each word.

1. Key the drill once SS at an easy pace to gain control of all your reachstroke motions. DS between 2-line groups.

2. Key the drill again to speed up your motions and build continuity.

**Reach review**

```
1  ki fr jh ft lo de ik rf hj tf ol ed tear for short
2  for rod tea jet raid door tore hike joke hair foil
```

**o/t**

```
3  too too|took took|loot loot|oath oath|forth forth;
4  toe toe|sort sort|hot hot|forth forth|other other;
```

**h/e**

```
5  she she|her her|herd herd|earth earth|ashes ashes;
6  the the|held held|hear hear|heir heir|these these;
```

**i/t**

```
7  it it|tire tire|rite rite|riot riot|little little;
8  kite kite|site site|edit edit|toil toil|fits fits;
```

**All keys learned**

```
9   the jade; like a; see the desks; for the; hot oil;
10  half a jar; red kite; she took first; to the lake;
11  she asked; tell a joke; read a; the dress fits her
12  her desk; the jail; for his sake; did he take the;
```

For additional practice **MicroType** ✦ **Alphabetic Keyboarding** ✦ **Lesson 6**

OBJECTIVES

1. *To learn and practice these word processing features: columns and column breaks.*
2. *To format two-column documents.*

# TWO-COLUMN DOCUMENTS

## 2A | Conditioning Practice

Key each line twice SS; then key a 1' writing on line 3. Determine *gwam*.

Alphabet 1   Quinn, zip your jacket and fix her muffler to brave raging winds.

Figures/ 2   Jones & Lange, Inc. ordered #246-1 @ $15.45 and #350-8 @ $23.97.
Symbols

Speed 3   An auditor for the sorority cut the giant endowment goal by half.

GWAM 1' | 1 | 2 | 3 | 4 | 5 | 6 | 7 | 8 | 9 | 10 | 11 | 12 | 13 |

## 2B | Columns

Multiple-column documents, such as leaflets, brochures, and newsletters, may contain two, three, or four vertical columns placed side by side on a page. The columns may be top-, center-, or bottom-aligned.

To format a document into two or more columns:

1. Open a new or existing document that you want to format in columns. From the Format menu, select Page Settings. The Page Setting dialog box appears.

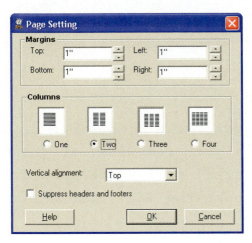

2. Click the number of columns desired in the Columns section. Click OK to apply the page settings.

### Practice What You Have Learned

1. Open the file *CD-U16L2Text*. Format the text as two columns. Change the settings, if needed, to display the document in portrait orientation. Save as *U16L2Text1*. Keep the document open.

2. Format the text in three columns. Change the settings to display the document in landscape orientation. Save as *U16L2Text2*. Keep the document open.

3. Format the text in four columns. Display the document in landscape orientation. Save as *U16L2Text3*.

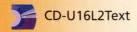

CD-U16L2Text

**OBJECTIVE**

*To learn reach technique for* **n** *and* **g**.

# NEW KEYS: n AND g

### 7A | Conditioning Practice

Key each line twice SS (slowly, then faster); DS between 2-line groups.

e/r 1  rare doer fear feet tire hire read ride rest after

o/t 2  toad told took other hotel total tools tooth torte

i/h 3  hits idle hail hiked their fifth faith heist hairs

### 7B | New Keys:  n and g

Key each line twice SS (slowly, then faster).  If time permits, key lines 7–9 again.

Follow the *Plan for Learning New Keys* outlined on page 12.

### Learn n

1  j n jn jn|njn njn|an an|on on|no no|in in|and and;
2  kind kind|none none|loan loan|find find|land land;
3  not till noon; not a need; not in; a national need

### Learn g

4  f g fg fg|gfg gfg|go go|dog dog|gas gas|goes goes;
5  age age|logs logs|glad glad|eggs eggs|legal legal;
6  great grin; large frog; gold dog; eight large eggs

### Combine n and g

7  gone gone|sing sing|king king|gnat gnat|ring rings
8  sing along; a grand song; green signs; long grass;
9  eight rings; a grand king; long gone; sing a song;

**n** Right index finger

**g** Left index finger

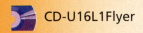
CD-U16L1Flyer

2. Make these formatting changes:

- Set top, bottom, and side margins to .75". Insert 12 points of space after paragraphs.

- Center-align the title in a 24-point, bold Arial font.

- Double-space and center-align paragraph 1 using a 14-point Arial font.

- In paragraph 2, use single spacing, a .5" left and right paragraph indentation, and a 12-point Arial font.

- Copy the paragraph 2 ruler settings and apply them to paragraphs 4 and 6. (Note that the font style is not copied as part of the ruler settings.)

- Insert a border around paragraphs 2, 4, and 6.

3. Save as *U16L1Poster1*; keep the file open.

- Delete the borders from paragraphs 2, 4, and 6 and then shade each of these paragraphs with a 10% fill of a color you choose. Use a White background.

- Change the title font color to one that matches the shading you used in paragraphs 4 and 6.

4. Save as *U16L1Poster2*.

## 1F | One-Column Flyer

1. Open *CD-U16L1Flyer*.

2. Design a one-column flyer. Include borders and shading. Insert at least one appropriate picture of food, if available. Apply other formatting features of your choice to make an attractive flyer.

3. Design and include a permission form at the bottom of the flyer that has space for student's name, name and period of the class to be missed, name of instructor whose class will be missed, and signature of the instructor granting permission.

4. Save as *U16L1Flyer*.

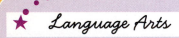

*Language Arts*

## 1G Writing: Number Expression

Read the following number usage rule. Key the Learn line, noting the number choices. Key the Apply lines, making the necessary corrections. Save as *U16L1Writing*.

**Rule 8:** Spell (capitalized) names of small-numbered streets and avenues (ten and under).

Learn 1 The new school will be located at 533 Fifth Avenue and 23rd Street.

Apply 2 Turn right on Fifteenth Street and go to 6th Avenue.

Apply 3 The stadium is located between 2nd Street and Center Street.

**Reach out and tap ENTER**

## Keying Cue

Keep up your pace to the end of line, tap the ENTER key quickly, and start a new line without pausing.

**Technique Goals**
- curved, upright fingers
- wrists low, but not resting
- quick-snap keystrokes
- down-and-in spacing
- eyes on copy as you key

### 7C | Technique: ENTER Key

1. Key the lines once SS.
2. Key the lines again at a faster pace.

```
1  large gold jar;
2  take the last train;
3  did he take the last egg;
4  she has to sing the last song;
5  join her for a hike at the lake at;
```

### 7D | New-Key Mastery

Key each line twice SS; DS between 2-line groups.

**Fingers curved**

**Fingers upright**

Reach Review
```
1  rf ik hj tf ol ed nj gf; lo fr ft jn de ki jh fgf;
2  get the; real ink; hang on; take the; their trees;
```

n/g
```
3  sing gone night seeing doing going ringing longest
4  sing one song; going along; long night; good angle
```

Space Bar
```
5  if he no as to it is so do at in so of did elk jet
6  It ask and the are let oil oar ill son odd fan sat
```

All keys learned
```
7  desk soil lark joke that done find join gold lake;
8  tank logs hand jade free toil seek said like tear;
```

All keys learned
```
9   oil free; did join; has half; go get; near the end
10  tell jokes; right here; ask her; fine desk; is it;
```

You can apply the same ruler settings more than once provided you have not copied different settings to the Clipboard.

## 1E | One-Column Poster

1. Using default settings, key the poster below and on the next page.

### Basic Document Design

Word processing gives you many opportunities to decide the format and appearance of your documents.  You should use the following guidelines to make your documents inviting and easy to read and understand.

Use a 12-point font for most of the text in a document because it is a notably readable size, preferred by most readers.  A font size that is too small strains the reader's eyes and makes the document look crammed and difficult to read.  A font that is too large uses more space than is necessary and causes readers to read too slowly (letter by letter rather than whole words and phrases).

Use margins of 1" to 2".  Long lines tend to tire the eye quickly.  Short lines tend to cause the eye to jump back and forth too often.  The use of a few long or short lines in a document is not likely to cause readers problems, however.

Use white space in the margins to keep a document from looking crowded and difficult to read.  Use white space between document parts to inform a reader where one part ends and another part begins.

Use a ragged right margin.  Varying line endings and consistent spacing between words is easier to read than justified text (even line endings, inconsistent spacing).

Use bold, italic, and small amounts of underlining to call attention to some parts of a document.  Avoid overusing one technique or using too many different techniques in a document.  When too many parts of a document are emphasized, no one part will seem especially important.  When too many different techniques are used, the document will appear cluttered.

Use color to enhance the message or appearance of the document.  Use darker shades of color for fonts and lighter shades of color for highlights and fills.

## 7E | Enrichment

Key each line twice SS; DS between 2-line groups; QS after lines 3, 7, and 12.

**Goal for lines 1–3:**
• curved, upright fingers

### Reach review

```
1  jh jh|jn jn|fg fg|fr fr|ft ft|de de|ki ki|lo lo|jh
2  no no|hot hot|oil oil|the the|gold gold|rest rest;
3  hold nest gone that nails there going alert radio;
```

**Goal for lines 4–7:**
• down-and-in motion of thumb

### Space Bar

```
4  is at if so no do as he of go it to an or is on in
5  of hen got ink and the ask jar let hit jet den far
6  no ink|on the go|hit it|ask her to|did not see the
7  he is to join her at the lake; she is not the one;
```

**Goal for lines 8–12:**
• Tap ENTER key quickly; start new line immediately.

### ENTER key

```
8   he is there;
9   ask if it is far;
10  the sign for the lake;
11  she still has three of the;
12  did he join her at the lake the;
```

**Goal for lines 13–16:**
• Reduce pause between lines.

### Short words and phrases

```
13  on on|do do|in in|it it|go go|or or|as as|are are;
14  see see|the the|and and|are are|for for|hire hire;
15  jet jet|kid kid|fit fit|ask ask|ton ton|risk risk;
16  he is to go see the lodge; he lost the three jars;
```

**For additional practice** MicroType ✦ Alphabetic Keyboarding ✦ Lesson 7

## 1C | Borders

A border can be added around a paragraph. Borders can be used to make text easier to read by emphasizing certain passages. Borders are most effective when they are used sparingly.

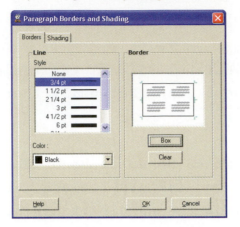

To add borders:

1. Position the cursor in the paragraph you want to format.

2. From the Format menu, select Borders and Shading.

3. Click the Borders tab.

4. Choose the line style and color for the border. In the Borders box, click Box to apply the border to all four sides.

5. Click OK to apply the borders around the paragraph.

### Practice What You Have Learned

CD-U16L1Border

1. Open *CD-U16L1Border*.

2. Select the first paragraph and apply a ¾-point black border around it.

3. Select the last paragraph and apply a ¾-point red border around it.

4. Save as *U16L1Border*.

## 1D | Shading

Shading can be added to a paragraph to focus the reader's attention on its contents. Like borders, shading is most effective when it is used sparingly.

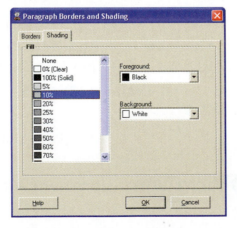

To add shading to a paragraph:

1. Position the cursor in the paragraph you want to shade. If you want to apply shading to more than one paragraph, select the paragraphs you want to change.

2. From the Format menu, select Borders and Shading.

3. Click the Shading tab.

4. Choose the desired fill pattern.

5. Choose the background and foreground colors.

6. Click OK to apply the borders and shading settings.

### Practice What You Have Learned

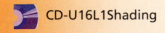

CD-U16L1Shading

1. Open *CD-U16L1Shading*.

2. Apply shading as directed in the paragraphs.

3. Save as *U16L1Shading*.

# LESSON 8

## OBJECTIVE

*To learn reach technique for **Left Shift** and **. (period)**.*

### ✦ Tips

1. Hold down the Left Shift key with the little finger on the left hand.
2. Tap the letter with the finger on the right hand.
3. Return finger(s) to home keys.

**Left Shift** Left little finger

**. (period)** Right ring finger

## 8A | Conditioning Practice

Key each line twice SS (slowly, then faster); DS between 2-line groups.

Reach review 1   ft jn fr jh de ki gf lo tf nj rf hj ed ik fg ol ng

Space Bar 2   so it if at or on is go do ask the and jar art lid

All keys learned 3   join the; like those; ask her to sing; define the;

## 8B | New Keys:  Left Shift and . (period)

Key each line twice SS (slowly, then faster); DS between 2-line groups.  If time permits, rekey lines 7–9.

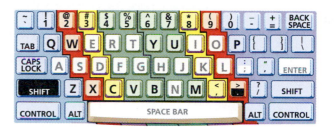

**Learn Left Shift key**

1   a J|a J|Ja Ja|Jan Jan|a K a K|Kate Kate|Hank Hank;
2   Idaho; Kansas; Ohio; Oregon; Indiana; Illinois; IL
3   Lane and I; Ida and Jane; Hal and Kate; John and I

**Learn . (period)**

4   l . l .|l. l.|a.l. a.l.|d.l. d.l.|j.l j.l|k.l. k.l
5   hr. hr.|ft. ft.|in. in.|rd. rd.|ea. ea.|ltd. ltd.;
6   fl. fl.|fed. fed.|alt. alt.|ins. ins.|asst. asst.;

**Combine Left Shift and . (period)**

7   I took Linda to Lake Harriet.  Lt. Kerns is there.
8   I did it.  Lana took it.  Jett Hill left for Ohio.
9   Karl and Jake got Ida and Janet to go to the fair.

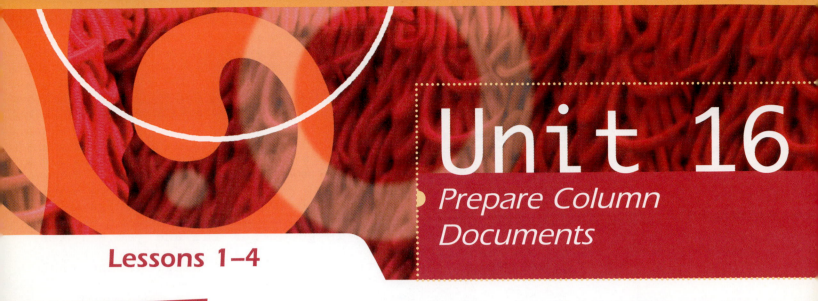

# Unit 16
## *Prepare Column Documents*

### Lessons 1–4

---

## ONE-COLUMN DOCUMENTS

### OBJECTIVES

1. *To learn and practice the copy and apply ruler word processing feature.*
2. *To format one-column documents.*

### 1A | Conditioning Practice

Key each line twice SS; then key a 1' writing on line 3. Determine *gwam*.

Alphabet 1 Marvi and Frank saw the xylophone at the quaint jazz nightclub.

Figures 2 Deb sold 105 shirts, 47 belts, 94 skirts, 36 suits, and 28 coats.

Speed 3 The bushels of corn by the cornfield on the burlap are for Lauri.

**GWAM** 1' | 1 | 2 | 3 | 4 | 5 | 6 | 7 | 8 | 9 | 10 | 11 | 12 | 13 |

### 1B | Copy and Apply Ruler

Format
- Font...
- Paragraph...
- Tabs...
- Borders and Shading...
- Page Settings...
- Format Picture...

- Header
- Footer

- Copy Ruler
- Apply Ruler
- Copy Style
- Apply Style

Use the Copy Ruler and Apply Ruler commands to copy ruler settings (tabs, indents, alignment, and spacing) from one paragraph to one or more paragraphs in the same or a different document.

To copy ruler settings:

1. Position the insertion point anywhere in the paragraph that has the ruler settings you want to copy. From the Format menu, select Copy Ruler.

2. Select one or more paragraphs to which you want the ruler settings applied. From the Format menu, select Apply Ruler.

**Practice What You Have Learned**

1. Open the file *CD-U16L1Ruler*.

2. Copy the paragraph 1 ruler settings and apply them to paragraph 2. Verify that the paragraphs have the same left, right, and hanging indentations.

3. In paragraph 1:
   - Set the vertical line spacing to 2.5.
   - Change the hanging indent to a first line 0.5" indent.
   - Set the horizontal alignment to center.

4. Copy the ruler settings from paragraph 1 to paragraphs 3 and 4. Save as *U16L1Ruler*.

CD-U16L1Ruler

## 8C | New-Key Mastery

Key each line twice SS; DS between 2-line groups.

Abbreviations/initials
1  J. Hart and K. Jakes hired Lila J. Norton to sing.
2  Lt. Karen I. Lane took Lt. Jon O. Hall to the jet.

3rd row emphasis
3  I told her to take a look at the three large jets.
4  Iris had three of her oldest friends on the train.

Key words
5  if for the and old oak jet for oil has egg jar oar
6  told lake jade gold here noon tear soil goes fade;

Key phrases
7  and the|ask for|go to the|not so fast|if he|to see
8  If there is|to go to the|for the last|none of the;

All letters learned
9  Jodi and Kendra Jaeger are in the National finals.
10  Jason Lake did not take Jon Hoag for a train ride.

## 8D | Technique:  Space Bar and ENTER Key

1. Key each line twice SS; DS between 2-line groups.

2. Key the drill again at a faster pace if time permits.

1  Linda had fish.
2  Jan is on the train.
3  Nat took her to the lake.
4  He is here to see his friends.
5  Kathleen sold the large egg to her.
6  Kate and Jason hired her to do the roof.
7  Lane took all eight of the girls to the lake.

## Math Activities

**2F ▪ Math Challenge 13**

### FIND THE LOAN AMOUNT ON A SIMPLE INTEREST LOAN

1. Key a sentence to explain how you find the loan amount on a simple interest loan problem like this: *What is the loan amount if the interest is $30, the interest rate is 6%, and the time is 1 month?*

2. Find the loan amount for the following problems and key your answers in sentence form. For example, an appropriate sentence for the answer to the problem stated above is: *The loan amount on a loan that charges $30 interest at the rate of 6% for 1 month is $500.*

   2a. Interest amount is $200; interest rate is 5%; time is 2 years.

   2b. Interest amount is $6.25; interest rate is 5%; time is ½ year.

   2c. Interest amount is $3,000; interest rate is 6%; time is 20 years.

   2d. If Susie's three-month loan at 8% cost her $400 interest, how much did she borrow?

3. Save your answers as *U15L2Math*.

---

### Careers ..................

**2G ▪ Career Exploration Portfolio – Activity 13**

▪ You must complete Career Activities 1-3 before completing this activity.

1. Retrieve your Career folder and the information in it that relates to the three career clusters that you have chosen.

2. If your interests have changed as a result of completing the first 12 Career Exploration activities, identify the career cluster that is now your first choice, second choice, and third choice.

3. Using the career cluster that is now your first choice and the Internet, search for schools that you could attend after you are graduated from high school to pursue an occupation in this cluster. Write a paragraph or two describing what kind of school it is, where it is, the cost to enroll, whether it has resident students and/or commuter students, and other information that interests you. Print your file, save it as *U15L2Career13*, and keep it open.

4. Exchange papers with a classmate and have the classmate offer suggestions for improving the content and correcting any errors he or she finds in your paragraph(s). Make the changes that you agree with and print a copy to turn in to your instructor. Save your file as *U15L2Career13* and close it.

5. Return your folder to the storage area. When your instructor returns your paper, file it in your Career folder.

## 8E | Enrichment

1. Key each line once SS; DS between 3-line groups.
2. Rekey the drill at a faster pace if time permits.

### Technique Goals
- curved, upright fingers
- finger-action keystrokes
- quiet hands/arms
- out-and-down shifting

**Tip**

Keep your eyes on the copy except when you lose your place.

### Shifting

1 Kellee and I did see Jed and Jonathan at the lake.
2 Jane and Hal are going to London to see Joe Hanks.
3 Lee left for the lake at noon; Kenneth left later.

### Keying sentences

4 Jessie is going to talk to the girls for the kids.
5 Harold Lett took his friends to the train station.
6 Lon and Jen are going to see friends at the lodge.
7 Natasha and Hansel are taking the train to London.

For additional practice ▶ **MicroType** ✦ **Alphabetic Keyboarding** ✦ **Lesson 8**

## 2E | Speed Building

1. Key two 1' timings on each paragraph.
2. Key two 3' timings on paragraphs 1–3 combined; find *gwam*.

GWAM 3'

|  |  |
|---|---|
| Attitude is the way people communicate their feelings or | 3 / 72 |
| moods to others.  A person is said to have a positive attitude | 8 / 77 |
| when he or she anticipates successful experiences.  A person | 12 / 81 |
| such as this is said to be an optimist.  The best possible | 16 / 85 |
| outcomes are expected.  The world is viewed as a great place. | 20 / 89 |
| Good is found in even the worst situation. | 23 / 92 |
| Individuals are said to have negative attitudes when they | 26 / 95 |
| expect failure.  A pessimist is the name given to an individual | 31 / 100 |
| with a bad view of life.  Pessimists emphasize the adverse | 35 / 104 |
| aspects of life and expect the worst possible outcome.  They | 39 / 108 |
| expect to fail even before they start the day.  You can plan on | 43 / 112 |
| them to find gloom even in the best situation. | 46 / 115 |
| Only you can ascertain when you are going to have a good or | 50 / 119 |
| bad attitude.  Keep in mind that people are attracted to a | 54 / 123 |
| person with a good attitude and tend to shy away from one with a | 58 / 127 |
| bad attitude.  Your attitude quietly determines just how | 62 / 131 |
| successful you are in all your personal relationships as well as | 66 / 135 |
| in your professional relationships. | 69 / 138 |

GWAM 3' | 1 | 2 | 3 | 4 |

# LESSON 9

## OBJECTIVES

1. *To improve use of Space Bar, **Left Shift** key, and **ENTER (RETURN)** key.*
2. *To improve keying speed on words, phrases, and sentences.*

### Technique Goals

- curved, upright fingers
- low wrists, but not resting
- hands and arms steady

## 9A | Conditioning Practice

Key each line twice SS (slowly, then faster); DS between 2-line groups. If time permits, practice each line again.

Reach review 1   tft iki olo hjh gfg ede njn rfr njt frlo kide fgjh

Spacing 2   in of do at or and the ask jar oil hot get sir tea

Left Shift 3   I see the lake.  Jane took the fan.  Kent is here.

## 9B | Keyboard Mastery

Key each line twice SS; DS between 2-line groups.

h/e
1 share shell heard heart hello ahead death fishnet;
2 Hal left the fish in the old red shed at the lake.

i/r
3 fire risk ring tire iris ride iron hire heir right
4 Iris tried to hire Jason to fight the three fires.

o/t
5 toad toil told oath total other often token toilet
6 Jonathan told the others to take the toast to Lon.

n/g
7 gnat gang king gain grand linger ringing negligent
8 Jorge Lang sang a song to the king on the gondola.

Left Shift
9 Jake Lane; Hans Linton; Kate I. Jeter; Jan O. Nash
10 Karl left for Oregon.  Jan is engaged to Hal King.

## 2C | Speed Forcing Drill

Key each line once at top speed. Then try to complete each sentence on the 15", 12", or 10" call, as directed by your teacher. Force speed to higher levels as you move from line to line.

**Emphasis: high-frequency balanced-hand words**

| | | GWAM | 15" | 12" | 10" |
|---|---|---|---|---|---|
| 1 | The small ornament on their oak mantle is a whale. | | 40 | 50 | 60 |
| 2 | Ann is apt to yell when they cut down the big oak. | | 40 | 50 | 60 |
| 3 | Their box with the emblem of the duck is on the mantle. | | 44 | 55 | 66 |
| 4 | The city map may aid the six men when they do the work. | | 44 | 55 | 66 |
| 5 | Sign the forms for the firm to pay the girls for their work. | | 48 | 60 | 72 |
| 6 | The city official may make it to the big social at the lake. | | 48 | 60 | 72 |

★ *Language Arts*

## 2D Writing: Word Choice

Study the spelling and definitions of the following words. Key the Learn lines, noting the word choices. Key the Apply lines, selecting the correct words. Save as *U15L2Writing*.

**loose** (adjective)  not fixed tight; not restrained

**lose** (verb)  have pass from one's possession; be defeated in

Learn 1  Harry will **lose** the air in his tire if he has a **loose** valve.

Learn 2  They are more apt to **lose** the tug-of-war if they have a **loose** grip.

Apply 3  My cows are (loose, lose) and I may (loose, lose) them if I don't get them.

Apply 4  The hockey team does not expect to (loose, lose) on Saturday.

## 9C | Technique: Return

Key each line twice SS; DS between 2-line groups.

1 Jordan is here.

2 He left for Indiana.

3 Jared has the large jars.

4 Jessie said to take the shelf.

5 Jon left to take the girls to sing.

6 Jan left to take the rings to the girls.

**Technique Goals**

• **Reduce the pause between words.**

• **Reduce the time taken to shift/tap key/release when making capital letters.**

## 9D | Technique: Space Bar and Left Shift

Key each line twice SS; DS between 2-line groups.

**Down-and-in-spacing**

**Space Bar (Space immediately after each word.)**

1 do the and are not ask jet oil tea sea got had ton

2 salt frog jail knot tree dent lake gain this dress

3 to see|he is|ask her|of it|to go|for the|and it is

**Left Shift key (Shift; tap key; release both quickly.)**

4 Lee and Ida are in the den; Nathan is at the lake.

5 Lila took Jake to Lake Ontario to see Jon J. Kent.

6 Indiana lost to Illinois and Idaho lost to Oregon.

## OBJECTIVES

1. *To improve keying techniques.*
2. *To improve keying speed and control.*

**Technique Goals**
- curved, upright fingers
- quick-snap keystrokes
- quiet hands and arms

# SKILL BUILDING

### 2A | Conditioning Practice

Key each line twice SS; then key a 1' writing on line 3. Determine *gwam*.

| | | |
|---|---|---|
| Alphabet | 1 | Paul quickly indexed a dozen jokes for his big comedy act review. |
| Figures/Symbols | 2 | Policy (#321-04-5) paid me $29.67 interest and a $54.85 dividend. |
| Speed | 3 | My maid is to rush the antique bowl to the girls in the dorm. |

**GWAM** 1' | 1 | 2 | 3 | 4 | 5 | 6 | 7 | 8 | 9 | 10 | 11 | 12 | 13 |

### 2B | Technique:  Response Patterns

1. Key each line twice SS (slowly, then faster); DS between 2-line groups.
2. Take 1' timings on each even-numbered line.

| | | |
|---|---|---|
| Alphabet | 1 | zebra extra vicious dozen happen just quick forgot way limp exact |
| | 2 | Everyone except Meg and Joe passed the final weekly biology quiz. |
| Figures/Symbols | 3 | Account #2849 \| 10% down \| for $6,435.70 \| Lots #8 & #9 \| $250 deductible |
| | 4 | The fax machine (#387-291) is on sale for $364.50 until March 21. |
| Bottom Row | 5 | modem zebra extinct moving backbone moon vacate exam computerized |
| | 6 | Zeno's vaccine injection for smallpox can be given in six months. |
| Third row | 7 | you tip rip terror yet peer quit were pet tire terrier pepper out |
| | 8 | Our two terrier puppies were too little to take to your pet show. |
| Double letters | 9 | footnote scanner less process letters office cell suppress footer |
| | 10 | Jill, my office assistant, will process the four letters by noon. |
| Balanced hand | 11 | wish then turn us auto big eight down city busy end firm it goals |
| | 12 | If the firm pays for the social, the eight officials may also go. |
| Shift keys | 13 | The New York Times \|Gone with the Wind \|Chicago Tribune \|WordPerfect |
| | 14 | Alan L. Martin finished writing "Planning for Changing Technology." |
| Adjacent keys | 15 | were open top ask rest twenty point tree master merge option asks |
| | 16 | The sort option was well received by all three new group members. |
| Space Bar | 17 | it is fix and fox go key do by box men pen six so the to when big |
| | 18 | Did they use the right audit form to check the new city bus line? |

**GWAM** 1' | 1 | 2 | 3 | 4 | 5 | 6 | 7 | 8 | 9 | 10 | 11 | 12 | 13 |

## 9E | Speed Building

Key each line twice SS (slowly, then faster); DS between 2-line groups.

**Key words (Think, say, and key the words.)**

1 aid did end rod sit ten too for got off doe title;
2 held lake good fish food land sign also hand eight
3 risk girl odor shelf signs their aisle flake right

**Key phrases (Think, say, and key the phrases.)**

4 to the|dial the|half of the|if he is|an odor|is it
5 is it|for the|she is|go to the|good sign|it is the
6 to go to the|and for the|the lake is|held the fish

**Key sentences (Tap keys at a brisk, steady pace.)**

7 Kate said she has ten disks; all the disks are old.
8 Kristi has an old red dress that she does not like.
9 Jennifer and Jonathan are to sing three old songs.

**For additional practice** MicroType♦**Alphabetic Keyboarding♦Lesson 9**

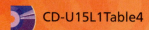
CD-U15L1Table4

**Table 4**

1. Open the data file *CD-U15L1Table4*.

2. Insert a row above row 9. Key **2 p.m.** in column 1 of this row.

3. Insert a row above row 1. Merge the cells in the row into one cell. Key **APPOINTMENT SCHEDULE** in row 1.

4. Apply a grid table format with borders around all cells.

5. Right-align column 1; center-align and bold all headings and the title. Center the table horizontally and vertically on the page.

6. Use Times New Roman, 10 point for all cells. Delete row 4 that begins with *8 a.m.*

7. Save as *U15L1Table4*.

**Letter with Table**

1. Key the following letter with a table that is to be printed on letterhead stationery. Use block format and mixed punctuation for the letter.

2. You decide all formatting features for the table, but it must be centered horizontally. Leave one blank line above and below the table.

3. Save as *U15L1Letter1*.

January 4, 20--

Ms. Janet Young
647 Main Street
Moorcroft, WY 82721-7514

Dear Ms. Young:

The values of your investments at the end of last year are given in the table below. The table also shows the values at the beginning of the year. The percent of change for the year is shown in the last column.

| Janet Young Portfolio | | | |
|---|---|---|---|
| Investment | Beginning of Year | End of Year | % of Change |
| EXS Growth | $25,678.92 | $29,123.56 | 13.41% |
| Landmark Mixed | $19,568.20 | $21,076.84 | 7.71% |
| Morris Foreign | $7,012.67 | $7,492.86 | 6.85% |
| Redbank Bond Fund | $45,690.00 | $48,362.90 | 5.85% |
| Totals | $97,949.79 | $106,056.16 | 8.28% |

Your growth fund had a very good year and the remaining funds did well. My suggestion is to "stay the course" for the coming year. I think that the foreign fund will have a strong year. Interest rates are expected to remain stable or go lower. This means the bond fund should continue to do well.

If you have any questions or need to discuss your portfolio, please do not hesitate to call me.

Sincerely,

Dick Herndon
Certified Financial Advisor

xx

# LESSON 10

## OBJECTIVE

*To learn reach technique for **u** and **c**.*

**u** Right index finger

**c** Left middle finger

### 10A | Conditioning Practice

Key each line twice SS (slowly, then faster); DS between 2-line groups.

Reach review 1  hjh tft njn gfg iki .l. ede olo rfr it go no or hi

Space Bar 2  so ask let jet his got ink are and the kid off did

Left Shift 3  Jason and I looked for Janet and Kate at the lake.

### 10B | New Keys: u and c

Key each line twice SS (slowly, then faster); DS between 2-line groups. If time permits, repeat lines 7–9.

Follow the *Plan for Learning New Keys* outlined on page 12.

**Learn u**

1  j u|juj juj|uju uju|us us|due due|jug jug|sun sun;

2  suit suit|dusk dusk|four four|fund fund|huge huge;

3  just for fun; under the rug; unusual fur; found us

**Learn c**

4  d c|dcd dcd|act act|cash cash|card card|ache ache;

5  Jack Jack|sack sack|lock lock|calf calf|rock rock;

6  acted sick; tic toc goes the clock; catch the cat;

**Combine u and c**

7  duck duck|accuse accuse|cruel cruel|actual actual;

8  crucial account; cute cousin; chunk of ice; juice;

9  such success; rustic church; no luck; count truck

**Table 2**

1. Key the following table. Make each column 1" wide.

2. Center the title in ALL CAPS and bold above the table. Use a 12-point font for the title and for the rest of the table.

3. Center-align the entries in columns 1–3 and left-align column 4. Use bold and center alignment for the column heads.

4. Apply a 1½-point, black, single-line border to all sides of all cells. Center the table vertically and horizontally. Save as *U15L1Table2*.

### FRACTION & DECIMAL EQUIVALENTS

| 4ths | 8ths | 16ths | Decimal |
|:---:|:---:|:---:|:---|
|  |  | 1 | 0.0625 |
|  | 1 | 2 | 0.125 |
|  |  | 3 | 0.1875 |
| 1 | 2 | 4 | 0.25 |
|  |  | 5 | .3125 |
|  | 3 | 6 | 0.375 |
|  |  | 7 | 0.4375 |
| 2 | 4 | 8 | 0.5 |

**Table 3**

1. Key the following table. Format column 1 to 1.25" wide and columns 2–6 to 1" wide. Merge cells as shown.

2. Use a 12-point font for the title and rest of the table.

3. Left-align column 1. Right-align the other columns. Use a .25" hanging indent in column 1. Right-align *Totals* in row 9. Use center alignment and bold for all headings and the title.

4. Apply a ¾-point, black, single-line border around all cells. Apply shading to rows 3 and 6. Use 10% fill, black foreground, and white background for the shading.

5. Center the table vertically and horizontally. Save as *U15L1Table3*.

| TOP FUNDRAISERS | | | | |
|:---|:---:|:---:|:---:|:---:|
| **Student** | **March** | **April** | **May** | **Total** |
| **Sophomore Class** | | | | |
| Singleton Elizabeth | $525 | $510 | $893 | $1,928 |
| Kitterman Alexander | $475 | $457 | $614 | $1,546 |
| **Junior Class** | | | | |
| Gethsemane Constance | $513 | $627 | $739 | $1,879 |
| Biddlestone Christopher | $458 | $761 | $568 | $1,787 |
| Totals | $1,971 | $2,355 | $2,814 | $7,140 |

## 10C | New-Key Mastery

Key each line twice SS; DS between 2-line groups.

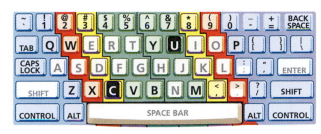

**3rd/1st rows**
1 run car nut nice cute noon touch other clean truck
2 Lincoln coin; strike three; cut the cards; four or
3 Jack and Nicholas are going to Otter Lake in Ohio.
4 Lucille took a truck to Ohio.  Janet sold her car.

**Key words**
5 call fund kind race neck golf half just toil lunch
6 cause guide hotel feast alike joins; laugh; judge;

**Key phrases**
7 if she can|he can do the|it is the|and then|all of
8 till the end|tie the knot|faster than|a little red

**All keys learned**
9 Either Jack or Lance said the four girls are here.
10 Hugh likes to run on the lakefront; Jack does not.

## 10D | Technique:  Space Bar and Left Shift

Key each line twice SS; DS between 2-line groups.

### Space Bar

1 Lucas asked the girls to get the dogs at the lake.
2 Lance said he can go to Oregon to get the old car.
3 Janice and her three dogs ran along the shoreline.

### Left Shift

4 Jack and Joe Kern just left to go to Lake Ontario.
5 Jo thinks it takes less than an hour to get there.
6 Kanosh and Joliet are cities in Utah and Illinois.

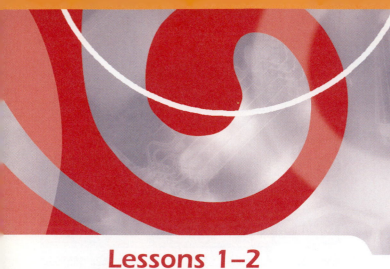

# Unit 15
## Assess Tables and Build Skill

**Lessons 1–2**

**LESSON**

# 1

## OBJECTIVE

*To assess your ability to prepare tables.*

### 1A | Conditioning Practice

Key each line twice SS; then key a 1' writing on line 3. Determine *gwam*.

Alphabet 1  If they study, Kami and Jeb expect high scores on every law quiz.

Figures 2  Rooms 1398 and 2076 were used for the 7:45 p.m. parents' meeting.

Speed 3  The six men in the red bus may go to the downtown chapel with me.

**GWAM** 1' | 1 | 2 | 3 | 4 | 5 | 6 | 7 | 8 | 9 | 10 | 11 | 12 | 13 |

### 1B | Tables

**Table 1**

1. Create the table shown below. Format column 1 to 1.75" wide and columns 2–4 to 1" wide.

2. Center the title in ALL CAPS. Use a 16-point font and bold for the title. Use a 12-point font for the rest of the table. Left-align the entries in column 1. Center-align the entries in columns 2–4.

3. Center the table vertically and horizontally on the page. Save as *U15L1Table1*.

### GAME STATISTICS FOR NOEL FORD

| Opponent | Tackles | For Loss | Sacks |
|---|---|---|---|
| James Madison | 5 | 2 | 1 |
| Woodward | 6 | 2 | 3 |
| Jennings | 5 | 3 | 2 |
| East Ford | 5 | 3 | 1 |
| Jones Mill | 4 | 1 | 1 |
| South Harris | 7 | 4 | 3 |
| Mapleton | 6 | 2 | 2 |
| Sussex | 8 | 3 | 4 |
| Totals | 46 | 20 | 17 |

**Tip**

Try to reduce hand movement and the tendency of unused fingers to fly out or follow the reaching finger.

Key each line twice SS; DS between 2-line groups.

**u/c**

1 cut luck such cuff lunch crush touch torch justice
2 Okichi Kinura had juice.  Lucius caught the judge.

**n/g**

3 gone ring fang long eggnog length; sing sang song;
4 Glen thinks Glenda Leung can sing the eight songs.

**Left Shift**

5 Julian and Hector left a note for Leticia Herrera.
6 Juan and Luisa took Jorge and Leonor to the dance.

**All keys learned**

7 Jack Lefstad said to take the road through Oregon.
8 Janet and Linda caught eight fish in Lake Ontario.

For additional practice MicroType + Alphabetic Keyboarding + Lesson 10

### Job 10 • December 6

Dr. Newton was very pleased with the report you prepared. She was impressed with the number of students involved and the amount of money raised. She suggested that you write a thank-you letter to the businesses that participated. Compose a letter for her to sign. Some information that you should include in your letter follows. Save your letter.

- Thank the business for participating in Ridge School's fundraising project for Carrie Lewis.

- State how the funds will be used and where they were deposited.

- Give the total amount raised and mention how many students and businesses were involved in the project.

- Express a desire to involve the business in future school projects in which students learn the importance of providing service to others or the community.

### Job 11 • December 7

Dr. Newton has informed Ms. Johnson that the school assembly is going to be held on December 17 at 1:15 p.m. in the school auditorium. At the beginning of the assembly, the principal, Ms. Johnson, and you will present a check for $1,743.25 to the Lewis family. A reporter from your local newspaper has been invited.

Compose a letter for Principal Newton (see Job 5 for her name, degree, and title) inviting Carrie and her parents to the assembly. Be sure to tell them the purpose of the invitation and other important details they need to know to make arrangements to attend. Be sure to have them telephone Ms. Johnson at 951-555-0168 or e-mail her at ljohnson@ridge.net to inform her how many family members will be attending.

Carrie's father is Henry and her mother is Ida. They live at 2010 Rosewood Place, Riverside, CA 92506-6528. Save your letter.

© BLEND IMAGES

## LESSON
# 11

### OBJECTIVE

*To learn reach technique for **w** and **Right Shift**.*

**w** Left ring finger

---

### Tip

1. Hold down the Right Shift key with the little finger on the right hand.

2. Tap the letter with the finger on the left hand.

3. Return finger(s) to home key.

---

**Right Shift** Right little finger

---

### 11A | Conditioning Practice

Key each line twice SS (slowly, then faster); DS between 2-line groups.

Reach review 1  jn de ju fg ki ft lo dc fr l. jtn ft. cde hjg uet.

u/c 2  cut cue duck luck cute success accuse juice secure

All keys learned 3  Jake and Lincoln sold us eight large ears of corn.

### 11B | New Keys:  w and Right Shift

Key each line twice SS (slowly, then faster); DS between 2-line groups.  If time permits, repeat lines 7–9.

Follow the *Plan for Learning New Keys* outlined on page 12.

**Learn w**

1  s w sw sw|we we|saw saw|who who|wet wet|show show;

2  will will|wash wash|work work|down down|gown gown;

3  white gown; when will we; wash what; walk with us;

**Learn Right Shift Key**

4  ;A ;A;|Al; Al;|Dan; Dan;|Gina; Gina;|Frank; Frank;

5  Don saw Seth Green and Alfonso Garcia last August.

6  Trish Fuentes and Carlos Delgado left for Atlanta.

**Combine w and Right Shift**

7  Will Wenner went to show the Wilsons the two cars.

8  Wes and Wade want to know who will work this week.

9  Willard West will take Akiko Tanaka to Washington.

The Project

The students agreed to place collection cans in ~~local~~ businesses for (4) [sp]
weeks. A student ~~will be~~ [was] assigned to each business to get permission to
place the cans and to collect the donations each week. All cans were
removed at the end of November. All money collected was put in an account
at National Trust Bank. Only Ms. Johnson has the authority to make
deposits and with drawals.

The Participants

(Insert your name here) served as the leader of the project and these
six students served as co-captains of student teams. Each team had three
students plus a co-captain. The co-captains and team members are listed in
the table below.

| Carrie Lewis Fundraising Participants | | | |
|---|---|---|---|
| Co-captain | Team Members | | |
| Joe Brown | Zakir Shaheed | Donna Matessi | Christine Cheripka |
| Mary Kite | Jennifer Rey | Charles John | Camerica Quan |
| Lou Forde | Renny Varghese | David Ziran | Juan Vardez |
| Sue Rouse | Brian Dodd | Robin Alwine | Andy Glover |
| Jerry Blair | Keith Ardash | Aida Varner | Sharon Pratt |
| Greta Veri | Kathie Kredel | Gregg Oslosky | Betty Konchock |

The Results

As the table below shows, $1,743.25 was raised during the four
weeks. Joe Brown's team collected the most money. Individually, Donna
Matessi collected the most. Others raising the highest amount for the
team and the businesses where collections were highest for each team
are reported in the table below. The member of each team who collected
the most will receive $5 gift certificates that were donated by Pizza
Palace.

(Insert Table U14J8 here)

The money collected will be given to the Lewis family before the
end of December. Carrie and her parents will be invited to a school
assembly and will be presented with a check for $1,743.25.

## Technique Goals

- quick finger-action reaches
- quiet hands and arms
- eyes on copy

**Tip**

Key at a steady pace; space quickly after each word.

**Tip**

Do not space after an internal period in an abbreviation.

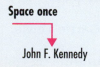

| **No space** |
| Ed.D. |

Space once after a period following initials.

| **Space once** |
| John F. Kennedy |

## 11C | New-Key Mastery

Key each line twice SS; DS between 2-line groups.

w and Right Shift
1  Alaska; Wisconsin; Georgia; Florida; South Dakota;
2  Dr. Wick will work the two weekends for Dr. Woods.

n/g
3  eight or nine|sing the songs again|long length of;
4  Dr. Wong arranged the song for singers in Lansing.

Key words
5  wet fun ask hot jar cot got use oil add run are of
6  card nice hold gnaw join knew face stew four feat;

Key phrases
7  will see|it is the|as it is|did go|when will|if it
8  I will|where is the|when can|use it|and the|of the

All keys learned
9  Nikko Rodgers was the last one to see Jack Fuller.
10  Alfonso Garcia and I took Taisuke Johns to Newark.

## 11D | Technique:  Spacing with Punctuation

Key each line once DS.

1  Ron F. Cano used ck. for check and cr. for credit.
2  Dr. West said to use wt. for weight; in. for inch.
3  Jason F. Russell used rd. for road in the address.
4  Dr. Tejada got her Ed.D. degree at Colorado State.

**Job 8 • December 3**

You have received the Record of Collections forms prepared by the co-captains. Your handwritten table uses data from that table to show the information you want to announce.

1. Create a table for the information shown. Merge cells as needed.

2. Insert a Totals row at the bottom and report the total for each dollar column. Align the dollar amounts with a decimal tab.

3. Format the table attractively and center it on the page.

4. Save the table.

| CARRIE LEWIS FUNDRAISING RESULTS | | | | |
|---|---|---|---|---|
| Co-captain | Amount Team Raised | Highest Amount Raised | | |
| | | Amount | Team Member | Business |
| Jerry Blair | $245.17 | $101.65 | Aida Varner | Stefano Convenience Store |
| Joe Brown | $332.87 | $145.45 | Donna Matessi | Better Home Center |
| Lou Forde | $317.59 | $133.59 | David Ziran | Mama Leone's Pizza |
| Mary Kite | $287.45 | $122.56 | Charles John | Designs by Deanna |
| Sue Rouse | $265.13 | $105.67 | Robin Alwine | Parkview Credit Union |
| Greta Veri | $295.04 | $117.45 | Betty Konchock | Lake Vue Restaurant |

**Job 9 • December 4**

The collections phase of the fundraising project is complete. Ms. Johnson has requested that you create a report to describe the project and its results. The report will be given to Ms. Johnson, Dr. Newton, and the students who were involved with the project.

1. Format the information in standard report format.

2. Insert the table you prepared in Job 8 where indicated. You can use the Copy/Paste command to place the table in the report. Change the font and font size to match the first table in the report.

3. Save the report.

CARRIE LEWIS FUNDRAISING RESULTS

Twenty-one students volunteered in early October to participate in a service project to raise funds to help pay the medical bills for Carrie Lewis. Carrie is the sister of Dean Lewis, a classmate of ours. The ~~fundraising~~ project was approved in early October and completed in ~~late~~ December. Ms. Johnson, our teacher, agreed to supervise the project, and Dr. Newton, our principal, approved it.

*(continued)*

**Position Reminder**

As you key each line:

• Keep hands/arms steady.

• Use finger-action keystrokes.

• Keep unused fingers curved, upright over home keys.

• Keep your eyes on the copy.

© FRANKSITEMAN.COM 2007

## 11E | Enrichment

1. Key each pair of lines once SS.

2. Key each even-numbered line again to increase speed.

**u/c**

  1  cute luck duck dock cure junk clue just cuff ulcer

  2  Luci could see the four cute ducks on the counter.

**w and Right Shift**

  3  Wade and Will; Don W. Wilson and Frank W. Watkins.

  4  Dr. Wise will set the wrist of Sgt. Walsh at noon.

**Left Shift and .**

  5  Julio N. Ortega|Julia I. Santiago|Carlos L. Sillas

  6  Lt. Lou Jordan and Lt. Jan Lee left for St. Louis.

**n/g**

  7  gain gown ring long range green grind groan angle;

  8  Last night Angie Nagai was walking along the road.

**o/t**

  9  foot other tough total tooth outlet outfit notice;

 10  Todd took the two toddlers towards the other road.

For additional practice **MicroType** ✦ **Alphabetic Keyboarding** ✦ **Lesson 11**

**Job 6 • October 20**

You decide to prepare a table to record the collections as they are tallied at the end of each week.

1. Create a table as shown below. Include all the businesses involved in the project in column 1 (see Job 4).

2. Format column 1 to 2.5" and the remaining columns to 0.75".

3. Merge and align cell entries as shown. You decide all other formatting features to make the information easy to read.

4. Save the table.

| RECORD OF COLLECTIONS | | | | | |
|---|---|---|---|---|---|
| Business | Amount Collected | | | | |
| | Week 1 | Week 2 | Week 3 | Week 4 | Total |
| China Buffet | | | | | |
| Lake Vue Restaurant | | | | | |
| Monticello Savings and Loan | | | | | |
| | | | | | |

**Job 7 • October 22**

You decide to send a copy of the table (created in Job 6) to the co-captains. They will use the table to record the amount of money collected at their respective businesses. Key a final copy of the following memo to send with the table. Save the memo.

TO:          Co-captains

FROM:        (Student Name)

DATE:        October 22, 20--

SUBJECT:     RECORD OF COLLECTIONS FORM

Please use the enclosed form to record the amount of money your team members collect at each business. Remind your team members to make their collections weekly and to give the money to you.

Record the amount by store on the form. Then give the money collected and a completed form for the week to Ms. Johnson. Thank you for helping make this project a success.

Enclosures: Four copies of Record of Collections form

## LESSON 12

### OBJECTIVE

*To learn reach technique for **b** and **y**.*

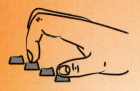

**Fingers curved**

### 12A | Conditioning Practice

Key each line twice SS.

Reach review 1   sw ju ft fr ki dc lo .l jh fg ce un jn o. de gu hw

c/n 2   cent neck dance count clean niece concert neglect;

All letters learned 3   Jack and Trish counted the students on the risers.

### 12B | Technique: ENTER Key

1. Key each line twice SS; at the end of each line quickly tap the ENTER key and immediately start new line.

2. On line 6, see how many standard words you can key in 30 seconds (30"). (See Standard Word at the left.)

1   Jan left Ken at the lake.
2   Justin said she will be there.
3   Ashton could see the thin red line.
4   Sarah cooked lunch for all of the girls.
5   Jose told us to take his new car to the lake.
6   Glenda took the left turn at the fork in the road.

**GWAM** 1' |   1   |   2   |   3   |   4   |   5   |   6   |   7   |   8   |   9   |   10   |

### Standard Word

A *standard word* in keyboarding is five characters or any combination of five characters and spaces, as indicated by the number scale under line 6. The number of standard words keyed in 1' is called gross words a minute (*gwam*).

### Job 4 • October 15

You need to key the names of the co-captains and team members in the table you created in Job 2. You took notes at the meeting using the table you created earlier. Your notes show the co-captain and team members assigned to each business. Businesses that will not be used are marked *Delete*. Businesses to be added are listed below the table.

 CD-U14J4

1. Open and print the file *CD-U14J4*, which contains the table and the names of the co-captains and team members you wrote at the meeting.

2. Create an attractive table with merged cells that lets the reader quickly see each co-captain and his/her team members. Center the table on the page. You decide all other formatting features.

3. Save the table.

### Job 5 • October 16

Ms. Johnson has received a handwritten draft of a letter from the principal. Each team member must give this letter to a responsible person at each business. Format the letter to be printed on school letterhead stationery. Dr. Newton will sign it. The letter should be available for you to give to your co-captains on October 18. Because there is no letter address, vertically center the letter on the page. Use a 14-point font. Save the letter.

October 18, 20--

Dear Member of the Business Community:

Your help is needed with a school service project. Students from Ridge School are seeking donations to help pay medical expenses for Carrie Lewis. Carrie is a student at Ridge School. She was seriously injured in an accident recently.

You can help by allowing students to place a donation container in your business. The student assigned to your business will collect the donations at the end of each week.

The project will end on November 31. Please contact Ms. Lori Johnson if you have any questions about the project. She is the teacher who is supervising this service project. Her telephone number is 951-555-0168, and her e-mail is ljohnson@ridge.net.

Thank you for helping our students in this worthwhile endeavor. Learning to help others is an important lesson for students.

Sincerely,

Patricia Newton, Ed.D.
Principal

**Note:**

If you are using *MicroType* software, you can use the Timer feature. Instructions are given on page 44.

**To find 1-minute (1') *gwam*:**

1. Note on the scale the number beneath the last word you keyed. That is your 1' *gwam* if you key the line partially or only once.

2. If you completed the line once and started over, add the number determined in step 1 to the number 10. The resulting number is your 1' *gwam*.

**To find 30-second (30") *gwam*:**

1. Find 1' *gwam* (total words keyed).

2. Multiply 1' *gwam* by 2. The resulting number is your 30" *gwam*.

## 12C | New Keys: b and y

Key each line twice SS (slowly, then faster); DS between 2-line groups. If time permits, rekey lines 7–9.

Follow the *Plan for Learning New Keys* outlined on page 12.

### Learn b

1   f b fb fb|fob fob|tub tub|bug bug|bat bat|bus bus;
2   bfb bfb|boat boat|boot boot|jobs jobs|habit habit;
3   blue bus; big bat; brown table; a bug; big hubbub;

### Learn y

4   j y jy jy|yet yet|eye eye|dye dye|say say|day day;
5   yjy yjy|yell yell|stay stay|easy easy|style style;
6   Sunday or Friday; buy or bye; fly away; any jockey

### Combine b and y

7   by by|baby baby|bury bury|lobby lobby|gabby gabby;
8   bay bridge|blue eyes|busy body|noisy boys|baby toy
9   Tabby and Barry had a baby boy with big blue eyes.

GWAM 1'|  1  |  2  |  3  |  4  |  5  |  6  |  7  |  8  |  9  |  10  |

**b** Left index finger

**y** Right index finger

### Job 1 • October 7

Ms. Johnson has prepared a handwritten list of twenty or so local businesses that have a high volume of customers from the community. You will key these names in the last two columns of a table.

CD-U4J1

1. Open and print the data file *CD-U14J1*, which contains the names and locations.

2. Create a table that has four columns and 25 rows. Make column 1 1", columns 2 and 3 1.5", and column 4 2". Key the names and locations in the last two columns of the table. Key appropriate column headings. List the names in alphabetical order by the business name. Leave the first two columns blank for the moment.

3. Format the table attractively by using a table format.

4. Save the table.

### Job 2 • October 10

Ms. Johnson has reviewed your draft of a memo you plan to send to the co-captains. Her revisions follow. The table you will create in Job 3 is the enclosure. Prepare a final copy of the memo.

TO:  Co-captains

FROM:  (Insert Your Name)

DATE:  October 10, 20--

SUBJECT:  Selection of Businesses and Assignments

All co-captains and I will meet on October 14 at 2:45 p.m. in Ms. Johnson's room. We will identify the businesses we ~~want to~~ *will* use as fund raising sites. We will also decide which co-captain and team member will work with each business. A tentative list of businesses is enclosed. Please review it.  List the name and street address of any business you ~~feel~~ *think* should be added at the bottom of the page.  *Delete* ~~Cross out~~ any of the businesses I listed that you do not believe should be used in our fundraising activity. Be prepared to select three businesses for your team at the meeting. We must finalize our list and assignments at the meeting.

Enclosure

### Job 3 • October 10

You need to complete the table of the businesses you created in Job 1 so you can enclose it with the memo Ms. Johnson returned to you. You need to revise it so you can write in the names of the co-captains and team members at the meeting.

1. Open the table you created in Job 1. Key **Co-captain** as the column 1 heading and **Team Member** as the column 2 heading.

2. Insert a row above row 1 and key **CO-CAPTAIN AND TEAM MEMBER ASSIGNMENTS BY LOCATION**.

3. Save the revised table.

## 12D | Technique: Space Bar

Key each line once.

1  Bobby took us to the lake to see the new ski show.
2  Bo will take the test when he gets back to school.
3  Anne will see her son after the first of the week.
4  Chad left his horn on the chair by the front door.

## 12E | New-Key Mastery

1. Key each line twice SS; DS between 2-line groups.
2. Key the lines again at a faster pace.

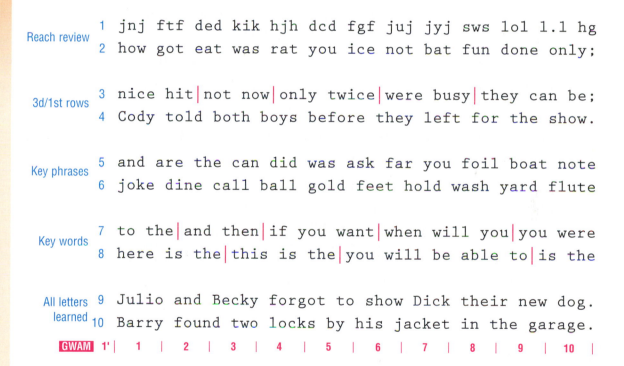

Reach review
1  jnj ftf ded kik hjh dcd fgf juj jyj sws lol 1.1 hg
2  how got eat was rat you ice not bat fun done only;

3d/1st rows
3  nice hit|not now|only twice|were busy|they can be;
4  Cody told both boys before they left for the show.

Key phrases
5  and are the can did was ask far you foil boat note
6  joke dine call ball gold feet hold wash yard flute

Key words
7  to the|and then|if you want|when will you|you were
8  here is the|this is the|you will be able to|is the

All letters learned
9   Julio and Becky forgot to show Dick their new dog.
10  Barry found two locks by his jacket in the garage.

GWAM  1' |  1  |  2  |  3  |  4  |  5  |  6  |  7  |  8  |  9  |  10 |

# Unit 14

## Project 2—Carrie Lewis Fundraising

**Lessons 1–2**

## LESSONS

# 1–2

### OBJECTIVES

1. *To format tables, memos or e-mail messages, business letters, and reports.*

2. *To make appropriate formatting decisions and follow instructions.*

3. *To use previously learned word processing commands, particularly those used to create tables.*

### 1-2A | Conditioning Practice

Complete this drill each day that you work on Project 2. Key each line twice SS. Then key a 1' timed writing on line 3; determine *gwam*.

Alphabet 1   The very quick jaunt to the new frog zoo was excluded by my pals.

Figures 2   Call 555-0179 by 12:45 p.m. to arrange the meeting for 11:30 a.m.

Speed 3   Their neighbor by the island may pay Sue for the giant ivory pan.

GWAM 1' | 1 | 2 | 3 | 4 | 5 | 6 | 7 | 8 | 9 | 10 | 11 | 12 | 13 |

### 1-2B | Project 2

#### Project Assignment

Assume that you are the leader of a fundraising project. The purpose of the project is to help pay medical expenses for Carrie Lewis, the sister of one of your classmates. Carrie was seriously injured in an accident. Your teacher, Ms. Lori Johnson, agrees to supervise the project. You and six co-captains who report to you decide to raise funds by placing donation containers in local businesses.

The project will take about eight weeks, and the ten jobs in this unit fall within that time frame. Use the month and day shown and the current year for each job. (You will actually complete the jobs in two or three class periods.)

You will provide leadership for the project by working with co-captains of three teams of students and your teacher. You will design and prepare documents that are needed for the project. Follow all instructions and apply what you have learned in your keyboarding and word processing class to complete the jobs.

Use block format with mixed punctuation for letters. Assume the letters will be printed on school letterhead stationery. Use the standard format you have learned for memos. All tables should be centered horizontally and vertically on the page, unless they are part of a larger document such as a report.

If you have access to e-mail, your teacher may instruct you to send e-mail messages rather than memos. Name all the files you create with *U14J* and the job number (*U14J1, U14J2,* etc.).

# MicroType
## Word Processing
### Timer Feature

Use the Timer feature when you key timed writings. The Timer "counts down" the amount of time you indicate and displays the timing results.

## MicroType
### TIP

Click the Timer button to access the Timer feature quickly.

## 12F | Timer Feature

**Learn to Use the Word Processing Timer Feature**

To use the word processing Timer:

1. Open the Word Processor in *MicroType 4*.

2. Click Edit on the menu bar. Click Timer. The Timer dialog box appears.

3. Click the Count-down timer option if it is not already selected.

4. Click the desired time or key a time in the Variable minutes or seconds box. Click OK.

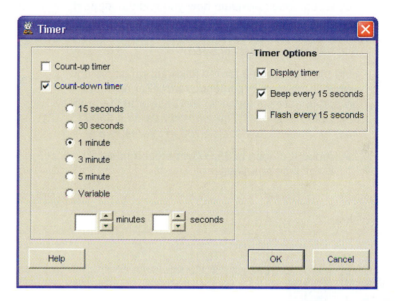

5. Notice that the time indicated in the Timer dialog box appears on the lower-right corner of the screen and counts down during the timing.

**Practice What You Have Learned**

1. Access the Timer feature.

2. Set the Timer for 30 seconds.

3. Key the drill lines of **12D** until the time elapses.

4. Review the Timing Results box and click OK to close the box.

5. Close the document without saving.

For additional practice ▶ MicroType + Alphabetic Keyboarding + Lesson 12

## Math Activities

### 4H ▪ Math Challenge 12

## FIND THE INTEREST RATE ON A SIMPLE INTEREST LOAN

1. Key a sentence to explain how you find the interest rate on a simple interest loan problem like this: *What is the interest rate on a $500 loan for 3 years that has interest costs of $180?*

2. Find the interest rate for the following problems and key your answers in sentence form. For example, an appropriate sentence for the answer to the problem stated above is: *The interest rate on a $500 loan for 3 years that costs $180 in interest is 6%.*

   2a. Amount of loan is $5,000; interest amount is $200; time is ½ year.

   2b. Amount of loan is $2,500; interest amount is $750; time is 3 years.

   2c. Amount of loan is $600; interest amount is $4; time is 1 month.

   2d. If the interest on a $15,000 loan for 2 years is $2,100, what is the interest rate?

3. Save your answers as *U13L4Math*.

## Careers ...........

### 4I ▪ Career Exploration Portfolio – Activity 12

▪ You must complete Career Activities 1-3 before completing this activity.

1. Retrieve your Career folder and the information in it that relates to the career cluster that is your third choice.

2. Use the Internet to search for the education that is recommended for occupations in this career cluster and then compose a paragraph or two explaining what you have learned. Print your file and then save it as *U13L4Career12* and keep it open.

3. Exchange papers with a classmate and have the classmate offer suggestions for improving the content and correcting any errors he or she finds in your paragraph(s). Make the changes that you agree with and print a copy to turn in to your instructor. Save your file as *U13L4Career12* and close the file.

4. Return your folder to the storage area. When your instructor returns your paper, file it in your Career folder.

# LESSON 13

## OBJECTIVES

1. *To improve use of* **Space Bar, Left** *and* **Right Shift keys,** *and* **ENTER** *key.*
2. *To improve keying speed on words, phrases, and sentences.*

### Position Reminder

**Before you begin each lesson:**

- Position your body directly in front of the keyboard; sit erect, with feet on the floor.
- Curve your fingers deeply and place them in an upright position over the home keys.
- Position the textbook for easy reading.

**Proper keying position**

### Technique Goals

- Reduce the pause between words.
- Reduce the time taken to shift/tap key/release when making capital letters.

### 13A | Conditioning Practice

Key each line twice SS (slowly, then faster); DS between 2-line groups. If time permits, practice each line again.

Reach review 1  bet run ice now boy hit oil you the grin were race

b/y 2  buy boy bay say big toy bag yes bug eye bear baby;

Shift keys 3  Dr. Barton got his Ed.D. at Utah State in English.

### 13B | Technique: Space Bar and Left Shift

Key each line twice SS; DS between 2-line groups.

**Down-and-in-spacing**

**Out-and-down shifting**

**Space Bar (Space immediately after each word.)**

1  it is to be he go of if no at as in on ice and the
2  when card nice back hand joke tear yard used again
3  to find|all day|if it is|the end|be able|to see it
4  she will be|as you can|if you are|when will you be

**Shift keys (Shift; tap key; release both quickly.)**

5  J. R. Reyes will be in Kansas on Friday or Sunday.
6  Dr. Rios went to Boston in June and again in July.
7  Jay toured Sweden and Norway during June and July.
8  Ken Norris and Clark Barns were in Salt Lake City.

© FRANKSITEMAN.COM 2007

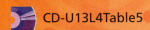

CD-U13L4Table5

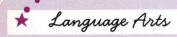

## 4E | Extend Table Formatting Skills

1. Open the file *CD-U13L4Table5*. Read the MicroType Tip at the left.

2. Select the cells in column 1, rows 3–5. Set a .25" hanging indent for these cells.

3. Select the cells in column 2, rows 3–5. Set a .25" first-line paragraph indentation for these cells.

4. Select the cells in column 3, rows 3–5. Set a decimal tab at .75" in these three cells to align the numbers at the decimal points. Save as *U13L4Table5*.

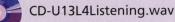

★ *Language Arts*

## 4F Writing: Number Expression

Read the following number usage rule. Key the Learn lines, noting number choices. Key the Apply lines, making the necessary corrections. Save as *U13L4Writing*.

**Rule 7:** Capitalize nouns preceding numbers (except *page* and *line*), and use figures for numbers that follow nouns.

Learn 1   I believe line 4 on page 16 of Chapter 2 has a punctuation error.

Learn 2   Her office is in Suite 400 of Schneider Hall.

Apply 3   You should go to room five of Davies Center.

Apply 4   Dr. Smith's article is in volume one of the BE Forum.

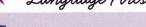

★ *Language Arts*

CD-U13L4Listening.wav

## 4G Listening: Mental Math

1. Open the sound file *CD-U13L4Listening.wav*. It contains three mental math problems.

2. Each problem starts with a number followed by several addition, subtraction, multiplication, and division steps. Key or handwrite the new answer after each step, but compute the answer mentally.

3. Record the last answer for each problem. After you listen to Problem 3, close the file.

4. Check the accuracy of your work with your instructor. If you made an error, repeat the activity.

- curved, upright fingers
- quiet hands/arms
- quick spacing—no pause between words
- finger-reach action to Shift keys

**Goal**

At least 15 *gwam.*

## 13C | Speed Building

Key each line twice SS (slowly, then faster); DS between 2-line groups.

**Key words (Think, say, and key the words.)**

1 if but sir and oak the for row dog she rug key did
2 lake owns with rush turn when worn city busy chair
3 also hall disk eight goals fight shake world their

**Key phrases (Think, say, and key the phrases.)**

4 in the│it can be│you will see│if there is│when can
5 when you are│he will do the│to go to the│and it is
6 when will you│she can take the│it is not│they will

**Key sentences (Tap keys at a brisk, steady pace.)**

7 Justin took the coat to the cleaners on Wednesday.
8 Nancy can ride the horse to the lake with Willard.
9 Jose and Julia took both of the boys to the store.

## 13D | Speed Check

1. Key each line once DS.

2. Key a 20" timed writing on each line. If you finish a line, tap ENTER and key it again. Your *gwam* rate is shown word for word above the lines.

3. Key another 20" writing on each line. Try to increase your keying speed.

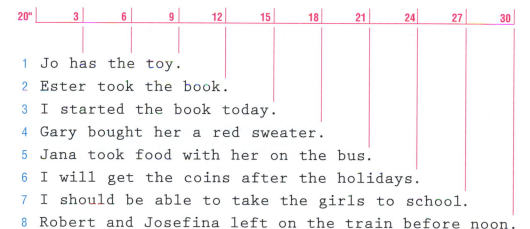

| 20" | 3 | 6 | 9 | 12 | 15 | 18 | 21 | 24 | 27 | 30 |

1 Jo has the toy.
2 Ester took the book.
3 I started the book today.
4 Gary bought her a red sweater.
5 Jana took food with her on the bus.
6 I will get the coins after the holidays.
7 I should be able to take the girls to school.
8 Robert and Josefina left on the train before noon.

## 4D | Tables

### Letter with Table

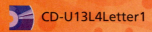

CD-U13L4Letter1

1. Open the file *CD-U13L4Letter1*. Read the business letter.

2. Create the following table, placing it where indicated in the letter. Leave one blank line above and one blank line below the table. Choose and apply formatting features to include borders and shading in the table.

| CENTURY COLLEGE School of Applied Sciences | | | | |
|---|---|---|---|---|
| Program | Students Enrolled | | | |
| | This Year | | Last Year | |
| | Females | Males | Females | Males |
| Actuarial Sciences | 10 | 14 | 12 | 11 |
| Operations Management | 33 | 28 | 37 | 30 |
| Sport Management | 56 | 54 | 50 | 62 |
| Health Services Management | 27 | 31 | 32 | 35 |
| Logistics Engineering | 12 | 10 | 14 | 14 |
| Software Engineering | 22 | 24 | 20 | 26 |
| Applied Math | 14 | 16 | 10 | 12 |

3. Delete *(Place table here.)* Center the table horizontally on the page. Save as *U13L4Letter1*.

### Table

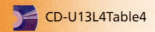

CD-U13L4Table4

1. Open the file *CD-U13L4Table4*. Delete column 9.

2. Insert the statistics for Juan Tajeda at the correct place so the numbers in column 8 will be in descending order.

   Tajeda          205     24     56     8     43     18     .317

3. Delete the row that contains information about the player with the lowest batting average (in column 8).

4. Preview and apply a table format that presents this data clearly. Save as *U13L4Table4*.

The insertion point can be quickly moved from one location to another in a document by using keys or key combinations.

MicroType

**TIP**

You can also use the mouse to move the insertion point. Click on the location in a line of text where you want to place the insertion point.

**13E | Move Insertion Point**

### Learn to Move the Insertion Point

To move the insertion point, use the keys or key combinations shown below:

| To move: | Keys |
|---|---|
| One letter to the right | → |
| One letter to the left | ← |
| One line up | ↑ |
| One line down | ↓ |
| One word to the right | CTRL + → |
| One word to the left | CTRL + ← |
| To the end of the line | END |
| To the beginning of the line | HOME |

### Practice What You Have Learned

Using the text lines you keyed for 13D and the insertion point moves chart above, quickly move the insertion point to the location of the red arrow. Make the changes indicated for each line.

Line 1: Key **new**

Line 2: Key **and I**

Line 3: Key **reading**

Line 4: Key **and Kate**

Line 5: Key **ride**

Line 6: Key **for her**

Line 7: Key **four**

Line 8: Key **on Tuesday**

1  Jo has the ▲ toy.

2  Ester ▲ took the book.

3  I started ▲ the book today.

4  Gary ▲ bought her a red sweater.

5  Jana took food with her on the bus ▲.

6  I will get the coins ▲ after the holidays.

7  I should be able to take the ▲ girls to school.

8  Robert and Josefina left on the train ▲ before noon.

## 4C | Borders and Shading

The Borders feature allows you to outline parts of the table with various line styles and colors. The Shading feature allows you to fill in areas of the table with varying shades of gray or with color. Shading and borders cover the selected area. This area may be the entire table or one or more cells, rows, or columns.

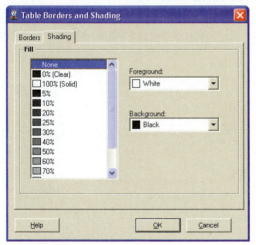

To apply borders or shading to a table:

1. Select the cells, rows, or columns you want to format. To apply the borders and shading to an entire table, place the cursor inside the table without selecting any rows, columns, or cells.

2. From the Table menu, select Borders and Shading.

3. Click the Borders tab to apply a border.

   • Choose the line style and color.

   • In the Borders box, click Box to apply the border to all four sides. Or click in the preview area to apply the border to selected sides. To remove a border from a side, click it again. You can apply different style borders to each side.

4. Click the Shading tab to apply shading.

   • Choose the desired fill pattern.

   • Choose the desired background and foreground colors.

5. Click OK to apply the borders and/or shading settings.

### Practice What You Have Learned

1. Create a table with five columns and five rows. Make all columns 1" wide. Use the default row height.

2. Apply a 2¼-point solid dark blue border around row 1. Shade the cells in row 1 with a solid blue color.

3. In column 1, rows 2–5, place a ¾-point double-line, red border on the left and right sides of the cells. Place the same border on the bottom of the cell in column 1, row 5.

4. In column 3, rows 3–5, place a 1½-point single-line, dark green border around all sides of each cell. Shade these cells with a foreground of 30% green and a white background.

5. In column 5, row 5, place a 1½-point single-line, dark green border on the bottom of the cell. Save as *U13L4Table3*.

## 13F | Enrichment

1. Key each line twice SS (slowly, then faster); DS between 2-line groups.
2. Rekey the drill for better control of reachstrokes.

1  Donald took Anna to see the beautiful fall colors.
2  Nick and I will not be able to be there on Friday.
3  Jose and I went to the bank to get a check cashed.
4  Erika has one week left before she takes the test.
5  Erin will be in town on Friday for the conference.

**For additional practice** MicroType ✦ **Alphabetic Keyboarding ✦ Lesson 13**

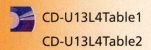

CD-U13L4Table1

CD-U13L4Table2

## 4B | Insert Rows and Delete Rows and Columns

The Table feature can be used to change existing tables. Common changes include the insertion of rows, the deletion of rows and columns, or the deletion of an entire table.

To insert a row or column:

1. Place the cursor in the row below where you want to insert a row or to the right of where you want to insert a column. Select the column if you are inserting a new column.

2. From the Table menu, choose Insert Rows or Insert Columns. Rows will be inserted above the selected row. Columns will be inserted to the left of the selected column.

To delete a row or a column:

1. Select the row(s) or column(s) to be deleted.

2. From the Table menu, choose Delete Rows or Delete Columns.

To delete an entire table:

1. Select the table.

2. From the Table menu, choose Delete Rows.

### Practice What You Have Learned

1. Open the file *CD-U13L4Table1*. Insert a new column to the right of column 2.

2. Key **A3**, **B3**, **C3**, **D3**, and **F3** in the new column, beginning in row 1.

3. Insert a new row above row 5. Key **E1**, **E2**, **E3**, **E4**, **E5**, and **E6** in the new row beginning in column 1.

4. Delete column 6 and row 6. Save the table as *U13L4Table1*.

5. Open *CD-U13L4Table2*. Insert a new row below the column headings. Key this text, beginning in column 1:

   **2006 Miami Heat Detroit Pistons 4-2**

6. Delete the bottom row. Adjust the alignment of the cells in the new row to match the other rows. Save the table as *U13L4Table2*.

## OBJECTIVE

*To learn reach technique for **m** and **x**.*

### 14A | Conditioning Practice

Key each line twice SS (slowly, then faster); DS between 2-line groups.  If time permits, practice each line again.

Reach review 1  car hit bus get ice not win boy try wait knit yarn

b/y 2  body obey baby busy bury bully byway beauty subway

All letters learned 3  Jerry will take the four cans of beans to Douglas.

### 14B | New Keys:  m and x

Key each line twice SS (slowly, then faster); DS between 2-line groups.  If time permits, rekey lines 7-9.

Follow the *Plan for Learning New Keys* outlined on page 12.

**m** Right index finger

**x** Left ring finger

**Learn m**

1  j m jm jm|jam jam|arm arm|aim aim|man man|ham hams
2  lamb some game firm come dome make warm mark must;
3  more magic; many firms; make money; many mean men;

**Learn x**

4  s x|sx sx|six six|axe axe|fix fix|box box|tax tax;
5  Lexi Lexi|oxen oxen|exit exit|taxi taxi|axle axle;
6  fix the axle; extra exit; exact tax; excited oxen;

**Combine m and x**

7  Max Max|mix mix|exam exam|axiom axiom|maxim maxim;
8  tax exams; exact amount; maximum axles; six exams;
9  Max Xiong took the extra exam on the sixth of May.

## 3F  Writing:  Word Choice

Study the spelling and definitions of the following words.  Key the Learn lines, noting the word choices.  Key the Apply lines, selecting the correct words.  Save as *U13L3Writing*.

**who's** (contraction)  who is

**whose** (adjective)  of or relating to whom or which

Learn 1  **Who's** going to go to the school social this week?

Learn 2  The teacher asked if we knew **whose** paper was printing.

Apply 3  I asked Juan to make a list of (who's, whose) absent today.

Apply 4  (Who's, Whose) parents are coming to open house on Tuesday?

★ *Language Arts*

## 3G | Composition:  Research Computer Ethics

A computer is a very powerful tool that has many uses.  Unfortunately, all people do not use the computer for good and ethical purposes.  Use a search engine to research ethics related to using computers.  Write a paragraph describing what you have learned about computer ethics.  Include the website address for at least one website that is a good resource for this activity.  Save as *U3L3Internet*.

## LESSON

# 4

## TABLES WITH SHADING AND BORDERS

### 4A | Conditioning Practice

## OBJECTIVES

1. *To learn and practice these word processing features:  insert and delete rows, columns, borders, and shading.*
2. *To format tables using borders and shading.*

Key each line twice SS; then key a 1' timed writing on line 2.  Determine *gwam*.

Alphabet 1  David saw pilots quickly taxi many big jets from the dozen gates.

Figures 2  With a discount (20%), Item #6359 will cost your business $1,784.

Speed 3  The goal is to fix the auto, bicycle, and rifle for my neighbor.

**GWAM**  1' | 1 | 2 | 3 | 4 | 5 | 6 | 7 | 8 | 9 | 10 | 11 | 12 | 13 |

## 14C | New-Key Mastery

Key each line twice SS; DS between 2-line groups.

3rd/1st row

1 no cut not toy but cow box men met bit cot net boy
2 torn core much rime only time next yarn into north

Space Bar

3 as ox do if go oh no we of is he an to by in it at
4 jar ask you off got hit old box ice ink man was in

Key words

5 mend game team card exam back hold join form enjoy
6 were time yarn oxen four dent mask when dark usual

Key phrases

7 she can|go to the|if they will|make the|at the end
8 When will|we will be able|need a|take a look|I can

All letters learned

9 Fabio and Jacki said you would need the right mix.
10 Glen said that he would fix my bike for Jacob Cox.

## 14D | Technique:  Spacing with Punctuation

Key each line twice SS; DS between 2-line groups.

1 Dr. Smythe and Dr. Ramos left for St. Louis today.
2 Dr. Chen taught us the meaning of f.o.b. and LIFO.
3 Keith got his Ed.D. at NYU; I got my Ed.D. at USU.
4 Sgt. J. Roarke met with Lt. Col. Christina Castro.

---

**Tip**

Do not space after an internal period in an abbreviation, such as Ed.D.

## 3E | Tables

### Table 1

1. Create a table (3 columns by 11 rows). Make all columns about 1.25" wide. Apply a table format to display borders around the cells (such as Grid 1).

2. Merge cells as needed. Key the text as shown, inserting the missing values in each row.

3. Format the title in a 24-point bold font. Format the column headings in a 16-point bold font. Format the cell entries in rows 3–10 in a 14-point font. Format row 11 in a 10-point font.

4. Center the table horizontally and vertically on the page. Save the document as *U13L3Table7*.

| FRACTIONS, DECIMALS, AND PERCENTS | | |
|---|---|---|
| Fraction | Decimal | Percent |
| 1/8 | | 12.5% |
| 1/4 | .25 | |
| 3/8 | .375 | 37.5% |
| 1/2 | | 50% |
| 5/8 | .625 | |
| | .75 | 75% |
| 7/8 | | 87.5% |
| 1 | 1.0 | 100% |

To find the equivalent of a fraction in decimal form, divide the numerator by the denominator. To change from a decimal to a percent, multiply by 100 and add the % sign. To change from a percent to a decimal, divide by 100 and drop the % sign.

### Table 2

1. Create a table that has two columns and five rows.

2. Marge and split cells to replicate the table below.

3. Key the table.

4. Preview various table formats. Select and apply the one that you think best displays the contents of the table. Save the document as *U13L3Table8*.

| Refreshment Booth Staffing--Saturday, August 15 | | | | |
|---|---|---|---|---|
| Morning | | Afternoon | | |
| Sarah Jones | Sam Gillan | Nacy Tambellini | | |
| Nancy Bashforth | Di White | Juanita Menendez | | Jen Youngman |
| Thomas and Gretchen Holliday | | | | |

**Tip**

Keep the insertion point moving steadily across each line (no pauses).

1. Key each line twice SS (slowly, then faster); DS between 2-line groups.

2. Key each line once more at a faster pace.

**m/x**

1 Mary Fox and Maxine Cox took all six of the exams.

**b/y**

2 Burly Bryon Beyer barely beat Barb Byrnes in golf.

**w/Right Shift**

3 Carlos DeRosa defeated Wade Cey in the last match.

**u/c**

4 The clumsy ducks caused Lucy Lund to hit the curb.

**Left Shift**

5 Keith and Mike went to St. Louis to see Mr. Owens.

**n/g**

6 Glen began crying as Ginny began singing the song.

**o/t**

7 Tom bought a total of two tons of tools yesterday.

**i/r**

8 Rick and Maria tried to fix the tire for the girl.

**h/e**

9 Helen Hale heard her tell them to see the hostess.

For additional practice ▶ MicroType ✦ Alphabetic Keyboarding ✦ Lesson 14

## 3C | Merge and Split Cells

While working with tables, you can merge (join) adjacent cells that are in the same row or the same column. This is useful when information in a table spans more than one column or row. You can split (divide) a cell into two cells.

To merge cells in a table:

1. Select two or more adjacent cells that you want to merge into one cell.

2. From the Table menu, select Merge Cells to combine the selected cells.

To split a cell in a table:

1. Select the cell that you want to split.

2. From the Table menu, select Split Cells to divide the cell into two cells.

### Practice What You Have Learned

1. Create a table with six columns and four rows. Make each column 1.1" wide and use the default row height.

2. Use the Merge Cells and Split Cells commands to make your table look like the one below. Then key the text as shown. Use a 10-point font and center alignment within cells.

3. Format the table using Grid 1 Table Format. Apply the format to borders only.

4. Center the table horizontally and vertically on the page. Save as *U13L3Table6*.

| All cells in row 1 were merged. The first and last cells in rows 2 and 4 were split into two cells. | | | | | | | |
|---|---|---|---|---|---|---|---|
| | | | | | | | |
| | | | Four adjacent cells in rows 3 and 4 were merged. | | | | |
| | | | | | | | |

## 3D | Superscripts and Subscripts

The Font command allows you to insert superscript and subscript numbers or text into a document.

To format text as a superscript or a subscript:

1. Select the text you want to format or position the cursor at the location where you want to key the superscript or subscript.

2. From the Format menu, select *Font*. Click the superscript or subscript box. Click OK.

### Practice What You Have Learned

1. Open a blank document.

2. Key the following lines using a 14-point font. Format the superscripts and subscripts as shown. Save as *U13L3Scripts*.

This formula, $d = -16t^2 + v_o t + a$, is often used to find the distance of falling objects.

If a and b are numbers or variables, then $a^x a^y = a^{x+y}$.

If a is a positive number and c is a real number, then $\log_a (a^c) = c$.

# LESSON 15

## OBJECTIVE

To learn reach technique for **p** and **v**.

**Proper keying position**

**p** Right little finger

**v** Left index finger

### 15A | Conditioning Practice

Key each line twice SS (slowly, then faster); DS between 2-line groups. If time permits, practice each line again.

| | | |
|---|---|---|
| One-hand words | 1 | rare gear seed hill milk lion bare moon base onion |
| Balanced-hand words | 2 | town wish corn fork dish held coal owns rich their |
| All letters learned | 3 | Gabe Waxon may ask us to join him for lunch today. |

### 15B | New Keys: p and v

Key each line twice SS; DS between 2-line groups. If time permits, rekey lines 7–9.

Follow the *Plan for Learning New Keys* outlined on page 12.

**Learn p**

1 ; p ;p ;p|put put|pin pin|pay pay|pop pop|sap sap;
2 pull pull|park park|open open|soap soap|hoop hoops
3 a purple puppet; pay plan; plain paper; poor poet

**Learn v**

4 f v fv fv|van van|vain vain|very very|value value;
5 over over|vote vote|save save|move move|dove dove;
6 drive over; seven verbs; value driven; viable vote

**Combine p and v**

7 cave push gave pain oven pick jive keep very river
8 have revised; river view; five to seven; even vote
9 Eva and Paul have to pick papa up to vote at five.

## 3B | Table Format

You can use table formats to give your tables a professional look. Table formats include settings such as alignment, borders, shading, and font styles.

Using table formats can save time. Table formats can be applied to specific rows or columns or the entire table.

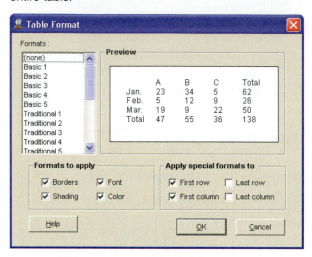

To apply a format to a table you have already created:

1. Position the cursor anywhere within the table. From the Table menu, select Table Format.

2. Choose an option from the Formats list. (Use the Preview box to see the table format.)

   • If desired, choose options in the Formats to Apply box. These options allow you to change the predefined format. For example, you can turn off borders or shading, leaving all of the other formats as they are.

   • If desired, choose options in the Apply Special Formats To box. You can selectively apply the format settings to the first row, first column, last row, and last column.

3. Click OK.

### Practice What You Have Learned

1. Open the file *CD-U13L3Table1*. Format the table with Grid 1; apply formats only to borders. Save as *U13L3Table1*.

2. Format the table with 3D Professional 1. Under Formats to Apply, select Borders, Shading, Font, and Color. Select First row and Last row under Apply Special Formats To. Save as *U13L3Table2* and close the file.

3. Open the file *CD-U13L3Table1*. Choose two formats that you want to use. Apply the desired formats and special options. Save the first format as *U13L3Table3* and the second as *U13L3Table4*.

4. Open a blank document. Center the title **MONTHLY SALES REPORT** about 2" from the top. Insert a new table that will have five columns and five rows. Apply the Traditional 2 format as you create the table. Select all format and special formats options. Key the following information in the cells. Right-align cells in columns 2, 3, 4, and 5. Save as *U13L3Table5*.

| Salesperson | January | February | March | April |
|---|---|---|---|---|
| Jim Jones | 750 | 654 | 807 | 504 |
| Helen Goins | 689 | 546 | 913 | 605 |
| Janet Perez | 582 | 631 | 768 | 604 |
| Totals | 2,021 | 1,831 | 2,488 | 1,713 |

CD-U13L3Table1

### MicroType
**TIP**

To apply a format to a new table, in the Insert Table dialog box, click Format when you create a new table.

## 15C | New-Key Mastery

Key each line twice SS; DS between 2-line groups.

**Technique Goals**

• Reach up without moving hands away from you.

• Reach down without moving hands toward your body.

• Use finger-action keystrokes.

• Keep hands and arms quiet.

Reach review
1 fv fr ft fg fb jn jm jh jy ju l. lo sx sw dc de ;p
2 free kind junk swim loan link half golf very plain

3rd/1st rows
3 oven cove oxen went been nice more home rice phone
4 not item river their newer price voice point crime

Key words
5 pair pays pens vigor vivid vogue panel proxy opens
6 jam kept right shake shelf shape soap visit visual

Key phrases
7 pay them|their signs|vote for|when will|if they go
8 you will be|much of the|when did they|to see their

Key sentences
9 Crew had seven of the votes; Brooks had only five.
10 They just left the park and went to see Dr. Nixon

## 15D | Technique:  Shift and ENTER Keys

Key each 2-line sentence once SS as enter is called every 30 seconds (30").  Leave a DS between sentences.

**Goal:**

To reach the end of each line just as the 30" (20") guide (enter) is called.

The 30" (20") *gwam* scale shows your gross words a minute if you reach the end of each line as the 30" (20") guide is called.

**Tip**

Keep your eyes on the copy as you shift and as you tap the ENTER key.

|  |  | gwam | 30" | 20" |
|---|---|---|---|---|
| 1 | Justin took Kate and Roger to |  | 12 | 18 |
| 2 | the new theatre last Saturday. |  | 12 | 18 |
| 3 | You will be able to see the column |  | 14 | 21 |
| 4 | when you turn right on Wilson Road. |  | 14 | 21 |
| 5 | Felipe bought eight of the shirts after |  | 16 | 24 |
| 6 | the old manager accepted his last offer. |  | 16 | 24 |
| 7 | Dane McDowell will compete in six more races |  | 18 | 27 |
| 8 | before the year ends the last weekend of May. |  | 18 | 27 |

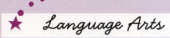

## 2F Writing: Number Expression

Read the following number usage rule. Key the Learn line, noting the number choices. Key the Apply lines, making the necessary corrections. Save as *U13L2Writing*.

**Rule 6:** Use figures to express weights and measures.

Learn 1    The 2 ft. tall box weighed 17 lbs. and 7 oz.

Apply 2    Which President was six ft. four in. tall?

Apply 3    Does a pound equal twelve oz. or sixteen oz.?

## 2G Reading: Soccer Championship

CD-U13L2Read

Open the file *CD-U13L2Read*. Read the document carefully and close the file. Let your instructor know when you are ready to answer questions covering the content of the file.

## LESSON 3

# TABLES WITH GRIDLINES

### 3A | Conditioning Practice

**OBJECTIVES**

1. *To learn and practice these word processing features: table format, merge cells, split cells, superscript, and subscript.*

2. *To format tables using predefined formats.*

Key each line twice SS; then key a 1' timed writing on line 2. Determine *gwam*.

Alphabet 1    If Marje has extra help, the jigsaw puzzle can be quickly solved.

Figures 2    The two club meetings will be on 9/28 and 10/7 at 4:30-6:15 p.m.

Speed 3    Cissy is to visit the auditor to fix the problem with the profit.

**GWAM**   1' | 1 | 2 | 3 | 4 | 5 | 6 | 7 | 8 | 9 | 10 | 11 | 12 | 13 |

## 15E | Enrichment

1. Key each line once at a steady, easy pace to master reachstrokes.

2. Key each line again at a faster pace.

**m/p**

1 plum bump push mark jump limp camp same post maple
2 Pam sampled the plums; Mark sampled the apricots.

**b/x**

3 box exact able except abide job expand debt extend
4 Dr. Nixon placed the six textbooks in the taxicab.

**y/v**

5 very verb eyes vent layer even days save yard vast
6 Darby Vance may take the gray van to Vivian today.

For additional practice MicroType + Alphabetic Keyboarding + Lesson 15

## 2E | Table with Source Note

Source notes are keyed at the bottom left of a table. Key **Source:** followed by the reference, single-spaced. If the table is center- or right-aligned, use a tab to position the note even with the left of the table.

1. Key the title and the table shown below. Click outside the table below column 1. Tap ENTER to leave one blank line. Key the source note, using Arial 10-point font.

2. Center-align the title. Use Arial, 14-point bold font for the title.

3. Change the text in the table to a 12-point Arial font. Insert hard returns to make the headings for columns 2 and 4 two lines as shown.

4. Change the width of column 1 to 2.3", column 2 to 1.5", column 3 to 1.2", and column 4 to 1.3". Left-align column 1; center-align columns 2, 3, and 4.

5. Make each row at least 24 points high. Use Bottom alignment for all rows.

6. Center-align and bold the column headings. Underline the column headings (last line only) as shown.

7. Center the table horizontally. Center the page vertically. Adjust the position of the source note. Save as *U13L2Table5*.

### AREA AND POPULATION OF THE WORLD

| Continent or Region | Area (1,000 sq. mi.) | % of Earth | % of World Population |
|---|---|---|---|
| North America | 8,209 | 16.3 | 7.9 |
| South America | 6,765 | 13.4 | 5.8 |
| Europe | 8,779 | 17.4 | 11.1 |
| Asia | 11,875 | 23.6 | 60.6 |
| Africa | 11,508 | 22.8 | 14.0 |
| Oceania, including Australia | 3,253 | 6.5 | 0.5 |
| Antarctica | 5,405 | 10.7 | 0.0 |

Source: *The World Almanac and Book of Facts 2007*. New York: World Almanac Books, 2007.

## LESSON 16

### OBJECTIVE

*To learn reach technique for **q** and **,** (comma).*

**q** Left little finger

**,** (comma) Right middle finger

### Tip

Space once after **,** (comma) used as punctuation.

---

### 16A | Conditioning Practice

Key each line twice SS (slowly, then faster); DS between 2-line groups. If time permits, practice each line again.

| | | |
|---|---|---|
| All letters learned | 1 | dash give wind true flop comb yolk joke hunt gain; |
| p/v | 2 | prove vapor above apple voted super cover preview; |
| All letters learned | 3 | Mary forced Jack to help move six big water units. |

### 16B | New Keys: q and , (comma)

Key each line twice SS; DS between 2-line groups. If time permits, rekey lines 7–9.

**Learn q**

1 a q aq|quit quit|aqua aqua|quick quick|quote quote
2 quest quest|quart quart|quite quite|liquid liquid;
3 quite quiet; quick squirrel; chi square; a quarter

**Learn , (comma)**

4 , k ,k ,k one, two, three, four, five, six, seven,
5 Akio, Baiko, Niou, and Joji are exchange students.
6 Juan, Rico, and Mike voted; however, Jane did not.

**Combine q and , (comma)**

7 Quota, square, quiche, and quite were on the exam.
8 Quin can spell Quebec, Nicaragua, Iraq, and Qatar.
9 Joaquin, Jacque, and Javier sailed for Martinique.

## 2C | Table Horizontal Alignment

Tables can be aligned horizontally at the left margin (the default), the right margin, or the center of a page.

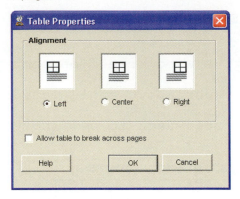

To align a table horizontally:

1. Position the insertion point inside the table.

2. From the Table menu, select Table Properties. Click the desired horizontal alignment button. Click OK.

**Practice What You Have Learned**

1. Open the file *U13L2Table1* that you created earlier.

2. Change the horizontal alignment for the table to Center. Center-align the table title. Save the file as *U13L2Table2*. Leave it open.

3. Change the horizontal alignment of the table to Right. Right-align the table title. Save the file as *U13L2Table3*.

## 2D | Table Row Height

You can change the height of rows in a table. The height of all rows can be changed to the same height, or each row can be a different height. The vertical alignment of text in cells can also be changed. The text can be top-, center-, or bottom-aligned.

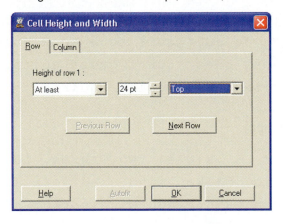

1. Select the row you want to change. From the Table menu, choose Cell Height and Width.

2. On the Row tab, in the drop-down list, select At Least; enter a row height in points (72 points = 1 inch). The row will be formatted to at least that height, regardless of the amount of text in the row. The row height will expand, if needed, to hold all the text you key in the row.

3. Select the text alignment option (top, center, or bottom) from the drop-down list.

4. If needed, click Next Row (or Previous Row) to change the height of other rows.

5. Click OK when all row heights have been set.

**Practice What You Have Learned**

1. Open the data file *CD-U13L2Table4*.

2. Change the width of columns 1 and 2 to 1.75". Underline the column headings.

3. Change the row 1 height to 28 points and choose Center alignment.

4. Change the height of all other rows to 24 points and choose Bottom alignment.

5. Center-align the table horizontally on the page. Center-align the document vertically on the page.

6. Save the file as *U13L2Table4*.

### MicroType
**TIP**

Click and drag the horizontal gridline of a table up or down to change row height.

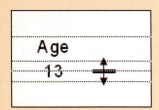

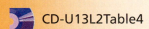
CD-U13L2Table4

## 16C | New-Key Mastery

Key each line twice SS; DS between 2-line groups.

Reach review
1 jh fg l. o. k, i, ft sw aq de ;p fr jn jb fv jn jm
2 We can leave now.  Take Nancy, Michael, and Jorge.

3rd/1st rows
3 nice bond many when oxen come vent quit very prom;
4 drive a truck|know how to|not now|when will you be

Key words
5 have jail wept quit desk from goes cave yarn boxer
6 brand extra cycle event equip know fight made show

Key phrases
7 when will you|may be able to|if you can|he will be
8 ask about the|need to be|where will|as you can see

All letters learned
9 The quaint old maypole was fixed by Jackie Groves.
10 Vera fixed the job growth plans quickly on Monday.

## 16D | Technique:  Spacing with Punctuation

Key each line twice; DS between 2-line groups.

1 Jay asked the question; Tim answered the question.
2 Ann, Joe, and I saw the bus; Mark and Ted did not.
3 I had ibid., op. cit., and loc. cit. in the paper.
4 The Mets, Dodgers, Cardinals, and Padres competed.

**Tip**

Space once after , (comma) or ; (semicolon) used as punctuation.

## TABLES WITH UNEQUAL COLUMN WIDTHS

### OBJECTIVES

1. *To learn and practice these word processing features: table column width, table row height, and table horizontal alignment.*

2. *To format tables with unequal column widths.*

### MicroType

Click and drag the vertical gridlines of a table to the left or right to change column widths.

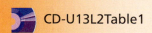

| Name | Age |
|------|-----|
| Tomas Perez | 15 |
| Heidi Smith | 18 |
| Larry Rogers | 13 |
| May Bridge | 24 |

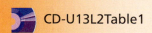
CD-U13L2Table1

### 2A | Conditioning Practice

Key each line twice SS; then key a 1' timed writing on line 2. Determine *gwam*.

Alphabet 1    Zelda was quite naive to pack fresh yams into just two big boxes.

Figures/ 2    He needs to pay $3,798 by May 8 to get 15% off on Model #460-12.
Symbols

Speed 3    Nell paid the men for the work they did in the field by the lake.

GWAM   1' | 1 | 2 | 3 | 4 | 5 | 6 | 7 | 8 | 9 | 10 | 11 | 12 | 13 |

### 2B | Table Column Width

You can change the width of one or more columns in a table to accommodate cell entries of unequal widths.

To change the width of a table column:

1. Select the column you want to change. From the Table menu, choose Cell Height and Width.

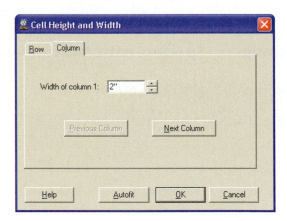

2. On the Column tab, key the width for the column (in inches) in the Width of column box.

3. Click Next Column (or Previous Column) as needed to change the cell width of other columns.

4. To format the table into equal column widths that begin and end at the side margins, click Autofit.

5. Click OK when the desired settings have been keyed.

### Practice What You Have Learned

1. Open the file *CD-U13L2Table1*.

2. Change the width of column 1 to 0.5", columns 2 and 3 to 1.5", and column 4 to 0.6".

3. Left-align the table title. Save the document as *U13L2Table1*.

## 16E | Enrichment

1. Key each line once at a steady, easy pace to master reachstrokes.

2. Key each line again at a faster pace.

**Goal for lines 1–3:**
• fingers upright

### Adjacent keys

1  ew mn vb tr op iu ty bv xc fg jh df ;l as kj qw er
2  week oily free join dash very true wash tree rash;
3  union point extra river track water cover weapon;

**Goal for lines 4–6:**
• hands/arms steady

### Long direct reaches

4  ny many ce rice my myself mu mute gr grand hy hype
5  lunch hatch vouch newsy bossy yearn beyond crabby;
6  gabby bridge muggy venture machine beauty luncheon

**Goal for lines 7–9:**
• two quick taps of each double letter

### Double letters

7  book feet eggs seek cell jeer keep mall adds occur
8  class little sheep effort needle assist happy seem
9  Tennessee Minnesota Illinois Mississippi Missouri;

**For additional practice** ▶ **MicroType ✦ Alphabetic Keyboarding ✦ Lesson 16**

New Keys:  q and , (comma)

## 1G  Writing:  Word Choice

Study the spelling and definitions of the following words.  Key the Learn line, noting the word choices.  Key the Apply lines, selecting the correct words.  Save as *U13L1Writing*.

**passed** (verb)  moved past, over, through

**past** (adjective)  some time ago, just gone by

Learn 1  Jim **passed** Jane's video game score this **past** week.

Apply 2  I (passed, past) Jerry two times on the way to the library in the (passed, past) week.

Apply 3  Jerry (passed, past) Ben on the last lap of the championship race.

*Our World*

### 1H ▪ Employee Theft

Pretend that you own a fast food business.  You employ three students who do the following things while being paid.

- Pamela makes a long distance call once a week to her brother.  She normally talks for 10 minutes at $.07 per minute.

- Tom arrives and leaves on time.  However, he usually takes five minutes more for lunch than he is allowed.  He also takes two extra five-minute breaks each day.  He works four days a week.

- Jeffrey drinks two $.49 soft drinks each day.  (He is allowed only one.)  He works five days a week.

Are these individuals stealing from you?  Why or why not?  Calculate how much your business will lose each year as a result of these behaviors.  Each person earns $5.50 per hour and works 50 weeks a year.  If you make $.10 profit on each hamburger you sell, how many hamburgers must you sell to cover these losses?

Key your answers and save the document as *U13L1Math*.

## OBJECTIVES

1. *To learn to key block paragraphs.*
2. *To improve keying technique and speed.*

### 17A | Conditioning Practice

Key each line twice SS (slowly, then faster); DS between 2-line groups. If time permits, practice each line again.

Reach review 1   The projected costs would far exceed the benefits.

Shift keys 2   Rick lives in St. Paul; Charla lives in San Diego.

Easy 3   Jan did sign all the title work for the eight men.

### 17B | Block Paragraphs

Key each paragraph once SS; DS between paragraphs. Then key the paragraph again at a faster pace.

**Paragraph 1**

As more and more young people take up the sport of inline skating, safety should be a top priority of all those who are involved in the sport.

**Paragraph 2**

Areas that are designated just for skaters are the best place for someone who has never skated before to learn. Such areas are much safer than the city streets or bike paths.

GWAM   1' |   1   |   2   |   3   |   4   |   5   |   6   |   7   |   8   |   9   |   10   |

### 1E | Formatted Table

1. Open a new blank document. Use the default margins and center the page vertically.

2. Key the title as shown in bold, all caps, using a 16-point font. Center the title.

3. DS after the title. Change the font to a regular, 12-point font.

4. Insert a table (4 columns by 12 rows). Key the information shown in the table.

5. Left-align all cells in the table.

6. Format all paragraphs (including the table title) for 12 points of space after the paragraphs.

7. Format the column headings in bold underline and change the font size to 14 points. Center-align the column headings.

8. Bold all words in columns 1 and 3.

9. Save the table as *U13L1Table4*.

## FREQUENTLY USED FOREIGN PHRASES

| Phrase | Language | Pronunciation | English Meaning |
|---|---|---|---|
| apropos | French | ap-ruh-POH | relevant |
| c'est la vie | French | se lah VEE | that's life |
| en masse | French | ahn MAHS | in a large body |
| esprit de corps | French | es-PREE duh KAWR | group spirit |
| ex post facto | Latin | eks pohst FAK-toh | retroactively |
| fait accompli | French | fayt uh-kom-PLEE | an accomplished fact |
| faux pas | French | fowe PAH | a social blunder |
| in toto | Latin | in TOH-toh | totally |
| mea culpa | Latin | MAY-uh CUL-puh | through my fault |
| que sera sera | Spanish | keh sair-ah sair-ah | what will be will be |
| status quo | Latin | STAY-tus QWOH | existing order of things |

*Our World*

### 1F ▪ Common Elements

1. Open *CD-U13L1Table5*. This table contains information about five elements from the Periodic Table of the Elements. Using the information in columns 1 and 2, key the name of the element in column 3 that you know.

2. Format the table using what you have learned in this lesson. Save it as *U13L1Table5*.

CD-U13L1Table5

*Science*

## 17C | Technique: Space Bar and Shift Keys

Key each line twice SS; DS between 2-line groups.

Down-and-in spacing

Out-and-down shifting

**Space Bar (Space immediately after each word.)**

1 it to is do if wet and the are axe pay not bet see
2 exam card very back done free gone join quit large
3 You will be able to see the final game of the day.
4 They said to be there early to get the best seats.

**Shift keys (Shift; tap key; release both quickly.)**

5 Andres, Mario, Juan, Julia, Rosa, Julio, Jose, Rey
6 Mr. Ortega; Mrs. Lisko; Dr. Good; Mrs. J. W. Faust
7 Dr. Evans and Dr. Figueroa will work next Tuesday.
8 Ben Voss and Joy Rice will graduate next December.

## 17D | Speed Check

Key a 30" timed writing on each line. Your *gwam* rate is shown above and below the lines. If time permits, key another 30" timing on each line. Try to increase your keying speed.

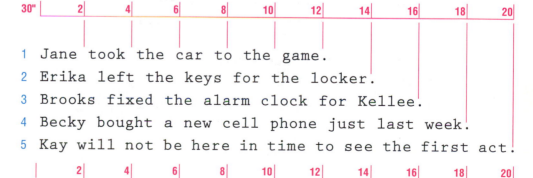

| 30" | 2 | 4 | 6 | 8 | 10 | 12 | 14 | 16 | 18 | 20 |

1 Jane took the car to the game.
2 Erika left the keys for the locker.
3 Brooks fixed the alarm clock for Kellee.
4 Becky bought a new cell phone just last week.
5 Kay will not be here in time to see the first act.

| 2 | 4 | 6 | 8 | 10 | 12 | 14 | 16 | 18 | 20 |

## 1C | Table with Even Columns

1. Open a new blank document. Use the default margins. Set the vertical alignment for the page to Center.

2. Key the table title as shown. Use all caps, bold, and center alignment for the title. DS after the title.

3. Change to left alignment and turn off bold. Insert a table (four columns by seven rows).

4. Key the following information in the table. Use bold and underline as shown for the column heads. Note that some lines will wrap within cells.

5. Save the document as *U13L1Table2*.

### BIRTHSTONES

| **Month** | **Birthstone** | **Month** | **Birthstone** |
|---|---|---|---|
| January | Garnet | July | Ruby |
| February | Amethyst | August | Sardonyx or Peridot |
| March | Bloodstone or Aquamarine | September | Sapphire |
| April | Diamond | October | Opal or Tourmaline |
| May | Emerald | November | Topaz |
| June | Pearl, Moonstone, or Alexandrite | December | Turquoise or Zircon |

## 1D | Select Row, Column, or Table

Information in a row, column, or an entire table can be selected quickly using options from the Table menu. Once text is selected, format changes can be made to all the text or cells in the row, column, or entire table.

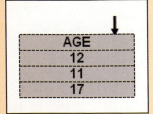

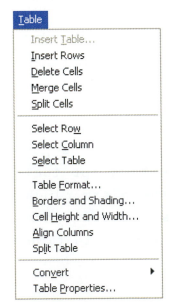

To select parts of a table:

1. Position the insertion point in the row, column, or table you want to select.

2. From the Table menu, choose the Select Row, Select Column, or Select Table option, whichever is appropriate.

### Practice What You Have Learned

1. Open the file *U13L1Table2* that you created earlier.

2. Select the table and insert 12 points of blank space after the paragraphs.

3. Select the table and change the font to Arial and the font size to 12 points.

4. Select row 1 and center-align all cell entries. Select column 2 and change the font style to italic. Then select column 4 and change the font style to italic.

5. Select the table title and format it in a Arial, 16-point bold font.

6. Save the document as *U13L1Table3*.

Technique Goals
- quick-snap keystrokes
- quick joining of letters to form words
- quick joining of words to form phrases

## 17E | Speed Building

Key each line twice SS (slowly, then faster); DS between 2-line groups.

**Key words and phrases (Think, say, and key words and phrases.)**

1 rush town yard fuse mild park gave cabs jinx house
2 comb very hole wild unit keep just food gone extra
3 to be able|if you go|when will he|they may be able
4 if they are|this will be|you will see|when can you

**Key sentences (Tap keys at a brisk, steady pace.)**

5 Tim was able to make the grades he needed to pass.
6 Dr. Riana Nelson will see you next week on Friday.
7 I lost my ticket for the Yankee game on Wednesday.
8 Glenda is planning a big surprise party for Gavin.

## 17F | Enrichment

Key each line twice SS (slowly, then faster); DS between 2-line groups.

1 She may do the work on the dock for us on Tuesday.
2 The forms are in a large box by the kitchen stove.
3 Jay may go to the lake to fix the neighbor's door.
4 The girl did all of the lawn work before she left.
5 I took the title to city hall to have it recorded.

**For additional practice** MicroType + Alphabetic Keyboarding + Lesson 17

To insert a table into a document:

1. Position the cursor where you want to insert the new table.

2. From the Table menu, select Insert Table. Enter the number of columns and rows for the table. Click OK.

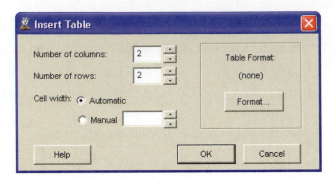

To key text or numbers in a table:

1. The cursor will be in column 1, row 1 when the table is created. Begin keying the text or numbers in this cell.

2. Use the TAB key or the arrow keys to move from cell to cell and row to row. (Tapping ENTER begins a new line in the cell.) The mouse may also be used to move the insertion point in a table by clicking the desired cell.

**Practice What You Have Learned**

1. Open a new blank document. Position the cursor about 2" from the top of the page. Key **NOTABLE INVENTIONS** in bold and all caps for the table title. Center-align the title. DS after the title.

2. Change the alignment to left and turn off bold. Insert a table with four columns and six rows.

3. Key the following column heads and entries in the table. Underline the column heads as shown. Save the table as *U13L1Table1*.

### NOTABLE INVENTIONS

| Invention | Date | Inventor | Nationality |
|---|---|---|---|
| Adding machine | 1642 | Pascal | French |
| Calculating machine | 1833 | Babbage | English |
| Electronic computer | 1942 | Atanasoff, Berry | United States |
| Mini computer | 1960 | Digital Corporation | United States |
| Laptop computer | 1987 | Sinclair | English |

## LESSON 18

### OBJECTIVE

To learn reach technique for **z** and **:** *(colon)*.

**z** Left little finger

**:** Left Shift and tab **:** key

### Tip

Space twice after **:** used as punctuation.

---

### 18A | Conditioning Practice

Key each line twice SS; then key a 1' timing on line 3.  Find *gwam*.

All letters learned  1  Jack quickly helped Mary Newton fix the big stove.

Spacing  2  it is | if you can | by the end | when will he | to be the

Easy  3  Helen may go to the city to buy the girls a shake.

GWAM  1' |  1  |  2  |  3  |  4  |  5  |  6  |  7  |  8  |  9  |  10  |

### 18B | New Keys:  z and : (colon)

Key each line twice SS (slowly, then faster); DS between 2-line groups.  If time permits, rekey lines 7–10.
Follow the *Plan for Learning New Keys* outlined on page 12.

**Learn z**

1  a z a z | az az | zap zap | zip zip | raze raze | size size;

2  daze daze | maze maze | lazy lazy | hazy hazy | zest zest;

3  Utah Jazz; hazel eyes; loud buzz; zoology quizzes;

**Learn : (colon)**

4  ;: ;: | a: b: c: d: e: f: g: h: i: j: k: l: m: n: o:

5  p: q: r: s: t: u: v: w: x: y: z: a:b:c d:e:f g:h:i

6  Dear Mr. Baker:  Dear Dr. Finn:  Dear Mrs. Fedder:

**Combine z and : (colon)**

7  Liz invited the following:  Hazel, Inez, and Zach.

8  Use these headings:  Zip Code:  Zone:  Zoo:  Jazz:

9  Buzz, spell these words:  size, fizzle, and razor.

10  Dear Mr. Perez:  Dear Ms. Ruiz:  Dear Mrs. Mendez:

# Unit 13
## Prepare Tables

### Lessons 1–4

---

**LESSON**

# 1

## OBJECTIVES

1. *To learn and practice these word processing features: insert table, select cells, and vertically align tables.*
2. *To format tables with equal column widths.*

## TABLES WITH EQUAL COLUMN WIDTHS

### 1A | Conditioning Practice

Key each line twice SS; then key a 1' timed writing on line 2. Determine *gwam*.

| Alphabet | 1 | Flo quickly realized the blue gown Meja wore was quite expensive. |
|---|---|---|
| Figures | 2 | The art sold for $75.49, $83.20, and $69.19 in three area stores. |
| Speed | 3 | Elena kept the antique handiwork in the ivory box by the cubicle. |

**GWAM** 1' | 1 | 2 | 3 | 4 | 5 | 6 | 7 | 8 | 9 | 10 | 11 | 12 | 13 |

### 1B | Insert Table

Tables are used to organize information. The Table feature allows you to arrange Information vertically in columns and horizontally in rows. The intersection of a row and a column is called a **cell**. When text is keyed in a cell, it wraps within that cell—instead of wrapping around to the next row. The gridlines displayed on the screen help organize the information; they do not print.

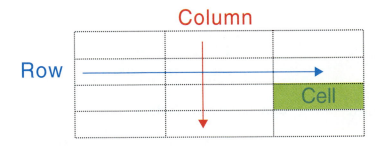

• curved, upright fingers
• quiet hands and arms
• steady keystroking pace

## 18C | New-Key Mastery

Key each line twice SS; DS between 2-line groups.

q/z
1 zoom hazy quit prize dozen freeze quizzed equalize
2 Zoe was quite amazed by the quaint city of La Paz.

p/x
3 pox expect example explore perplex explain complex
4 Tex picked six apples for a pie for Rex and Pedro.

v/m
5 move vase mean veal make vice mark very comb above
6 Mavis came to visit Mark, Vivian, Val, and Marvin.

Easy
7 Their maid may pay for all the land by the chapel.
8 The auditor may do the work for the big city firm.

Alphabet
9 Glenn saw a quick red fox jump over the lazy cubs.
10 Gavin quickly explained what Joby made for prizes.

## 18D | Word Wrap

### Learn to Use Wordwrap

To use wordwrap:

1. Key the paragraph. Tap ENTER at the end of the paragraph.

2. Tap ENTER again to leave a blank line before beginning to key the text of the next paragraph.

### Practice What You Have Learned

1. Key the paragraph below.

2. Tap ENTER twice at the end of the paragraph.

At the end of a full line, the copy and insertion
point move to the next line automatically.  This
is called wordwrap.  Use wordwrap when you key a
paragraph.  At the end of a paragraph, though, tap
the ENTER key twice to place a double space between it
and the next paragraph.

## MicroType

### Word Processing
#### Wordwrap

The Wordwrap feature causes text at the end of a full line to move or "wrap" to the next line without having to tap the ENTER key.

## Math Activities

**3G ▪ Math Challenge 11**

### FIND THE INTEREST ON A SIMPLE INTEREST LOAN

1. Key a sentence to explain how you find the interest on a simple interest loan problem like this: *What is the interest on a $500 loan at 6% interest for 2 years?*

2. Find the interest for the following problems and key your answers in sentence form. For example, an appropriate sentence for the answer to the problem stated above is: *The interest on a $500 loan at 6% for 2 years is $60.*

   2a. Amount of loan is $3,000; interest rate is 4%; time is 1.5 years.

   2b. Amount of loan is $2,500; interest rate is 8%; time is 6 months.

   2c. Amount of loan is $12,000; interest rate is 5%; time is 10.5 years.

   2d. If you borrow $20,000 for college at 6% on a simple interest loan for 10 years, how much interest will you need to pay?

3. Save your answers as *U12L3Math*.

---

### Careers

#### 3I ▪ Career Exploration Portfolio – Activity 11

- You must complete Career Activities 1–3 before completing this activity.

1. Retrieve your Career folder and the information in it that relates to the career cluster that is your second choice.

2. Use the Internet to search for the education that is recommended for occupations in this career cluster, and then compose a paragraph or two explaining what you have learned. Print your file, save it as *U12L3Career11*, and keep it open.

3. Exchange papers with a classmate and have the classmate offer suggestions for improving the content and correcting any errors he or she finds in your paragraph(s). Make the changes that you agree with and print a copy to turn in to your instructor. Save it as *U12L3Career11* and close the file.

4. Return your folder to the storage area. When your instructor returns your paper, file it in your Career folder.

## 18E | Key Block Paragraphs

1. Key each paragraph below once SS; DS between them.
2. Key a 1' timed writing on each paragraph.

**Paragraph 1**

*gwam* 1'

| | |
|---|---|
| A good team member is honest, does a fair share of | 10 |
| the work, and is eager to help another team member | 20 |
| if there is a need to do so.  Quite often the best | 30 |
| team member must be a superb follower as well as a | 40 |
| good leader. | 43 |

**Paragraph 2**

| | |
|---|---|
| There are several other skills that a person ought | 10 |
| to acquire in order to become a good leader.  Such | 20 |
| skills as the ability to think, listen, speak, and | 30 |
| write are essential for a good leader to possess. | 40 |

**GWAM** 1' | 1 | 2 | 3 | 4 | 5 | 6 | 7 | 8 | 9 | 10 |

## 18F | Enrichment

**Technique Goals**
- fingers upright
- hands/arms steady

1. Key each line once at a steady, easy pace to master reachstrokes.
2. Key each line again at a faster pace.

x/:

1 To:  Rex Cox, Tex Oxley|From:  Max Saxe|A:B as C:D
2 Spelling words:  extra, extract, exam, and explain

q/,

3 square square|quick quick|equip equip|squad squad;
4 Spelling words:  quartz, quiet, quote, and quickly

p/z

5 Lopez Lopez|pizza pizza|zephyr zephyr|Perez Perez;
6 Spelling words:  utilize, appeal, cozy, and pepper

m/v

7 velvet velvet|move move|remove remove|movie movie;
8 Spelling words:  Vermont, Vermillion, and Vermeil.

**For additional practice** ▶ **MicroType** + **Alphabetic Keyboarding** + **Lesson 18**

## 3F | Speed Building

1. Key one 1' unguided and two 1' guided timed writings on each paragraph.
2. Key two 3' unguided writings on paragraphs 1–2 combined; find *gwam*.

### Quarter-Minute Checkpoints

| gwam | 1/4' | 1/2' | 3/4' | Time |
|------|------|------|------|------|
| 16 | 4 | 8 | 12 | 16 |
| 20 | 5 | 10 | 15 | 20 |
| 24 | 6 | 12 | 18 | 24 |
| 28 | 7 | 14 | 21 | 28 |
| 32 | 8 | 16 | 24 | 32 |
| 36 | 9 | 18 | 27 | 36 |
| 40 | 10 | 20 | 30 | 40 |

GWAM | 3' | 5'

Appearance, which is often defined as the outward aspect of | 4 | 2 | 42

someone or something, is quite important to most of us and affects | 8 | 5 | 45

just about every day of our lives.  We like to be around people | 13 | 8 | 47

whom and things that we consider attractive.  Because of this | 17 | 10 | 50

preference, appearance is an important factor in almost every | 21 | 13 | 52

decision we make. | 22 | 13 | 53

Appearance often affects our selection of food, the place in | 26 | 16 | 55

which we live, the clothes we purchase, the car we drive, and the | 31 | 18 | 58

vacations we schedule.  For example, we usually do not eat foods | 35 | 21 | 61

that are not visually appealing or buy clothing that we realize | 39 | 23 | 63

will be unattractive to others who are important to us. | 43 | 26 | 65

Appearance is also important in business.  People in charge of | 47 | 28 | 68

hiring almost always stress the importance of good appearance. | 51 | 31 | 71

Your progress in a job or career can be affected by how others | 55 | 33 | 73

judge your appearance.  It is not uncommon for those who see but do | 60 | 36 | 76

not know you to evaluate your abilities and character on the basis | 64 | 39 | 78

of your personal appearance. | 66 | 40 | 80

GWAM 3' | 1 | 2 | 3 | 4
5' | 1 | 2 | 3

LESSON

# 19

OBJECTIVE

To learn reach technique for **CAPS LOCK** and **?** (question mark).

## NEW KEYS: CAPS LOCK AND ? (question mark)

### 19A | Conditioning Practice

Key each line twice SS; then key a 1' writing on line 3; find *gwam*.

Alphabet 1   Gus Javon quickly baked extra pizza for the women.

z/: (colon) 2   To:  Ms. Liza Guzzo  From:  Dr. Beatriz K. Vasquez

Easy 3   The firms paid for both of the signs by city hall.

**GWAM** 1' | 1 | 2 | 3 | 4 | 5 | 6 | 7 | 8 | 9 | 10 |

### 19B | New Keys: CAPS LOCK and ? (question mark)

Key each line twice SS (slowly, then faster); DS between 2-line groups. If time permits, rekey lines 7–9.

Depress the CAPS LOCK to key a series of capital letters. To release the CAPS LOCK to key lowercase letters, depress the CAPS LOCK key again.

**Learn CAPS LOCK**

  1  The CARDINALS will play the PHILLIES on Wednesday.

  2  Use SLC for SALT LAKE CITY and BTV for BURLINGTON.

  3  THE GRAPES OF WRATH was written by JOHN STEINBECK.

**Learn ? (question mark)**

Space twice.

  4  :? :? ;? ;? ?; ?; Who? What? When? Where? Why?

  5  When will they arrive?  Will you go?  Where is he?

  6  What time is it?  Who called?  Where is the dance?

**Combine CAPS LOCK and ?**

  7  Is CSCO the ticker symbol for CISCO?  What is MMM?

  8  MEMORIAL DAY is in MAY; LABOR DAY is in SEPTEMBER.

  9  When do the CUBS play the TWINS?  Is it on SUNDAY?

**Caps Lock** Left little finger

**? (question mark)** Left shift; then right little finger

### Tip

Space twice after **?** at the end of a sentence

## Language Arts

### 3D Writing: Number Expression

Read the following number usage rule. Key the Learn line, noting number choices. Key the Apply lines, making the necessary corrections. Save as *U12L3Writing*.

**Rule 5:** Use figures for house numbers except house number One.

Learn 1    The house at One Park Place is identical to the one at 9 Oak Street.

Apply 2    The hotel is located at 1 Huntington Boulevard.

Apply 3    My dentist lives at Ten Plaza Square.

*Our World*

### 3E ▪ Speaking: Democratic Society

Open the file that contains the paragraphs you keyed for Unit 9 Lesson 3G (*U9L3World*). Develop an outline from these paragraphs. Use the outline to make a brief presentation to three of your classmates. Perhaps you have found additional material or have new ideas since you wrote the paragraphs. If so, include that material in your presentation. Be prepared to answer questions from your classmates following your remarks. Save as *U12L3Speaking*.

*Social Studies*

©GETTY IMAGES/PHOTODISC

- **Reach up without moving hands away from you.**
- **Reach down without moving hands toward your body.**
- **Use CAPS LOCK to make ALL CAPS.**
- **Use finger-action keystrokes.**
- **Use quiet hands and arms.**

**To find 1' *gwam*:**

For each line you completed, add 10 to the scale figure beneath the point at which you stopped in a partial line.

## 19C | New-Key Mastery

1. Key each line twice SS; DS between 2-line groups.
2. Key a 1' writing on line 11 and then on line 12.

**CAPS LOCK/ ? (question mark)**
1 UTAH is the BEEHIVE state.  What is HAWAII called?
2 Who did Mark select to play CASSIE in CHORUS LINE?

**z/v**
3 Vince Perez and Zarko Vujacic wore velvet jackets.
4 Zurich, Zeist, Venice, and Pskov were on the quiz.

**q/p**
5 Paula, Pepe, and Peja took the quiz quite quickly.
6 Quincy Pappas and Enrique Quin were both preppies.

**Key words**
7 very exam calf none disk quip wash give just zebra
8 lazy give busy stop fish down junk mark quit exact

**Key phrases**
9 if you can|see the|when will you|it may be|when he
10 where will|and the|as a rule|who is the|to be able

**Alphabet** 11 Jeff Pevey may send a box with a big quartz clock.
**Easy** 12 A complex theory was rejected by Frank G. Vizquel.

**GWAM** 1' | 1 | 2 | 3 | 4 | 5 | 6 | 7 | 8 | 9 | 10 |

### 3B | Technique: Letter Keys

1. Key each line twice SS (slowly, then faster); DS between 2-line groups.
2. Take 30" timings on selected lines.

**Emphasize continuity and rhythm with curved, upright fingers.**

N 1 Norman's niece and nephew can be tended by a new nanny on Monday.

O 2 One of our boys opposed opening more offshore moorings for boats.

P 3 Peter's playful puppies pulled the paper wrapping off the apples.

Q 4 Quinten quit questioning the quantity of bouquets at the banquet.

R 5 Robert and Rae arrived after a carriage ride over the rural road.

S 6 Sue sat still as soon as Sam served his sushi and sashimi dishes.

T 7 Ty took title to two tiny cottages the last time he went to town.

U 8 Uko usually rushes uptown to see us unload the four sugar trucks.

V 9 Val voted to review the vivid videos when she visits the village.

W 10 Will was waving wildly when a swimmer went wading into the water.

X 11 Six tax experts explained that he was exempt from the excise tax.

Y 12 Your younger boy yearns to see the Yankees play in New York City.

Z 13 Zeno puzzled over a zealot who seized a bronze kazoo at a bazaar.

GWAM 1' | 1 | 2 | 3 | 4 | 5 | 6 | 7 | 8 | 9 | 10 | 11 | 12 | 13 |

### 3C | Speed Forcing Drill

Key each line once at top speed. Then try to complete each sentence on the 15", 12", or 10" call, as directed by your instructor. Force speed to higher levels as you move from line to line.

**Emphasis: high-frequency balanced-hand words**

| | GWAM | 15" | 12" | 10" |
|---|---|---|---|---|
| 1 Nancy is to make an official bid on the land. | | 36 | 45 | 54 |
| 2 The sign for the city spa is by the city bus. | | 36 | 45 | 54 |
| 3 Bob's dog slept by the big chair on the city dock. | | 40 | 50 | 60 |
| 4 Ruth may go with us to the city to sign the forms. | | 40 | 50 | 60 |
| 5 The six girls in the sorority may pay to go on the bus. | | 44 | 55 | 66 |
| 6 Helen paid the men for the work they did on the shanty. | | 44 | 55 | 66 |
| 7 Jana and Rich are to fix the big problem with the tax forms. | | 48 | 60 | 72 |
| 8 He may bid on the field by the lake for land for the chapel. | | 48 | 60 | 72 |

### 19D | Block Paragraphs

1. Key each paragraph once.
2. If time permits, key a 1' timing on each paragraph.

**Paragraph 1**

*gwam* 1'

Dance can be a form of art or it can be thought of   10
as a form of recreation.  Dance can be utilized to   20
express ideas and emotions as well as moods.   29

**Paragraph 2**

One form of dance that is quite common is known as   10
ballet.  The earliest forms of ballet are believed   20
to have taken place in Western Europe.   28

**Paragraph 3**

To excel at ballet, you must take lessons when you   10
are very young.  It is not uncommon to see a three   20
year old in a dance studio taking ballet lessons.   30

**Paragraph 4**

In addition to starting at a very young age, hours   10
and hours of practice are also required to develop   20
into a skilled performer of ballet.   27

GWAM  1' |  1  |  2  |  3  |  4  |  5  |  6  |  7  |  8  |  9  |  10  |

For additional practice  MicroType ◆ Alphabetic Keyboarding ◆ Lesson 19

New Keys:  CAPS LOCK and ? (question mark)

## 2F | Speed Building

1. Key one 1' unguided and two 1' guided timed writings on each paragraph.
2. Key two 3' unguided writings on paragraphs 1–2 combined; find *gwam*.

**MicroType**
*Timed Writing*
A

**All letters used**

### Quarter-Minute Checkpoints

| gwam | 1/4' | 1/2' | 3/4' | Time |
|------|------|------|------|------|
| 16 | 4 | 8 | 12 | 16 |
| 20 | 5 | 10 | 15 | 20 |
| 24 | 6 | 12 | 18 | 24 |
| 28 | 7 | 14 | 21 | 28 |
| 32 | 8 | 16 | 24 | 32 |
| 36 | 9 | 18 | 27 | 36 |
| 40 | 10 | 20 | 30 | 40 |

| | GWAM | 3' | 5' |
|---|---|---|---|
| If you plan to purchase a computer, determine what you will | | 4 | 2 | 37 |
| use it for before you buy it. Will you need to key documents using | | 9 | 5 | 40 |
| word processing? Will you need to key worksheets and keep large | | 13 | 8 | 43 |
| databases? Will you need to create presentations using sound and a | | 17 | 10 | 45 |
| large amount of graphics? | | 19 | 11 | 46 |

Are there other requirements? For example, if you want to use handwriting or speech recognition software on your computer, you will need a computer that has the zip to run the software. You will also need to purchase these software programs and special hardware such as a microphone and digital pen.

Do you require a desktop or a laptop personal computer? If you plan to use handwriting recognition, you may want to consider purchasing a computer that has a writing tablet. Other major items you need to consider are whether you need a printer that will also serve as a copier and scanner.

GWAM 3' | 1 | 2 | 3 | 4
5' | 1 | 2 | 3

---

**LESSON**

# 3

**OBJECTIVES**

1. *To improve keying techniques.*
2. *To improve keying speed and control.*

# SKILL BUILDING

## 3A | Conditioning Practice

Key each line twice SS; then key a 1' timed writing on line 3. Determine *gwam*.

Alphabet 1  Marvin will expect to judge the best quality of the seven kazoos.
Figures 2  My team averaged 81 on test scores of 94, 82, 72, 65, 80, and 93.
Speed 3  Helena is to dismantle the shanty down by the dock on the island.

GWAM 1' | 1 | 2 | 3 | 4 | 5 | 6 | 7 | 8 | 9 | 10 | 11 | 12 | 13 |

## NEW KEYS: BACKSPACE AND TAB

### OBJECTIVES

**1.** *To learn reach technique for the **BACKSPACE** key and **TAB** key.*

**2.** *To improve and check keying speed.*

### 20A | Conditioning Practice

Key each line twice SS; then key a 1' writing on line 3. Find *gwam*.

Alphabet 1   Zelda Majewski quickly bought four expensive cats.

CAPS LOCK 2   Rebecca used LXX for SEVENTY, and LXXX for EIGHTY.

Easy 3   Diana and I paid the man for the antique ornament.

**GWAM** 1' | 1 | 2 | 3 | 4 | 5 | 6 | 7 | 8 | 9 | 10 |

### 20B | New Key: BACKSPACE Key

The BACKSPACE key is used to delete text to the left of the insertion point.

1. Locate the BACKSPACE key on your keyboard.

2. Reach up to the BACKSPACE key with the right little finger (be sure to keep the index finger anchored to the j key); tap the BACKSPACE key once for each letter you want deleted; return the finger back to the ; (semicolon) key.

3. Key lines 1–9 below.

**Backspace key** Right little finger; keep right index finger anchored to **j** key.

= Delete

**This symbol means to delete.**

#### Learn Backspace

Line 1   v   [backspace]   g   [backspace]   b   [enter]

Line 2   c   [backspace]   s   [backspace]   a   [enter]

Line 3   d   [backspace]   x   [backspace]   c   [enter]

Line 4   j   [backspace]   l   [backspace]   k   [enter]

Line 5   d   [backspace]   a   [backspace]   s   [enter]

Line 6   o   [backspace]   i   [backspace]   p   [enter]

Line 7   s   [backspace]   d   [backspace]   a   [enter]

Line 8   x   [backspace]   v   [backspace]   c   [enter]

Line 9   r   [backspace]   w   [backspace]   e   [enter]

## 2C | Speed Forcing Drill

Key each line once at top speed. Then try to complete each sentence on the 15", 12", or 10" call, as directed by your instructor. Force speed to higher levels as you move from line to line.

**Emphasis: high-frequency balanced-hand words**

| | | GWAM | 15" | 12" | 10" |
|---|---|---|---|---|---|
| 1 | The proficient man was kept busy with the problem. | | 40 | 50 | 60 |
| 2 | Glen and the girls may handle the problems for us. | | 40 | 50 | 60 |
| 3 | She may blame the girls for the problem with the cycle. | | 44 | 55 | 66 |
| 4 | The auditor did not sign six key elements on the audit. | | 44 | 55 | 66 |
| 5 | The haughty widow and the maid may go to visit the neighbor. | | 48 | 60 | 72 |
| 6 | He may make the panel suspend the pay of the city officials. | | 48 | 60 | 72 |

★ *Language Arts*

## 2D  Writing:  Word Choice

Study the spelling and definitions of the following words. Key the Learn lines, noting the word choices. Key the Apply lines, selecting the correct words. Save as *U12L2Writing*.

**choose** (verb)  to select; to decide

**chose** (verb)  past tense of choose

Learn 1  Gregory will **choose** the winning English essay.

Learn 2  He **chose** to write an essay on patriotism.

Apply 3  Did you know they (choose, chose) Sandy for treasurer?

Apply 4  Who do you think the director will (choose, chose) to lead the choir?

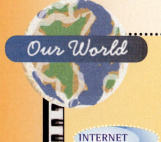

*Our World*

INTERNET

## 2E ▪ Research a College or University

Many colleges and universities have Internet sites that provide information about the schools. Use an Internet search engine to find the website for a college or university you are interested in learning more about. Access the website and find answers to the following questions. Save as *U12L2Internet*.

- What does the institution charge each year for tuition and fees? If the school is not in your home state, you will need to know how much nonresident tuition costs.

- What is the cost for room and board per year?

- What are the admission requirements?

- What test(s) is required in order to be accepted?

## 20C | Speed Check: Sentences

1. Key a 30" writing on each line. Your rate in *gwam* is shown word for word above the lines.

2. Key another 30" writing on each line. Try to increase your keying speed.

```
1  Karl did not make the ski team.
2  Jay shared his poem with all of us.
3  Doris played several video games online.
4  Their next game will be played in four weeks.
5  She will register today for next semester classes.
6  She quit the team so she would have more time to study.
```

| GWAM | 30" | 2 | 4 | 6 | 8 | 10 | 12 | 14 | 16 | 18 | 20 |
|------|-----|---|---|---|---|----|----|----|----|----|----|

## 20D | New Key: TAB Key

The TAB key is used to indent the first line of paragraphs. Word processing software has preset tabs called default tabs. Usually, the first default tab is set 0.5" to the right of the left margin. This tab is used to indent paragraphs (see copy below).

1. Locate the TAB key on your keyboard (usually at upper left of alphabetic keyboard).

2. Reach up to the TAB key with the left little finger; tap the key firmly and release it quickly. The insertion point will move 0.5" to the right.

3. Key each paragraph once SS. DS between paragraphs. As you key, tap the TAB key firmly to indent the first line of each paragraph. Use the BACKSPACE key to correct errors as you key.

**Tab** key Left little finger

```
Tab→The Tab key is an important key.  It is used to indent
blocks of copy such as these.

Tab→The Tab key can also be used to create tables.  Tables
are used to arrange data quickly and neatly into columns.

Tab→Learn now to use the Tab key by touch.  By doing so,
you will add to your keying skill.

Tab→Tap the Tab key firmly and release it very quickly.
Begin the line without a pause.

Tab→If you hold the Tab key down, the insertion point
will move from tab to tab across the line.
```

## OBJECTIVES

1. *To improve keying techniques.*
2. *To improve keying speed and control.*

### 2A | Conditioning Practice

Key each line twice SS; then key a 1' timed writing on line 3. Determine *gwam*.

Alphabet 1   Amy realizes we need five expert judges to check the unique book.

Figures/Symbols 2   Her dress costs $486.97 (20% off), and she has saved only $97.60.

Speed 3   The neighbor may dismantle the dock by the lake in the coalfield.

GWAM 1' | 1 | 2 | 3 | 4 | 5 | 6 | 7 | 8 | 9 | 10 | 11 | 12 | 13 |

### 2B | Technique:  Letter Keys

1. Key each line twice SS (slowly, then faster); DS between 2-line groups.
2. Take 30" timings on selected lines.

**Emphasize continuity and rhythm with curved, upright fingers.**

A 1   After Diana Aaron ate the pancake, she had an apple and a banana.

B 2   Barbi Bilbrey became a better batter by batting big rubber balls.

C 3   Chi Chang from Creekcrest Circle can catch a raccoon for Chelcia.

D 4   Did Dave and Don decide to delay the date of departure for a day?

E 5   Ed and Eileen were elected to chaperone every late evening event.

F 6   Fred figured fifty fast rafts floated from Fairfax to Ford Falls.

G 7   Gary and Gregg glanced at the gaggle of geese on the green grass.

H 8   His haphazard shots helped them through half of the hockey match.

I 9   I think Ike insisted on living in Illinois, Indiana, or Missouri.

J 10   Jackie just objected to taking Jay's jeans and jersey on the jet.

K 11   Ken kept Kay's knickknack in a knapsack in the back of the kayak.

L 12   Large and small holes in the lane by her dwelling will be filled.

M 13   Mike meets my mom most mornings at the mall in the summer months.

GWAM 1' | 1 | 2 | 3 | 4 | 5 | 6 | 7 | 8 | 9 | 10 | 11 | 12 | 13 |

## 20E | Keyboard Reinforcement

1. Key lines once SS; DS between 2-line groups.
2. Key the lines again at a faster pace.
3. Key a 1' writing on lines 10–12.

### Position Reminder

As you key each line:

- Keep fingers curved and upright.
- Keep forearms parallel to slant of keyboard.
- Keep your body erect, sitting back in chair.
- Place feet on floor for balance.

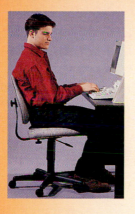

**Reach review (Keep the fingers that are not used for reaching on home keys.)**

```
1  open moon exam coat bear very quit huge when ozone
2  when can|juice box|next exam|before long|long gone
3  Henry chews his gum so loud that it annoys others.
```

**Space Bar emphasis (Think, say, and key the words.)**

```
4  the and can fit hat bit dot pan zoo for ham jam or
5  in the|it is|and she|may see|the end|of our|off of
6  The big sign down by the city hall is for Orlando.
```

**Shift key emphasis (Reach up and reach down without moving the hands.)**

```
7  Stan and Doris Benson are here to se Dr. Marshall.
8  Mark moved to Ogden from Salt Lake City on Friday.
9  He got his Ph.D. last Friday from San Diego State.
```

**Easy sentences (Think, say, and key the words at a steady pace.)**

```
10  I am to make a plan to buy a firm in the old town.
11  The maid paid the eight men for the work they did.
12  Pamela may do the work for us if the pay is right.
```

**GWAM** 1' | 1 | 2 | 3 | 4 | 5 | 6 | 7 | 8 | 9 | 10 |

## 1G | Business Letter

1. Key the following information as a business letter.  Use block format and open punctuation.  Assume the letter will be printed on letterhead paper.  Place the date about 2" from the top of the page.

2. Spell-check the letter and proofread carefully.  Correct all errors.  Save the letter as *U12L1Letter3*.

November 26, 20--

Mrs. Evelyn M. McNeil

4582 Campus Drive

Fort Worth, TX 76119-1835

Dear Mrs. McNeil

You are invited to visit our exciting gallery of gifts.  With our help, gift-giving can be a snap at any time of the year.  Our store has a vast wide array of gifts "for kids of all ages."

What's more, many of our gifts are prewrapped for presentation.  All can be packaged and shipped from our store to all most anywhere in the world.

A catalog of our hottest gift items and a schedule of our store hours are enclosed.  Please stop in and let us help you select that special gift.  You will receive information about our new website soon.

Sincerely

Ms. Carol J. Suess, Manager

xx

Enclosure

# Math Activities

## 20F ▪ Math Challenge 1

## REWRITE FRACTIONS AS DECIMALS AND PERCENTS

1. Write one or more sentences to explain how you rewrite fractions in their decimal and percent equivalents.

2. Using a pencil and paper, rewrite the following fractions as their decimal equivalents, rounded to hundredths if needed. Compare your answers with those provided by your instructor.

   2a. 2/5    2b. 7/25    2c. 13/30
   2d. 5/11   2e. 5/6

3. Using a pencil and paper, rewrite the following fractions as their percent equivalents, rounded to tenths if needed. Compare your answers with those provided by your instructor.

   3a. 3/4    3b. 3/8    3c. 63/85
   3d. 93/98  3e. 67/37

## Careers

## 20G ▪ Career Exploration Portfolio – Activity 1

There are many different career opportunities available to you once you graduate from high school. Some careers require no additional education, while others require many years of additional education. The 15 career exploration activities at the end of all units except the Project units will help you understand the requirements for some of the careers in which you may have an interest. Begin your exploration by completing the following steps.

1. Access http://www.careerclusters.org.

2. Complete the Career Clusters Interest Survey Activity. Your instructor will provide you with a copy of the survey or you can click on Free Career Clusters Interest Survey Activity and then click on View/Print Now. Print a copy of the survey and the Sixteen Career Clusters pages that follow the Interest Survey.

3. Obtain a folder for your Career Exploration Portfolio from your instructor, write your name and class period on it, place your completed Interest Survey and descriptions of the career clusters in the folder, and file the folder as instructed.

For additional practice ▶ MicroType + Alphabetic Keyboarding + Lesson 20

## 1F | Business Letter

1. Key the following information as a business letter. Use block format and mixed punctuation. Assume the letter will be printed on letterhead paper. Place the date about 2" from the top of the page.

2. Spell-check the letter and proofread carefully. Correct all errors. Save as *U12L1Letter2*.

3. Create a large envelope for the letter. (Assume the return address is preprinted.) Save the envelope as *U12L1Env2*.

February 23, 20--


Dr. Bonnie Klingensmith
Science Department
East Tulsa High School
10916 N. Garnett Road
Tulsa, OK 74116-1016

Dear Dr. Klingensmith

Our company has laboratory furniture and equipment that we would like to donate to your high school. We feel certain that your science teachers and students will benefit from what we are offering.

A list of the major items we can donate is enclosed. All items will be available before the end of July. They can be delivered and installed before school starts in late August.

Please call me at 918-555-0155. We will arrange a meeting for your personnel to see the furniture and equipment.

Sincerely


Jose L. Domingo
Public Relations

xx

Enclosure

bc Principal, East Tulsa High School

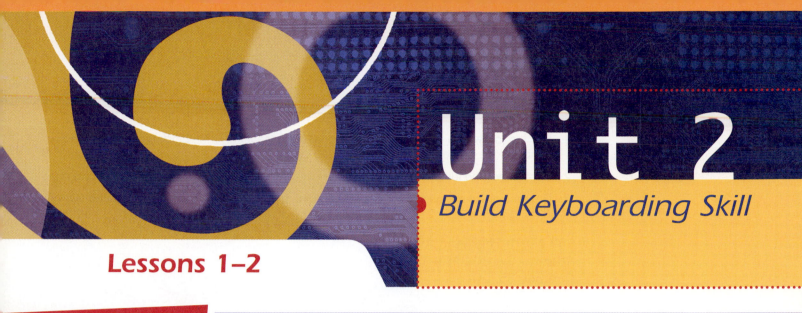

# Unit 2
## Build Keyboarding Skill

### Lessons 1–2

## LESSON
# 1

### OBJECTIVES

1. *To improve technique on individual letters.*
2. *To improve and check keying speed.*
3. *To learn to key script copy.*
4. *To learn the line spacing word processing feature.*
5. *To improve writing skills.*

### Technique Goals

- curved, upright fingers
- quick-snap keystrokes
- quiet hands and arms

## SKILL DEVELOPMENT 1

### 1A | Conditioning Practice

Key each line twice SS; then key a 1' timed writing on line 3.  Determine *gwam*.

| | | |
|---|---|---|
| Alphabet | 1 | Harv Zepow may get six jackets for Quigley's band. |
| Spacing | 2 | and the box yes was may you ice van zest paid quit |
| Easy | 3 | Kamela may work with the city auditor on the form. |

GWAM  1' | 1 | 2 | 3 | 4 | 5 | 6 | 7 | 8 | 9 | 10 |

### 1B | Technique:  Individual Letters

Key each line twice SS (slowly, then faster); DS between 2-line groups.

**Emphasize continuity and rhythm with curved, upright fingers.**

A 1  Ann Adams always wears an apron to wait on tables.
B 2  Barbara Babbitt said Bobby Gabel bobbled the ball.
C 3  Cody Cisco consciously circled the correct choice.
D 4  David and Donald did indeed divide instead of add.
E 5  Eileen and Ellen fed the seed to the three eagles.
F 6  Fifty-five took the final on Friday; five flunked.
G 7  Gregg giggled at the gang gathering the gray eggs.
H 8  Hans helped the hotheaded hitchhiker with his hat.
I 9  Iris finished itemizing items five, six, and nine.
J 10  Joy, Jay, Jane, and Jill just took a jet to Japan.
K 11  Kay knew Jack kicked the knickknack off the kayak.
L 12  Lillian will buy the ball and balloon at the mall.
M 13  Malcolm McMillan made minimum wage at Mammoth Zoo.

GWAM  1' | 1 | 2 | 3 | 4 | 5 | 6 | 7 | 8 | 9 | 10 |

## 1E | Personal-Business Letter

1. Key the following information as a personal-business letter. Use block format and open punctuation. Center the letter vertically on the page.

2. Spell-check the letter and proofread carefully. Correct all errors. Save as *U12L1Letter1*.

3. Create a small envelope with a return address for the letter. Save the envelope as *U12L1Env1*.

853 North Highland Avenue
Atlanta, GA 30306-0403
October 15, 20--


Ms. Amy Mazanetz
4505 Ashford Road
Atlanta, GA 30346-0346

Dear Ms. Mazanetz

Thank you for speaking to our Community Service Club. Your points on the importance of giving back to the community were very well received. They will help motivate us to do as much service work as we can.

I enjoyed learning about the projects you have supervised as a leader inour community. Our members plan to adopt at least two of the projectsyou described. We will choose the projects at our next meeting. Your insights into what it takes to plan, organize, manage, and evaluateservice projects will be helpful to us.

Again, thank you for sharing your expertise with our club and agreeing to work with us in the future.

Sincerely


Alex Neu
Secretary

## 1C | Speed Check: Sentences

If you finish a line before time is called and start over, your *gwam* is the figure at the end of the line *plus* the figure above or below the point at which you stopped.

1. Key a 30" writing on each line. Your rate in *gwam* is shown word for word above the lines.

2. Key another 30" writing on each line. Try to increase your keying speed.

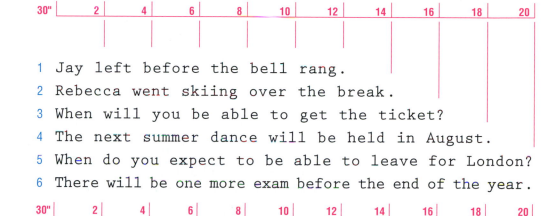

```
30"|    2  |    4  |    6  |    8  |   10  |   12  |   14  |   16  |   18  |   20

1  Jay left before the bell rang.
2  Rebecca went skiing over the break.
3  When will you be able to get the ticket?
4  The next summer dance will be held in August.
5  When do you expect to be able to leave for London?
6  There will be one more exam before the end of the year.

30"|    2 |    4 |    6 |    8 |   10 |   12 |   14 |   16 |   18 |   20 |
```

---

## ★ *Language Arts*

## 1D Writing: Word Choice

Study the spelling and definitions of the words below. Key the Learn lines, noting the word choices. Key the Apply lines, selecting the correct words. Save as *U2L1WordChoice.*

**than** (conj/prep) used in comparisons to show difference between items

**then** (noun/adverb) that time; at that time

Learn 1  She has higher grades **than** you have.

Learn 2  When your homework is done, you may **then** watch the game.

Apply 3  Felipe has more points (than, then) I on the exams.

Apply 4  After I count the votes, he will (than, then) announce the winner.

---

## 1E | Handwritten Copy (Script)

Key each line once DS.

1  *Occasionally the copy you will key is from script.*
2  *Script is copy that is written with pen or pencil.*
3  *Read script a few words ahead of the keying point.*
4  *Doing so will help you produce copy free of error.*
5  *With practice, you will key script at a good rate.*

## 1C | Memo

1. Key the following information in memo format. Use a 12-point font. Use paragraph spacing to insert vertical space between memo parts and paragraphs.

2. View the memo to verify correct format. Spell-check the memo and proofread carefully. Correct all errors. Save as *U12L1Memo*.

TO: Department Managers

FROM: Human Resources Manager

DATE: April 5, 20--

SUBJECT: FITNESS CLUB MEMBERSHIP

The Action Fitness and Exercise Center is offering a special plan to our employees. This plan includes membership for 90 days. The plan costs only $50, the regular monthly membership fee.

The plan includes a 90-day trial period. During this time, our employees can use the Center and all its equipment. The Center has an indoor running track, weight lifting stations, and exercise equipment (including treadmills, stair climbers, and rowing machines).

Our employees can also enroll in any of the aerobics, weight control, and healthy eating classes that are offered.

To take advantage of this offer, our employees must present one of the enclosed cards on their first visit. This offer applies to all members of the employee's immediate family.

xx

Enclosure

c Mary Parker

## 1D | E-mail (E-mail users only)

1. Key the following information as an e-mail message from you to your instructor. Use a 12-point font. Attach *U12L1List* to the e-mail message.

2. Spell-check the message and proofread carefully. Correct all errors. Save as *U12L1EMail*.

The attached list shows the value the portfolios for my clients as of the end of the first quarter. You can include them in the master list you are compiling for the office.

The Line Spacing command allows you to change the amount of white space between lines of text. Single spacing (SS) is the default line spacing. Other frequently used spacing options are 1.5 lines and double spacing (DS).

## 1F | Line Spacing

### Learn to Change Line Spacing

To change line spacing:

1. Place the insertion point on the line that is to be followed by the new line spacing.

2. On the menu bar, click Format. Click Paragraph. The Paragraph dialog box appears.

3. Click the down arrow for the Line spacing drop-down list and click a spacing option. Click OK.

**Single Spacing:** no blank lines between lines of text

**1.5 Lines Spacing:** ½ blank line between lines of text

**Double Spacing:** 1 blank line between lines of text

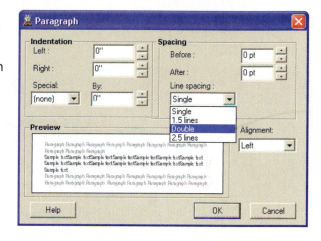

### Practice What You Have Learned

1. Set the line spacing to Double. Key the five lines of **1E** again.

2. Set the line spacing to 1.5 lines. Key **1E** a third time, trying to increase your script copy keying rate.

3. Compare the difference between SS, DS, and 1.5 spacing.

## 1G | Speed Check: Paragraphs

Key two 1' writings on each paragraph; determine *gwam* (the figure/dot above the last letter you keyed).

```
        •       2       •       4       •       6       •       8       •
      Being able to input at the keyboard is a very
   10        •      12       •      14       •      16       •      18       •
useful skill to learn.  It is one that you will be
   20        •      22       •      24       •      26       •      28       •
ble to use quite often during the next few years.
        •       2       •       4       •       6       •       8       •
      The computer keyboard is still the most common
   10        •      12       •      14       •      16       •      18       •
method used to input data.  Your job over the next
   20        •      22       •      24       •      26       •      28
few weeks is to learn to key the letters more
   •       30      •      32       •      34       •      36       •
quickly.  Key the letters with a lot of zest.
```

# Unit 12

## Assess Correspondence and Build Skill

### Lessons 1–3

## OBJECTIVE

*To assess your ability to format memos, e-mail messages, personal-business letters, and business letters.*

## CORRESPONDENCE FORMATTING SKILLS

### 1A | Conditioning Practice

Key each line twice SS; then key a 1' timed writing on line 3. Determine *gwam*.

Alphabet 1   Paul Carson just asked to survey the big tax quiz form in a week.

Figures 2   Check number 3597, 3608, 3612, and 3614 were cashed last Tuesday.

Speed 3   Jane is proficient when she roams right field with pep and vigor.

GWAM 1' | 1 | 2 | 3 | 4 | 5 | 6 | 7 | 8 | 9 | 10 | 11 | 12 | 13 |

### 1B | List

1. Key the following directory. Set a top margin at 2" and a left tab at 1.5", a center tab with dot leaders at 4.5", and a right tab with dot leaders at 6". Double-space the directory. Key the first two lines (title and headings).

2. Change the center tab at 4.5" to a decimal tab with dot leaders. Key the remaining lines.

3. View the list to verify correct format. Spell-check the list and proofread carefully. Correct all errors. Save as *U12L1List*.

#### Client Stock Value at End of First Quarter

| Name | Corporation | Shares | Dollar Value |
|---|---|---|---|
| Jerry Pacek | Packrone, Inc. | 656.875 | $25,104.79 |
| Robert Clohesty | Stoffer & Kiki, Inc. | 150.3 | $5,234.97 |
| Paul Naughton | National Life & Casualty, Inc. | 567 | $14,768.00 |
| Christine Eremiza | Stiffler Logistics International | 1,350.75 | $45,789.50 |

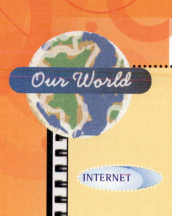

INTERNET

## 1H ■ Modern Wonders of the World.

Several of the modern wonders of the world are listed below. Use an encyclopedia or the Internet to learn about one of these wonders. Take notes and be prepared to share information about the wonder you research. Note the addresses of the Internet sites you use to learn about this topic.

- The Channel Tunnel
- Big Ben
- Eiffel Tower
- Mount Rushmore
- The Statue of Cristo Redentor
- Suez Canal

Your teacher may provide a world map to use with Our World activities. If directed, indicate the location of the modern wonder and label it on the map.

*Social Studies*

**For additional practice** ▶ **MicroType ✦ Keyboarding Skill Builder ✦ Lesson A**

## LESSON

# 2

### OBJECTIVES

1. To improve technique on individual letters.
2. To enhance keying technique.
3. To build straight-copy speed and control.
4. To improve writing skills.

# SKILL DEVELOPMENT 2

### 2A | Conditioning Practice

Key each line twice SS; then key a 1' timed writing on line 3. Determine *gwam*.

Alphabet 1   Nate will vex the judge if he bucks my quiz group.
CAPS LOCK 2   STACY works for HPJ, Inc.; SAMANTHA, for JPH Corp.
Easy 3   Nancy is to vie with six girls for the city title.
GWAM   1' |   1   |   2   |   3   |   4   |   5   |   6   |   7   |   8   |   9   |   10   |

**Job 8**

Prepare this letter to Larry Topolow from Mr. Sutter. Use the letterhead you designed in Job 3.

*(Insert current date)*

*Mr. Larry Topolow*
*400 Oak Street*
*Cincinnati, OH 45219-4010*

*Dear Larry:*

*On behalf of everyone at the Cleveland East Soccer Club, thank you for your years of service to our community. You have contributed greatly to the growth of our soccer programs. Your efforts have helped many boys and girls develop skills that helped them earn athletic grants. CESC currently has 16 boys and girls competing at the collegiate level. You should be proud of this achievement.*

*Please accept the enclosed certificate as a token of our appreciation for your leadership and service in our developing years. When you are in this area, please stop by and say hello your CESC friends and associates. We will enjoy your company and thoughts about what is best for CESC.*

*Sincerely,*

*Kyle Sutter*
*CESC President*

*xx*

*Enclosure*

**Job 9**

Create a personal-business letter to Mr. Sutter. Include the information below.

- Thank him for the opportunity to participate in your school's community service project and for selecting you to do his work.

- Tell him what you learned from this project.

- Request that he write you a letter of reference that you can include in your portfolio.

- Indicate that you are willing to help him in the future.

## 2B | Technique: Individual Letters

Key each line twice SS (slowly, then faster); DS between 2-line groups.

**Emphasize continuity and rhythm with curved, upright fingers.**

N 1  Nancy Kennan went downtown for a planning meeting.
O 2  Moorcroft is to oppose Upton in one football game.
P 3  Phillip wrapped the puppets in pink paper for Pam.
Q 4  Quinn Quayle quickly quoted the queen on the quiz.
R 5  Larry and Jarred hung the mirror right over there.
S 6  Bess sold subscriptions in Mississippi and Kansas.
T 7  Their estate battle took quite a bit of their time.
U 8  Spell untrue, unusually, unused, and usury for us.
V 9  Vivacious Vivian gave a vivid review of the video.
W 10  When will Wes work on Wilma Weston's two walkways?
X 11  Rex Baxter graded six extra tax exams for Dr. Cox.
Y 12  Gary may ask Cy to try to do a yard in Rapid City.
Z 13  The zero on Dr. Zacho's zoology quiz puzzled Zane.

GWAM  1' |  1 | 2 | 3 | 4 | 5 | 6 | 7 | 8 | 9 | 10 |

## 2C | Speed Check: Sentences

1. Key a 30" writing on each line. Your rate in *gwam* is shown word for word above the lines.
2. Key another 30" writing on lines 7–10. Try to increase your keying speed.

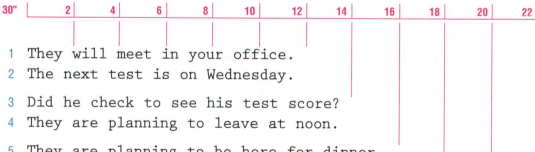

30" |  2 |  4 |  6 |  8 |  10 |  12 |  14 |  16 |  18 |  20 |  22

1  They will meet in your office.
2  The next test is on Wednesday.

3  Did he check to see his test score?
4  They are planning to leave at noon.

5  They are planning to be here for dinner.
6  Did you include her name on your report?

7  My exhibit placed first in the sales contest.
8  When we stop to get gas, we can buy some gum.

9  He is real excited to see the results of the test.
10  What time do you think Sheila will be ready to go?

11  Their best runner fell down going around the last turn.
12  The art exhibit featured work by Van Gogh and Da Vinci.

|  2 |  4 |  6 |  8 |  10 |  12 |  14 |  16 |  18 |  20 |  22 |

If you finish a line before time is called and start over, your *gwam* is the figure at the end of the line *plus* the figure above or below the point at which you stopped.

**Technique Goals**
- curved, upright fingers
- quick-snap keystrokes
- quiet hands and arms

All matches are played at the Soccer East Complex on Morgan Road. We can choose to sell refreshments from 8 a.m. to 11 a.m., from 11 a.m. to 2 p.m., or 2 p.m. to 5 p.m. They need three of us for each time slot. We would sell from the refreshment booth, and there will be adult supervision at all times.

We would be paid 15 percent of the revenues collected during our time or $15, whichever is greater. In the past most workers received $18 to $20 for their three-hour shift.

You can register as a worker by e-mailing Mrs. Mary Santori at msantori24@netpace.com. Give Mrs. Santori your name, telephone number, and the times and dates you want to work. She will get back to you to confirm your times and dates. Remember, the earlier you register, the more likely it is you will receive your preferred times and dates.

Sincerely,


Your Name

## Job 7

Format this tentative agenda for Mr. Sutter.

Cleveland East Soccer Club

Tentative Agenda—Executive Board Meeting

Tuesday, (Insert first Tuesday of next month date), 20--

   I.   Call to order

  II.   Approval of minutes

 III.   Reports

       A.  Vice President

       B.  Treasurer

       C.  Others

 IV.   Old business

       A.  Meeting date

## 2D Writing: Capitalization

Read the capitalization rules below. Study the Learn lines. Note how the rules are applied. Key the Learn lines and the Apply lines, making the necessary corrections in the Apply lines. Save as *U2L2Capitalization*.

**Rule 1:** Capitalize the first word of a sentence.

Learn 1 All of the games were cancelled due to the storm.

Learn 2 The next chapter will cover pronouns.

Apply 3 they will have pizza at the party.

Apply 4 he could not hear the teacher.

**Rule 2:** Capitalize personal titles and names of people.

Learn 5 I have an appointment with Dr. Ramirez.

Learn 6 They will meet with Ms. Nelson next week.

Apply 7 When did mr. baxter find his wallet?

Apply 8 mr. cox and dr. kubeck will be our keynote speakers.

## 2E | Insertion Point Moves Review

Review the insertion point moves on page 47. Use the text lines you keyed for **2C**. For each line shown below, move the insertion point to the location shown by the red arrow. Key the word(s) indicated.

Line 1: Key **old**

Line 2: Key **biology**

Line 3: Key **final**

Line 4: Key **for Miami**

Line 5 Key **later**

Line 6: Key **last**

```
1  They will meet in your  ▲ office.
2  The next  ▲ test is on Wednesday.
3  Did he check to see his  ▲ test score?
4  They are planning to leave  ▲ at noon.
5  They are planning to be here  ▲ for dinner.
6  Did you include her name on your  ▲ report?
```

**Job 5**

Prepare this memo to the executive board members.

TO:        Cleveland East Soccer Club Executive Board

FROM:      Kyle Sutter, President

DATE:      (Insert current date)

SUBJECT:   BOARD MEETING MINUTES

A copy of the minutes from the last meeting is enclosed.  Review them before the next meeting and bring any changes or corrections to the meeting.

I have surveyed the board members who were unable to attend our last meeting.  They all agree that Tuesday is a better meeting day than Wednesday.  Without exception, each suggested meeting on the first Tuesday of the month instead of the second Tuesday.  As I recall, all who attended the meeting indicated the first Tuesday was their second choice.  We will, therefore, change the meeting day from the first Wednesday to the first Tuesday.  I have reserved the Community Center so the meeting place and time will remain the same.

Please plan to attend.  A tentative agenda is enclosed.  If you want another item added to the agenda, please let me know by Friday before the meeting.

xx

Enclosures:  Meeting minutes and tentative agenda

**Job 6**

Compose a personal-business letter from yourself to send to your friends who might like to earn money selling refreshments at Saturday soccer matches.  Mr. Sutter has drafted a letter, but feel free to revise it.  Make a list of the names and addresses of your friends you want to receive the letter.

(Insert current date)


Your street address
Your city, state, and ZIP
Current date

Friend's name
Friend's street address
Friend's city, state, and ZIP

Dear (Insert the friend's name):

The Cleveland East Soccer Club is seeking our help to sell refreshments at their Saturday matches during May and June.  Each of us can select our times and dates on a first-come, first-serve basis.

(continued)

## 2F | Speed Check: Paragraphs

1. Key a 1' timed writing on each paragraph; determine *gwam* on each writing.

2. Using your better *gwam* as a base rate, select a goal rate and key two 1' guided writings on each paragraph as directed below.

3. Key two, 2' writings on paragraphs 1–2.

```
                •      2     •      4     •      6     •      8     •
    Do you realize just how important a keyboarding
  10     •     12    •     14    •     16    •     18    •     20
skill is?  No one can learn to keyboard for you.  You
    •     22    •     24    •     26    •     28    •     30    •
have to put in the time and effort yourself in order
    32     •     34     •
to learn this skill.
                •      2     •      4     •      6     •      8     •
    Once you learn the alphabetic keys, you should
  10     •     12    •     14    •     16    •     18    •     20
work to increase your speed.  If you put in the extra
    •     22    •     24    •     26    •     28    •     30
time and effort required, you will be able to key at
    •     32     •
a high rate.
```

GWAM 2' |     1    |    2    |    3    |    4    |    5    |

## Quarter-Minute Checkpoints

| gwam | 1/4' | 1/2' | 3/4' | Time |
|---|---|---|---|---|
| 16 | 4 | 8 | 12 | 16 |
| 20 | 5 | 10 | 15 | 20 |
| 24 | 6 | 12 | 18 | 24 |
| 28 | 7 | 14 | 21 | 28 |
| 32 | 8 | 16 | 24 | 32 |
| 36 | 9 | 18 | 27 | 36 |
| 40 | 10 | 20 | 30 | 40 |

## Guided (Paced) Writing Procedure

### Select a Practice Goal

1. Key a 1' timed writing on paragraph 1 of a set of paragraphs that contain word-count dots and figures above the lines, as in **2F** above.

2. Using the *gwam* as a base, add 4 *gwam* to determine your goal rate.

3. In column 1 of the table at the left, find the speed nearest your goal rate. In the quarter-minute columns beside that speed, note the points in the copy you must reach to maintain your goal rate.

4. Determine the checkpoint for each quarter minute from the dots and figures above the lines in paragraph 1. (*Example*: Checkpoints for 24 *gwam* are 6, 12, 18, and 24.)

### Practice Procedure

1. Key two 1' timed writings on paragraph 1 at your goal rate guided by the quarter-minute signals (1/4, 1/2, 3/4, time). Try to reach each of your checkpoints just as the signal is called.

2. Key two 1' writings on paragraph 2 of a set of paragraphs in the same way.

3. If time permits, key a 2' writing on the set of paragraphs combined, without the guides.

### Copy Difficulty

Copy used to measure skill is triple-controlled for difficulty:

E = easy

LA = low average

A = average

**Job 4**

Prepare a draft of this letter that the club will send to soccer clubs in the regional soccer association. Leona Fordyce, Tournament Director, will sign the letter. Use the letterhead you designed in Job 3. Also, change games to matches in the letter.

*(Insert current date)*

Mr. John Doe, President
St. Louis East Soccer Club
212 N. Kings Highway
St. Louis, MO 63108-5691

Dear President Doe:

The Cleveland East Soccer Club is sponsoring its 5th annual soccer tournament. The tournament is for Under 14 Boys and Girls traveling teams within our region. The tournament will be held on Friday, Saturday, and Sunday, June 5-7, 20--.

The first games on Friday will begin at 3 p.m. The championship games will begin at 4 p.m. on Sunday. Each team entering the tournament is guaranteed to play at least three games—one on each day. Our 4 full-size fields with lights and tournament schedule will accommodate up to 32 teams—16 boys and 16 girls—playing games with 35-minute halves.

A brochure is enclosed. Information about entry fees, food and lodging, tournament rules, trophies and awards, and an outline of a schedule is in the brochure. If you want to enter one or more teams, be certain to return the registration form from the last panel of the brochure. Times for first-round games will be drawn on June 1 and posted on our website at www.cesc.swep.org.

Sincerely,

Leona Fordyce
Tournament Director

xx

Enclosure

c Mr. Kyle Sutter, President

Our World

## 2G ▪ Research Weather

The Internet can be used to learn about current weather conditions and forecasts. Find information about weather conditions in your area.

INTERNET

1. Access the website http://asp.usatoday.com/weather/.

2. On the site, locate the section where you can personalize your weather forecast.

3. In the box that is provided, key the ZIP Code or name of your city.

4. Click the GO button to get the forecast.

5. Answer these questions:

- What is the current temperature of your city?
- When is the time of the sunset today?
- What is the humidity for today?
- What is tomorrow's projected high temperature?
- What is tomorrow's projected low temperature?

# Math Activities

## 2H ▪ Math Challenge 2

### REWRITE DECIMALS AS FRACTIONS AND PERCENTS

1. Key a paragraph to explain how you rewrite decimals as their fraction and percent equivalents.

2. Using a pencil and paper, rewrite the following decimals as a fraction, reduced to its lowest terms. Compare your answers with those provided by your instructor.

| | | |
|---|---|---|
| 2a. .45 | 2b. .068 | 2c. .333 |
| 2d. .875 | 2e. .0075 | |

3. Using a pencil and paper, rewrite the following numbers as percents, rounded to hundredths if needed. Compare your answers with those provided by your instructor.

| | | |
|---|---|---|
| 3a. .87 | 3b. 2.15 | 3c. .0024 |
| 3d. 5.035 | 3e. 105.55 | |

4. Save your answers as *U2L2Math*.

*Remember to replace "games" with "matches" throughout*

The president reported that lights have been installed on a new field. The field will be available for ~~games~~ *matches* beginning next week. Request for bids for new uniforms have *been* sent to area sporting goods stores. The response date is the *Friday* ~~Monday~~ before the next meeting. The approval of a contract will be on the agenda for the next meeting.

The president reported that we have more ~~than~~ children playing soccer this year than at any time in the past decade. Nearly 1,100 children from age 5 through 18 are on teams this season.

<u>Old Business</u>

The tournament brochure has been printed. It will be mailed to ~~the presidents of~~ the soccer clubs in the Eastern Ohio Region within the next few weeks. The class to train officials began last Saturday. Karl Moeller has recruited more than 25 parents and teenagers to attend the class. He expects at least 18 people to pass the class and be available for officiating matches this season.

<u>New Business</u>

The addition of three travel teams for the coming season were approved—Under 12 Boys and Girls and Under 18 Girls. Coaches and team managers will be appointed at the next meeting. Stacey Turnshek will find qualified volunteers.

The purchase of 50 tons of limestone for the parking lots was approved. Jim Turner, a local excavator and Club parent, will use his equipment to spread the stone.

The board accepted *with regret* the resignation of Larry Topolow, director of player development, who moved from the area.

The board discussed changing the meeting dates because *some* ~~many~~ board members cannot attend on Wednesday evenings. A motion was made to move the board meeting day to the second Tuesday of each month. This motion was tabled until the president is able to survey those who are absent to see if the second Tuesday is a good date. A vote will be taken at the next meeting.

<u>Next Meeting *and* Adjournment</u>

The next meeting date was set for 7 p.m. on the first Wednesday of next month. The meeting was adjourned at 9:15 p.m.

### Job 3

Mr Sutter has requested a new company letterhead. Design a letterhead for his review. The letterhead should include the club's e-mail address and website URL. The information you need is given below.

*Cleveland East Soccer Club*
*3450 Lee Road*
*Cleveland, OH 44120-3400*

*216-555-0199*
*cesc@invbox.net*
*www.cesc.swep.org*

### 21 ■ Career Exploration Portfolio – Activity 2

- You must complete Activity 1 on page 70 before completing this activity.

1. Retrieve your completed Career Clusters Interest Survey from your folder.

2. Determine your top three career clusters by adding the number of circled items in each box. Write the total number of items circled in the small box at the right of each section; then determine the boxes with the highest numbers. The box numbers correspond to the career cluster numbers on the pages you printed earlier.

For example, let's say you had 15 circles in Box 6, 11 circles in Box 7, and 12 circles in Box 11. You have shown an interest in Finance (Box 6), Government & Public Administration (Box 7), and Information Technology (Box 11).

3. Return your Career folder to the storage area.

**For additional practice** ▶**MicroType**✦**Keyboarding Skill Builder**✦**Lesson B**

**Job 1**

Mr. Sutter wants you to prepare a telephone directory of the CESC executive board arranged alphabetically by last name from the information below. Format the directory so the names begin at the left margin, the position titles are centered, and the telephone numbers end at the right margin. Use leaders to connect the information. Include a heading and column headings.

Kyle Sutter, President, 216-555-0101

Ken Gomez, Vice President, 216-555-0135

Beverly Gnieski, Treasurer, 216-555-0162

Shari Morakis, Director, 216-555-0115

Stacey Turnshek, Coaches and Managers, 216-555-0190

Leona Fordyce, Tournament Director, 216-555-0144

Sean O'Brien, Facilities and Equipment, 216-555-0127

Mary Santori, Field Services, 216-555-0108

Karl Moeller, Officials, 216-555-0149

**Job 2**

Mr. Sutter proofread the minutes from the last board meeting. Prepare a final copy. Arrange the minutes in a standard report format. Before saving, change all occurrences of *games* to *matches*.

Cleveland East Soccer Club    *all caps*

*DS*

Executive Board Meeting Minutes—(insert last Wednesday's date)

*DS*

The meeting at the Community Center was called to order at 7 p.m. by the president. A quorum was present.

Attendance

Kyle Sutter, President; Ken Gomez, Vice President; Beverly Gnieski, Treasurer; Shari Morakis, Director; Paula Sarti, Director; and Stacey Turnshek, Coaches and Managers attended the meeting. Leona Fordyce, Tournament Director; Sean O'Brien, Facilities and Equipment; Mary Santori, Field Services; and Karl Moeller, Officials were absent. *The director of player development position is vacant.*

Reports

*to date*

The treasurer submitted an income statement for the year. The club has a checkbook balance of $3,557 and savings certificates worth $7,500. The treasurer indicated that the club is operating within it's annual budget. The treasurer's report was accepted.

*(continued)*

# Unit 3
## Numeric Keyboarding

### Lessons 1–6

# 1

## OBJECTIVES

1. *To learn reach technique for 8 and 1.*
2. *To improve skill on straight-copy sentences and paragraphs.*

**8** Right middle finger

**1** Left little finger

### ✦ Tip

Keep eyes on copy as you key numbers.

## NEW KEYS:  8 AND 1

### 1A | Conditioning Practice

1. Key each line twice SS; DS between 2-line groups.
2. Key a 1' timed writing on line 3; determine *gwam*.

| Alphabet | 1 | Jack Valdez was quite eager for the next match to be played. |
| Spacing | 2 | Janice will be in town next week to go to the dance with us? |
| Easy | 3 | Henry and Jane may bowl with us; they may pay for all of us. |

**GWAM** 1' | 1 | 2 | 3 | 4 | 5 | 6 | 7 | 8 | 9 | 10 | 11 | 12 |

### 1B | New Keys:  8 and 1

Key each line twice SS (slowly, then faster); DS between 2-line groups.

**Learn 8**

1  k 8 k 8 k8 k8 8k8 8k8.  Reach up from the k to key 8 and 88.

2  Mary keyed 8.  Tom keyed 88.  Jeff keyed 888.  Kay keyed 88.

**Learn 1**

3  a 1 a 1 a1 a1 1a1 1a1.  Reach up from the a to key 1 and 11.

4  Only one student got an F out of 111.  The date is March 11.

**Combine 8 and 1**

5  I keyed May 81, 1881, rather than May 18, 1881 for the date.

6  Maxine missed Questions 8, 18, 81, and 88 on the final exam.

7  Out of 188 entries, only 88 runners competed on  November 18.

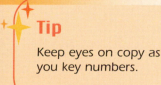

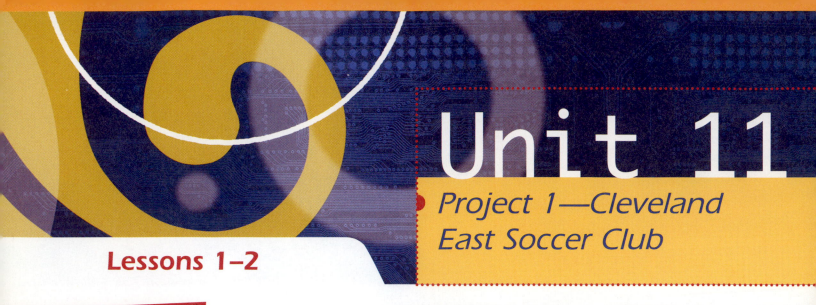

# Unit 11

## Project 1—Cleveland East Soccer Club

### Lessons 1–2

## LESSONS 1-2

### OBJECTIVES

1. *To format personal-business letters, business letters, memos, and e-mail messages.*
2. *To use Find, Find Again, and Replace word processing features.*

### 1–2A | Conditioning Practice

Complete this drill each day that you work on Project 1.  Key each line twice SS; then key a 1' timed writing on line 2.  Determine *gwam*.

Alphabet 1  The quiet crowd was amazed by the five goals Kip and Jaxi scored.

Figures 2  The 35 students in my ED4897 class meet in Nix Center Room 1026.

Speed 3  Ann and the girls are to land the dirigible in the big cornfield.

GWAM  1' | 1 | 2 | 3 | 4 | 5 | 6 | 7 | 8 | 9 | 10 | 11 | 12 | 13 |

### 1–2B | Project 1

#### Project Description

Assume that you are participating in a community service project in your keyboarding and word processing course.  You have been chosen to complete a series of jobs for Mr. Kyle Sutter, who is president of Cleveland East Soccer Club (CESC) and a social studies instructor in your school.

Mr. Sutter has given you several jobs to complete during the next two class periods.  Your main responsibility is to complete the jobs following his instructions.  If a formatting guide or instruction is not given, use your knowledge and judgment to complete the task.  Be alert to and correct errors in capitalization, punctuation, spelling, and word usage.

Use block format with mixed punctuation for letters.  Use the current date unless otherwise directed.  Name all the files you create with *U11J* and the job number (*U11J1*, *U11J2*, etc.).

When you are finished with each job, e-mail the document as an attachment to your instructor, who will verify that it is ready for Mr. Sutter's use.  Once your documents are verified by your instructor, or if you need to "speak" with Mr. Sutter, prepare an e-mail to him at sutterk@taftschool.net.  If you do not have permission to use e-mail, print and hand-deliver the documents to your instructor and Mr. Sutter.

## 1C Writing: Word Choice

Study the spelling and definition of the words below. Key the Learn lines, noting the word choices. Key the Apply lines, selecting the correct words. Save as *U3L1WordChoice*.

**their** (pronoun) belonging to them

**there** (adverb/pronoun) in or at that place; word used to introduce a sentence or clause

**they're** (contraction) a contracted form of *they are*

Learn 1  When will **their** house be completed?

Learn 2  **There** will only be six games in June.

Learn 3  If they don't hurry up, **they're** going to be late.

Apply 4  (Their, There, They're) going to release the next video soon.

Apply 5  Tomorrow is (their, there, they're) last opportunity to take the test.

Apply 6  Justin said he would meet me (their, there, they're).

## 1D | New-Key Mastery

1. Key lines 1–18 once SS; DS between 3-line groups.
2. Key a 1' timed writing on line 12, then on line 18. Determine *gwam* on each timing.

**Row Emphasis**

1  Your vacation is scheduled for August 11-18, not July 11-18.

Figures 2  I narrowed the list from 118 candidates to 81 and then to 8.

3  The population has gone from 8,818 in 1881 to 181,881 today.

4  cab cab | man man | van van | back back | madam madam | manage manage;

Home/1st 5  small cab | a van | a small vase | Jane and Jack | a ban | a small ham

6  Ms. Shank can call a cab.  Ms. Dallman can flag a small van.

7  when will | they are | who should | she will see | please  take | to us

Home/3rd 8  Pat took us to the theatre after we took Jay to the airport.

9  They will see Shirley Gillespie just after the July holiday.

**Tip**

- Reach up without moving the hand forward.
- Reach down without twisting the wrists or moving the elbows in and out.

## Math Activities

**9H ▪ Math Challenge 10**

### FIND THE PERCENT OF DISCOUNT

1. Key a sentence to explain how you find the percent of discount between two prices in problems like this: *What is the % of discount if the regular price is $100 and the discounted price is $70?*

2. Find the percent of discount for the following problems and key your answers in sentence form. Round answers to tenths if needed. For example, an appropriate sentence for the answer to the problem stated above is: *The percent of discount is 30% when the regular price is $100 and the discounted price is $70.*

2a. Regular price is $150; discounted price is $135

2b. Regular price is $20,750; discounted price is $2,490

2c. Regular price is $19.99; discount price is $13.99

2d. Jane has 25 candy bars that normally sell for $.75 each, but she is willing to sell them for $.50 each to reduce her inventory quickly. What percent of discount is she offering?

3. Save your answers as *U10L9Math*.

---

## Careers

### 9I ▪ Career Exploration Portfolio – Activity 10

▪ You must complete Career Activities 1–3 before completing this activity.

1. Retrieve your Career folder and the information in it that relates to the career cluster that is your first choice.

2. Use the Internet to search for the education that is recommended for occupations in this career cluster and then compose a paragraph or two explaining what you have learned. Print your file, save it as *U10L9Career10*, and keep it open.

3. Exchange papers with a classmate and have the classmate offer suggestions for improving the content and correcting any errors he or she finds in your paragraph(s). Make the changes that you agree with, and print a copy to turn in to your instructor. Save it as *U10L9Career10* and close the file.

4. Return your folder to the storage area. When your instructor returns your paper, file it in your Career folder.

**Response patterns**

Letter response

10 cedar plump tease imply treat union stage knoll beard kimono

11 Todd found a tortoise in his garage on West Dixon Boulevard.

12 He will be attending the University of Washington next year.

Word response

13 busy busy | goal goal | lake lake | rush rush | wish wish | soap soap;

14 dials dials | focus focus | digit digit | their their | shake shake;

15 profit profit | orient orient | island island | vivid vivid | do do;

16 Orlando works with vigor to dismantle the downtown chapel.

Easy 17 Keith and the dog slept on the big chair by the city chapel.

18 The maid is to go to the field to cut the wood for the city.

GWAM 1' | 1 | 2 | 3 | 4 | 5 | 6 | 7 | 8 | 9 | 10 | 11 | 12 |

*Social Studies*

## 1E | Speed Building

1. Key a 1' timed writing on each paragraph; determine *gwam* on each writing.

2. Add 2–4 *gwam* to your best rate in step 1 for a new goal.

3. Key two 1' guided writings on each paragraph at new goal rate. (See page 77 for procedures for setting goals.)

---

**MicroType**

*Timed Writing*

**A**

**All letters used**

**Quarter-Minute Checkpoints**

| gwam | 1/4' | 1/2' | 3/4' | Time |
|------|------|------|------|------|
| 16 | 4 | 8 | 12 | 16 |
| 20 | 5 | 10 | 15 | 20 |
| 24 | 6 | 12 | 18 | 24 |
| 28 | 7 | 14 | 21 | 28 |
| 32 | 8 | 16 | 24 | 32 |
| 36 | 9 | 18 | 27 | 36 |
| 40 | 10 | 20 | 30 | 40 |

GWAM 1'

The Arlington House is a place filled with the very | 11

interesting history of our country. The exquisite house | 23

built for the grandson of Martha Washington, George | 33

Custis, in time became the home of General Lee. The | 44

house was built in an amazing location which today looks | 55

out over the capital city of our nation. | 63

The home and land are also linked to other famous | 11

people of United States history. Soon after the Civil War | 23

started, the home became the headquarters of the Union | 34

army with much of the land to ultimately be used for what | 45

is today known as Arlington National Cemetery. President | 57

Kennedy and President Taft are just a few of the notables | 69

buried on the former estate of General Lee. | 77

GWAM 1' | 1 | 2 | 3 | 4 | 5 | 6 | 7 | 8 | 9 | 10 | 11 | 12 |

---

**Memo**

1. Key the following text in memo format. Use a 12-point font. Insert 12 points of vertical space after the paragraphs.

2. View the memo to verify that the format is correct. Spell-check and proofread carefully. Correct all errors. Save the document as *U10L9Memo*.

TO: All District Teachers

FROM: Marcus Ellerbee, Technology Director

DATE: October 25, 20--

SUBJECT: TECHNOLOGY NEEDS FOR NEXT SCHOOL YEAR

It's that time of year again when the ^school district's Technology committee must gather and consolidate all of your hardware and software requests, and then pass them on to the superintendent for consideration and then to the School Board for approval.

Any hardware items or software you need to assist you in preparing for, or in teaching, your classes should be requested now. The items you now request are for the next ^school year, and the approved items should be available for your use the beginning of the school year.

Hardware and software requests may be submitted for your office, the Technology Labs, or your classroom. ^Please Forward all requests in writing to me before Tuesday, Nov 28. The Technology Committee will consider your request early in January.

xx

## 9G | E-Mail (for e-mail users only)

1. Key the following text as an e-mail message to your instructor.

2. Attach *U10L9Memo* to the e-mail message.

TO: (Your instructor's e-mail address)

SUBJECT: MEMO TO ALL TEACHERS

Will you edit the attached memo I need to send to all faculty. Please send me any suggested changes in the next day or two. Thanks.

Use the notes you took on the modern wonders of the world for Unit 2, 1H, page 74. Prepare a list of the main points to use in presenting the information to three of your classmates. Your presentation will be one to two minutes in length. Consider informing your classmates about what the modern wonder is, when it was built, where it was built, and any other unique things you learned from your research.

Print a copy of your outline and take it home. Practice giving the speech to one or more of your family members. Come to class tomorrow prepared to present to three of your classmates. Your instructor may choose several students to give their speeches to the entire class.

As the speeches are given, note the locations and names of the modern wonders.

© PHOTODISC/GETTY IMAGES

**For additional practice** ▶ **MicroType** ✦ **Numeric Keyboarding** ✦ **Lesson 1**

---

## LESSON 2

### OBJECTIVES

1. *To learn reach technique for* **9** *and* **4**.
2. *To improve grammar skills and skill transfer.*

## NEW KEYS: 9 AND 4

### 2A | Conditioning Practice

Key each line twice SS; then key a 1' timed writing on line 3. Find *gwam*.

Alphabet 1  Kay McDonald gave us the quiz for the seven new export jobs.

Figures 2  April 18, May 18, June 8, and July 18 are the meeting dates.

Easy 3  She paid the girls for the work they did on the city chapel.

**GWAM** 1' | 1 | 2 | 3 | 4 | 5 | 6 | 7 | 8 | 9 | 10 | 11 | 12 |

**Personal-Business Letter**

1. Key the following information as a personal-business letter in block format with mixed punctuation.

2. View the letter to check the format. Spell-check and proofread carefully. Correct all errors. Save the letter as *U10L9Letter2*.

3. Prepare a small envelope. Include the return address from the letter as well as the delivery address. Save the document as *U10L9Env2*.

4. Open the file *U10L9Letter2*, which you created in step 2. Use the Replace feature to change *Valleybrook* to *Harris* and *major* to *program*.

5. Save the revised letter as *U10L9Letter3*.

335 Locust Street
Flushing, NY 11367-2379
January 16, 20--

Dr. Alyssa Simala, Principal
Valleybrook High School
2845 Melbourne Avenue
Flushing, NY 11367-2351

Dear Dr. Simala:

I want to commend you and your teachers for providing your students with an opportunity to earn college credits while they are in high school. As a parent of a daughter, Samantha, who was graduated last year from Valleybrook High, I want to let you know how much this opportunity means to our daughter, her father, and me.

Samantha earned nine credits from Chase Community College in her senior year at Valleybrook. All nine credits were accepted by Killington College and applied to the requirements in the Management Information Systems major she has selected.

This very worthwhile articulation agreement that you have with Chase is very valuable. It saves students money and time! For example, Samantha now has the opportunity to complete her major one semester early if she completes six credits during one or more summer sessions. If she elects to do this, she will save tuition, room, board, and fees for one semester. At today's prices, that translates into nearly $12,000! In addition, she will be able to enter the job market four months sooner, and that would provide even greater financial gain. If she gets a position paying $30,000 a year, that is another $10,000 that your articulation agreement earned her. What an opportunity for your students!

Thank you for making this available. If you ever need a parent to speak about the value of this program, just give me a call.

Sincerely,

Joanne H. Dunleavy

## 2B | New Keys: 9 and 4

Key each line twice SS (slowly, then faster); DS between 2-line groups.

### Learn 9

1  l 9 l 9 l9 l9 9l.  Jay was born on May 9, 1999, at 9:19 p.m.

2  How many of the 991 students joined before October 19, 1999?

### Learn 4

3  f 4 f 4 f4 f4 48.  I was born on March 4, 1944, at 4:14 a.m.

4  Questions 1 though 41 and 44 through 84 are multiple choice.

### Combine 9 and 4

5  Jamison bowled 49, 94, and 99; Travis bowled 99, 94, and 99.

6  May 9, June 4, and June 9 are the dates that work for James.

7  Fay had 14 hits in 49 at bats; I had 44 hits in 149 at bats.

## 2C | Figure-Key Mastery

Key each line twice SS (slowly, then faster); DS between 2-line groups.

1  Pete logged 891 miles on Tuesday and 948 miles on Wednesday.

2  I had 81 percent, 94 percent, and 89 percent on the quizzes.

3  Chad got 148 of the 199 votes that were cast on May 8 and 9.

4  Meg said that 481 students graduated at the May 19 ceremony.

**9** Right ring finger

**4** Left index finger

### Tip

Keep eyes on copy as you key numbers.

## 9F | Correspondence

**Business Letter**

1. Make an attractive letterhead using the following information. You decide font style, size, and color. Save as *U10L9Letterhead*.
   Valley Forge Mutual Funds
   P.O. Box 2600
   Valley Forge, PA 19482-2600
   www.valleyforge.swep.com

2. Open *U10L9Letterhead* (if it is not already open) and use the letterhead to key the following information as a business letter in block format with open punctuation. Use a 12-point font for the letter.

3. View the letter to check the format. Spell-check and proofread carefully. Correct all errors. Save the letter as *U10L9Letter1*.

4. Prepare a large envelope. (Assume the envelope has a preprinted return address.) Save the envelope as *U10L9Env1*.

January 5, 20--

Ms. Donna L. Martinez
673 Stockton Street
Salinas, CA 93970-2327

Dear Ms. Martinez:

We are responding to your telephone call requesting a valuation of Mr. James D. Hopson's Account 0908567-479 on November 15, 20--. Since that date was a Saturday and the stock markets were closed, we are providing information for the previous and next dates that the stock markets were open.

On both dates, Mr. Hopson's account held two funds—Equity Income and Explorer Growth. He had 1,342 shares of Equity Income and 275 shares of Explorer Growth on both dates. However, the value of each fund changed because there was a change in the price per share. These changes are as follows.

Equity Income increased from $25.78 per share on November 14 to $25.96 on November 17. As a result, the value of the fund changed from $34,596.76 to $34,838.32.

Explorer Growth increased from $78.95 per share on November 14 to $80.19 on November 17. As a result, the value of the fund changed from $21,711.25 to $22,052.22.

If you have any additional questions, please contact our Client Services Department at 1-888-555-0134. We are available Monday through Friday from 8 a.m. to 5 p.m. and Saturday from 9 a.m. to 4 p.m., Eastern time. An associate will be pleased to assist you.

Sincerely

James A. Herron

Client Services Representative

xx

## 2D  Writing: Capitalization

Read the capitalization rules below.  Study the Learn lines.  Note how the rules are applied.
Key the Learn lines and the Apply lines, making the necessary corrections.  Save as
*U3L2Capitalization*.

**Rule 3:** Capitalize days of the week.

Learn 1   Is the next game on Tuesday or Wednesday?

Learn 2   The lab is open on Tuesday, Thursday, and Friday.

Apply 3   Your appointment is on monday rather than on tuesday.

Apply 4   Mary planned on working monday through saturday.

**Rule 4:** Capitalize months of the year.

Learn 5   The tournament is in July, not August.

Learn 6   The next two meetings will be in April and May.

Apply 7   Spring semester runs from january through may.

Apply 8   The weather is better in july than it is in june.

## 2E | Rough Draft (Edited Copy)

### Proofreaders' Marks

$\land$ = insert

\# = add space

$\cup$ = transpose

$\gamma$ = delete

$\frown$ = close up

$\equiv$ = capitalize

1.  Study the proofreaders' marks illustrated at the left and in the sentences.

2.  Key each sentence DS, making all editing (handwritten) changes.

3.  Rekey the lines to improve your editing speed.

1  A first draft is a preleminary or tentative one. *(rough; i; revision)*

2  It is where the creator gets his thoughts on paper. *(writer; or her)*

3  After the draft is created, it will be looked over. *(rough; edited)*

4  Reviewing is the step where a person refines copy. *(Editing; writer; the)*

5  Proof readers marks are used edit the original copy. *(to; rough draft)*

6  The edting changes will be then be made to the copy. *(i; original)*

7  After the change have been made read the copy agian. *(s)*

8  more changes still may need to be made to the copy.

9  Edting proof reading does take a lottime and effort. *(i; and)*

10  error free copy is worth the trouble, how ever. *(An; message)*

## 9D | Replace

The Replace command allows you to find and replace specific text or a group of words within a document.

To replace text in a document:

1. From the Edit menu, select Replace. The Replace dialog box appears. Key the text you want to find in the Find what box and the replacement text in the Replace with box.

2. Set the search options.

   • If you want to find text that exactly matches the case of your search text, choose Match case.

   • Choose Find whole words only to locate only complete words.

   • Choose From cursor to have the program start searching from the location of the cursor.

   • If you don't want the program to confirm each replacement, turn off the Prompt to replace option.

3. Click Replace to replace only the first occurrence. Click Replace All if you want the program to find and replace all occurrences of the text.

### Practice What You Have Learned

1. Open the data file *CD-U10L9Replace*.

2. Use Replace to find all occurrences of the number *3* and replace with the word *three*. Use Replace to change all the other figures to words. Capitalize the words if appropriate.

3. Use Replace to change the name of the vice president from *Mary* to *Marie*.

4. Close all dialog boxes.

5. Save as *U10L9Replace*.

CD-U10L9Replace

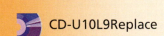

## *Language Arts*

## 9E Writing: Composition

Using the word processor, write a paragraph explaining how to use the Replace feature to replace text or a group of words. Write a second paragraph explaining how to set a tab with dot leaders. Save as *U10L9Composition*.

## 2F | Skill Transfer: Straight Copy, Script, Rough Draft

1. Key each paragraph once SS; DS between paragraphs.

2. Key a 1' timed writing on each paragraph; determine *gwam* on each writing. Compare the three rates.

3. Key one or two more 1' timed writings on the two slowest paragraphs to improve skill transfer.

**MicroType**
*Timed Writing*

### Straight Copy

GWAM 1'

Documents free of errors make a good impression. | 10
When a document has no errors, readers can focus on | 20
the content. Errors distract readers and can cause | 31
them to think less of the message. | 38

### Script

Therefore, it is important to proofread the final | 10
copy of a document several times to make sure it | 20
contains no errors before it leaves your desk. | 29
Readers of error-free documents form a positive image | 40
of the person who wrote the message. | 47

### Rough Draft

When a ~~negative~~ *positive* image of the per son who wrote the ~~the~~ | 10
*a* messge is formed the message is ~~less~~ *more* likely to succeed. | 22
remember, you never get a ~~another~~ *second* chance to make a good *first* | 34
impression. | 36

### Proofreaders' Marks

*stet* = no change

∧ = insert

⌅ = delete

# = add space

‿ = close up

∪ = transpose

⊙ = insert period

---

## 2G Reading: Women in History

Open the file *CD-U3L2Read*. Read the document carefully and close the file. Let your instructor know when you are ready to answer questions covering the content of the file.

CD-U3L2Read

For additional practice **MicroType** + **Numeric Keyboarding** + **Lesson 2**

## 9B | Find and Find Again

The Find and Find Again commands allow you to locate specific text or a group of words within your document.

To find text in a document:

1. From the Edit menu, select Find. Key the text you want to find in the Find what box.

2. Set the search options.

   • If you want to find text that exactly matches the case of your search text, choose Match case.

   • Choose Find whole words only to locate only complete words. When this option is not selected, the program will find all occurrences of the text, even partial words. For example, searching for *the* will find *the*, *there*, and *them*.

   • Choose From cursor to have the program start searching from the location of the cursor.

3. Click Find to begin the search.

To find same text again, from the Edit menu, choose Find Again.

### Practice What You Have Learned

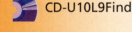
CD-U10L9Find

1. Open the data file *CD-U10L9Find*.

2. Find the first occurrence of *president* and change the text to bold.

3. Find all occurrences of *girls* and underline each occurrence.

4. Find all occurrences of *boys* and italicize each occurrence.

5. Save as *U10L9Find*.

---

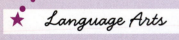
★ *Language Arts*

## 9C Writing: Number Expression

Read the following number usage rule. Key the Learn line, noting the number choices. Key the Apply lines, making the necessary corrections. Save as *U10L9Writing*.

**Rule 4:** Use figures to express time.

Learn 1   The game was supposed to start at 7:30 p.m.; it started at 7:42 p.m.

Apply 2   The meeting will start at three thirty p.m.

Apply 3   I had class at eight fifteen a.m. and ten fifteen a.m. on Tuesday and Thursday.

# LESSON 3

## OBJECTIVES

1. *To learn reach technique for **0** and **5**.*
2. *To improve grammar skills and skill transfer.*

**0** Right little finger

**5** Left index finger

### 3A | Conditioning Practice

Key each line twice SS; then key a 1' timed writing on line 3. Determine *gwam*.

Alphabet 1   Zack explained very quickly why most of those big jets left.

Figures 2   Dr. Cox began teaching here on May 4, 1988; he left in 1998.

Easy 3   The maid may go to the city for eight bushels of field corn.

**GWAM** 1' | 1 | 2 | 3 | 4 | 5 | 6 | 7 | 8 | 9 | 10 | 11 | 12 |

### 3B | New Keys: 0 and 5

Key each line twice SS (slowly, then faster); DS between 2-line groups.

**Learn 0**

1   ; 0 ; 0 | ;p0 ;p0 | ;j0 ;j0   Glenn had a 0.80 ERA and a .090 BA.

2   Raul keyed ;p0, ;p0, and ;p0 to practice the reach to the 0.

**Learn 5**

3   f 5 f 5 | fr5 fr5 | ft5 ft5   Larry had a 5.15 ERA and a .518 BA.

4   Anne keyed fr5, ft5, and r5t to practice the reach to the 5.

**Combine 0 and 5**

5   Jerry bowled 50, 55, and 105; Nick bowled 155, 150, and 105.

6   You did not deliver papers to 505 Bradford and 550 Bradford.

7   Marsha had 50 out of 50 and 50 out of 55 on the two quizzes.

CD-U10L8Plants

*Science*

## 8E | Business Letter

1. Open the data file *CD-U10L8Plants*.

2. Position the cursor between the first and second paragraphs in the body of the letter. Set a left tab at 1.5" and a right tab with dot leaders at 5". Key the following text using the tabs set.

| | | |
|---|---|---|
| TAB | Scientific Name | Common Name |
| TAB | Achillea ptarmica | Yarrow |
| TAB | Artemisia | Wormwood |
| TAB | Geranium | Geranium |
| TAB | Oenothera | Evening primrose |
| TAB | Sedum | Stonecrop |
| TAB | Trollius | Globeflower |

3. Format the letter in block format with mixed punctuation.

4. Spell-check the document. Proofread and correct all errors. Save the document as *U10L8Letter3*.

---

★ *Language Arts*

## 8F Writing:  Word Choice

Study the spelling and definitions of the following words.  Key the Learn line, noting the word choices.  Key the Apply lines, selecting the correct words.  Save as *U10L8Writing*.

**affect** (verb)  influence; produce an effect upon

**effect** (noun)  result

Learn 1  Prices can affect sales and have an effect on profits.

Apply 2  The students' school spirit had an (affect, effect) on the team.

Apply 3  Practice (affects, effects) our performance in our games.

---

## LESSON

## 9

### OBJECTIVES

1. *To format personal-business letters, business letters, memos, and e-mail messages.*

2. *To use Find, Find Again, and Replace word processing features.*

# CORRESPONDENCE

## 9A | Conditioning Practice

Key each line twice SS; then key a 1' timed writing on line 3.  Find *gwam*.

Alphabet 1  Paul quickly indexed a dozen jokes for his big comedy act review.

Figures 2  Lee was born 1/7/82, Sal was born 9/30/96, and I was born 5/4/92.

Speed 3  The eight men may do the work for us if Alicia pays for the land.

**GWAM** 1' | 1 | 2 | 3 | 4 | 5 | 6 | 7 | 8 | 9 | 10 | 11 | 12 | 13 |

## 3C | Figure-Key Mastery

Key each line twice SS (slowly, then faster); DS between 2-line groups.

1 The ZIP Code for 554 Hastings Boulevard is 50819, not 50918.

2 It was 118 degrees on Monday, 109 on Tuesday, and 104 today.

3 About 540 of the 891 students scored higher than 80 percent.

4 The population grew from 105,840 in 1989 to 150,504 in 1999.

★ *Language Arts*

## 3D Writing: Word Choice

Study the spelling and definitions of the words below. Key the Learn lines, noting the word choices. Key the Apply lines, selecting the correct words. Save as *U3L3WordChoice*.

**vary** (verb)  change; make different; diverge

**very** (adjective/adverb)  real; mere; truly; to a high degree

Learn 1 Grades are **very** important to Jason and Julie.

Learn 2 The amount you earn will **vary** from job to job.

Apply 3 The weather will (very, vary) from season to season.

Apply 4 Anna (very, vary) likely will be selected team captain.

## 3E | Technique:  Response Patterns

1. Key each line twice SS; DS between 2-line groups.

2. Key a 1' timed writing on lines 2, 4, and 6; determine *gwam* on each timing.

**Letter response**

1 beef beef | milk milk | area area | hymn hymn | wage wage | upon upon;

2 After we arrested a beggar on the estate, John regretted it.

**Word response**

3 busy busy | rock rock | half half | firm firm | sign sign | town town;

4 If Diane signs the form, I may dismantle the ancient chapel.

**Combination response**

5 extra bicycle | burnt cabbage | brass chair | great risk | city rate

6 Gregg and Edward may make Carter work for them on the barge.

**GWAM** 1' | 1 | 2 | 3 | 4 | 5 | 6 | 7 | 8 | 9 | 10 | 11 | 12 |

### Our World

## 8C ▪ Ethics

Helen agreed to watch her neighbor's three children from 3:30 to 5:00 p.m. Mondays through Thursdays for the next six weeks. Three weeks into this assignment, Helen has been asked to watch her aunt's two children from 3:30 to 5:30 p.m. Mondays through Fridays for eight weeks. Her aunt will pay her $.75 more per hour than her neighbor is paying.

Is it ethical for Helen to stop watching her neighbor's children to watch her aunt's children instead? Why or why not?

Use your word processor to key your response. Save as *U10L8World*.

*Social Studies*

## 8D | Leader Tabs

Leaders are a series of dots (…) or dashes (---) that lead the eyes across the page. The Leader Tab feature is used to place leaders from the left margin or a tab position to another tab position.

To set a leader tab:

1. Position the cursor in the paragraph in which you want to add a leader tab. If you want to insert a tab in more than one paragraph, select the paragraphs to change.

2. From the Format menu, select Tabs.

3. Key the Tab stop position (in inches) and set the desired alignment for the tab.

4. Select the Leader type desired. Click Set to insert the leader tab.

5. Repeat steps 3–4 to set additional tabs or leader tabs, if needed.

6. Click OK to exit the Tabs dialog box.

### Practice What You Have Learned

1. Open a new document.

2. Set a left tab at 2" and a left tab with dot leaders at 4".

3 Key the following information, using the tabs set.

| TAB | John Dunn ........................Right Field |
| TAB | Henrico Gomez .................Left Field |
| TAB | Jerry Tapper Center ...........Field |

4. Tap ENTER six times.

5. Set a left tab with dot leaders at 2", a center tab with an underline leader at 4", and a right tab with dash leaders at 6".

6. Key the following information, using the tabs set. Save as *U10L8Tabs*.

| TAB ..............Jim_____Pitcher ---------------------Throws left |
| TAB ..............Harry_____Pitcher -------------------Throws right |
| TAB ..............Jerry_____Catcher ------------------ Throws right |
| TAB ..............Junior_____First base -------------------Throws left |

## 3F | Speed Building

1. Key two 1' timed writings on each paragraph.
2. Key a 2' timed writing on paragraphs 1–2 combined.

|  | GWAM | 1' | 2' |
|---|---|---|---|

Make each of the fingers move quickly.    Hold the  10 | 5
hands    still.    Do not let either arm move in or out.    If  21 | 10
you keep your fingers curved, you will be able to add to  32 | 16
your speed as well as increase your accuracy.  41 | 21

You should be able to type with greater control  51 | 25
today than you did last week.    It is time to start  61 | 30
pushing yourself to key faster without worrying about  71 | 36
your errors.    You should be amazed at just how fast  81 | 41
you will be able to type when you work at it and put  92 | 46
in a little extra time.  96 | 40

| GWAM | 1' | 1 | 2 | 3 | 4 | 5 | 6 | 7 | 8 | 9 | 10 | 11 | 12 |
|---|---|---|---|---|---|---|---|---|---|---|---|---|---|
|  | 2' | | 1 | | 2 | | 3 | | 4 | | 5 | | 6 |

© BLEND IMAGES

**Business Letter 2**

1. Open the file *U10L7Letterhead* that you created in Lesson 7. Save the document as *U10L8Letter2*.

2. Key the following information as a business letter. Use block format with mixed punctuation.

3. View the letter to verify that the format is correct. Spell-check and proofread carefully. Correct all errors. Save the document again using the same name.

4. Key and print a large envelope. (Print on plain paper if your instructor so directs.) Assume that the envelope has a preprinted return address. Save the envelope as *U10L8Env2*.

March 6, 20--

Ms. Margo Johnson
24168 Squire Road
Columbia Station, OH 44028-0614

Dear Ms. Johnson:

Your satisfaction with our products is important to us. I'm sorry to learn that you are displeased with a few items in the last shipment of plants we delivered to your home last week.

We will refund your money or replace your plants if you are not fully satisfied with them. Our delivery person will pick up the plants you want to return. The driver will stop at your home between 10 a.m. and 1 p.m. next Wednesday. If you will not be at home then, place the plants by your garage door. The driver will leave a receipt for what you return.

You have 30 days to stop at our garden center to get replacement plants or a refund. Just present this letter and your receipt. A salesperson will be happy to take care of you.

Thank you for your business.

Sincerely,

Harry Piper, Owner

xx

bc Harriet Snowden

### 3G ▪ Research Driving Directions

The Internet can be used to get driving directions. Determine the directions, estimated distance, and estimated time to get to Mt. Rushmore from your house by following these steps:

INTERNET

1. Access the MapQuest website at http://www.mapquest.com/.

2. Key your address, city, state, and ZIP.

3. Key the place name, address, city, state, and ZIP of where you are going. (Key as much of the information as you can.)

   **Mt Rushmore National Memorial**
   **Keystone, SD 57751**

4. Click Get Directions.

5. If prompted, select an Ending Location from the choices offered.

6. Scroll down to see the directions for getting to Mt. Rushmore.

7. What is the total estimated time for this trip? What is the total distance for this trip?

8. Approximately how many MPH would you have to average in order to make it to Mt. Rushmore in the amount of time shown on MapQuest?

*Math*

For additional practice  **MicroType + Numeric Keyboarding + Lesson 3**

---

## LESSON

# 4

### OBJECTIVES

1. *To learn reach technique for 7 and 3.*
2. *To improve grammar skills and skill transfer.*

## NEW KEYS: 7 AND 3

### 4A | Conditioning Practice

Key each line twice SS; then key a 1' timed writing on line 3. Determine *gwam*.

| Alphabet | 1 | Jenny very quickly swam the dozen extra laps before leaving. |
| Figures | 2 | May 10, May 15, May 19, June 14, and June 18 were suggested. |
| Easy | 3 | Jan and Rich may pay us to go with them to work on the dock. |

| GWAM | 1' | 1 | 2 | 3 | 4 | 5 | 6 | 7 | 8 | 9 | 10 | 11 | 12 |
|------|----|----|----|----|----|----|----|----|----|----|----|----|----|

## LESSON

8

### OBJECTIVES

1. *To format business letters in block format with mixed punctuation.*
2. *To format large envelopes.*
3. *To learn leader tabs.*

---

**Tip**

If the letterhead is about 2" deep or deeper, begin the date a DS below the last line of the letterhead.

---

**Tip**

If more than one enclosure accompanies the letter, use *Enclosures*.

Enclosures and attachments are frequently identified so the receiver can verify that the correct one(s) were received.

---

## 8A | Conditioning Practice

Key each line twice SS; then key a 1' timed writing on line 3. Find *gwam*.

Alphabet 1 If they study, Kami and Jeb expect high scores on every law quiz.

Figures 2 Her sales were up 15% ($29,648) and profits were up 7% ($3,045).

Speed 3 Di's neighbor may fish off the dock at the lake by the coalfield.

GWAM 1' | 1 | 2 | 3 | 4 | 5 | 6 | 7 | 8 | 9 | 10 | 11 | 12 | 13 |

## 8B | Business Letters

**Business Letter 1**

1. Read the tips at the left. Open the file *U10L7Letterhead* that you created in Lesson 7. Save the document as *U10L8Letter1*.

2. Key the following information as a business letter. Use block format with mixed punctuation.

3. View the letter to verify that the format is correct. Spell-check and proofread carefully. Correct all errors. Save the document again using the same name.

4. Key and print a large envelope. (Print on plain paper if your instructor so directs.) Assume that the envelope has a preprinted return address. Save the envelope as *U10L8Env1*.

March 5, 20--

Mr. Edward Pudlowski
465 Saddler Drive
Bay Village, OH 44140-0465

Dear Mr. Pudlowski:

Thank you for allowing us to place an ad in your Spring Musical program. A check for $50 for the ad is enclosed. The ad should be a full page in the program booklet.

Please use the copy on the enclosed business card for the content of the ad. Also state in the ad that customers who present this ad at our Ohio Street garden center will get a 15 percent discount. (Place the discount information near the bottom of the ad.) This offer is valid until this coming June. If you have any questions about the content, please e-mail me at hlandscape@quickstar.com.

Our company is happy to support your booster group by placing this ad. Last year's ad generated many sales from first-time customers. I expect this year's ad and discount will do as well.

Sincerely,

Harry Piper, Owner

xx

Enclosures: Check and ad copy

## 4B | New Keys: 7 and 3

Key each line twice SS (slowly, then faster); DS between 2-line groups.

### Learn 7

1  j 7 j 7 | ju7 ju7 | u7j u7j  Only 7 of the 77 girls had pajamas.

2  Only about 77 percent of the 1,757 delegates actually voted.

### Learn 3

3  d 3 d 3 | de3 de3 | e3d e3d  Phone her at 353.3803 before 3 p.m.

4  A total of 313 students attended the 3:30 and 4:30 meetings.

### Combine 7 and 3

5  My cell phone number is 737.7733; my home phone is 373.3737.

6  Nestor scored 33 points on March 3 and 37 points on March 7.

7  Jacob lowered his ERA from 7.37 last year to 3.77 this year.

## 4C | Figure-Key Mastery

Key each line twice SS (slowly, then faster); DS between 2-line groups.

1  George Washington's term in office was from 1789 until 1797.

2  Thomas Jefferson served as President from 1801 through 1809.

3  Theodore Roosevelt was our President from 1901 through 1909.

4  Ronald W. Reagan served as President from 1981 through 1989.

**7** Right index finger

**3** Left middle finger

Social Studies

**Tip**

Keep eyes on copy as you key numbers.

## 7E Writing: Number Expression

Read the following number usage rule. Key the Learn line, noting the number choices. Key the Apply lines, making the necessary corrections. Save as *U10L7Writing*.

**Rule 3:** Use figures to express a day of the month following the month name.

Learn 1   The last game of the season is on March 9.

Apply 2   Rafael was born on September first.

Apply 3   Her last day of work was December tenth.

© BANANASTOCK

## 4D  Writing:  Capitalization

Read the capitalization rules below.  Study the Learn lines.  Note how the rules are applied.
Key the Learn lines and the Apply lines, making the necessary corrections.  Save as
*U3L4Capitalization*.

**Rule 5:** Capitalize cities, states, and countries.

Learn 1   The company is located in San Diego, California.

Learn 2   We have embassies in Brazil, Denmark, and Germany.

Apply 3   The finalists were from italy, france, and sweden.

Apply 4   Yes, the capital of hawaii is honolulu.

**Rule 6:** Capitalize the names of rivers, oceans, and mountains.

Learn 5   The Missouri River flows into the Mississippi River.

Learn 6   Part of the Colorado River is in the Rocky Mountains.

Apply 7   The american river starts in the sierra nevada mountains.

Apply 8   The pacific ocean is the largest; the arctic ocean is the smallest.

## 4E │ Technique:  Response Patterns

1.  Key each line twice SS; DS between 2-line groups.

2.  Key a 1' timed writing on lines 2, 4, and 6.

**Double-letter words**

1   bull need apple middle session illness Tennessee Mississippi

2   Kellee will keep all the books on Tennessee and Mississippi.

**Balanced-hand words**

3   eight blend flair handy panel shake theme vigor visit theory

4   Eight of the officials may go to the big social on the dock.

**One-hand words**

5   after cards draft craft mummy nylon trade union wages uphill

6   Greg Reese carved a pumpkin on a hill on my estate in Texas.

**GWAM** 1' │ 1 │ 2 │ 3 │ 4 │ 5 │ 6 │ 7 │ 8 │ 9 │ 10 │ 11 │ 12 │

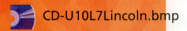
CD-U10L7Lincoln.bmp

## Practice What You Have Learned

1. Open a blank document. Position the cursor at the top left margin.

2. Insert the picture file *CD-U10L7Lincoln.bmp*. Change the size of the picture so it is 3" wide. Lock the aspect ratio.

3. Center-align the picture. Click outside to the right of the picture to position the cursor. Tap ENTER twice.

4. Key the following text below the picture. Use center alignment for the text. Use a 24-point font and bold for the first line of text. Use a 16-point font for the other lines.

**Abraham Lincoln**

Sixteenth President

1861-1865

Married to Mary Todd Lincoln

5. Tap ENTER as needed to leave about 2" of blank space.

6. Insert the picture file *CD-U10L7Flag.bmp*. Change the size of the picture to 1" wide. Remember to lock the aspect ratio. Center-align the picture.

7. Key the following text below the picture. Use center alignment and a 16-point font.

U.S. Presidents Project

8. Save the document as *U10L7Picture*.

## 7D | Letterhead

Follow the instructions below to create a letterhead that will be used in Lesson 8.

1. Open a blank document and change the top margin to .5".

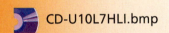
CD-U10L7HLI.bmp

2. Insert the picture file *CD-U10L7HLI.bmp* at the top margin using center alignment.

3. Change the size of the picture to a 1" height. Lock the aspect ratio.

4. Key the following information underneath the picture using SS and center alignment.

Harry's Landscape, Inc.

247 Ohio Street

Elyria, OH 44035-0280

Telephone: 442-555-0147

www.hlandscape.swep.com

5. Insert six points of blank space before the street address and before the telephone number.

6. Use a 16-point font for the business name and a 10-point font for the other lines.

7. Save as *U10L7Letterhead*.

## 4F | Speed Building

1. Key two 1' timed writings on each paragraph.
2. Key a 2' timed writing on paragraphs 1–2 combined.

**MicroType**

*Timed Writing*

**A**

**All letters used**

| | GWAM | 1' | 2' |
|---|---|---|---|
| New York City is a vibrant city with over eight | | 10 | 5 |
| million inhabitants. On a summer day the population is | | 21 | 10 |
| drastically increased with the many zealous tourists | | 31 | 16 |
| that come to view the many attractions that are part of | | 42 | 21 |
| this major city. Whether you are interested in sports, | | 53 | 27 |
| theatre, museums, or world government, you can find it | | 64 | 32 |
| all in the city of New York. | | 69 | 35 |
| Many tourists go to New York to see Broadway | | 78 | 39 |
| productions. Others go to see the Yankees and Mets | | 89 | 44 |
| play. Times Square, the place where many get together | | 99 | 50 |
| to bring in the new year, is another place people want | | 110 | 55 |
| to visit. The Statue of Liberty and Ellis Island, the | | 121 | 61 |
| place where millions of immigrants entered the United | | 132 | 66 |
| States, are also major attractions. However, Central | | 142 | 71 |
| Park is the area to go to relax and enjoy the beautiful | | 153 | 77 |
| view of the city away from the busy streets. | | 162 | 81 |

GWAM 1' | 1 | 2 | 3 | 4 | 5 | 6 | 7 | 8 | 9 | 10 | 11 | 12
2' | 1 | 2 | 3 | 4 | 5 | 6

*Language Arts*

## 4G Listening: The World Around You

1. Listen carefully to the sounds around you for three minutes.
2. As you listen, key a list of all the different sounds you hear.
3. Identify the three loudest sounds you heard. Key **1** by the loudest sound. Key **2** by the second loudest sound. Key **3** by the third loudest sound.
4. Save as *U3L4Listening*.

**For additional practice** MicroType + **Numeric Keyboarding** + **Lesson 4**

## MicroType
### TIP

The file types for the pictures to be inserted will vary with the word processing program. With some word processing software, you can insert clip art, sounds, video clips, and drawings from various sources.

## MicroType
### TIP

Drag the handles on a selected picture to change the size of the picture.

Pictures can be inserted in documents and adjusted to any desired size.

To insert a picture:

1. Position the cursor at the location where you want to insert the picture. You can use the Left, Center, and Right Align buttons on the toolbar to position the picture horizontally.

2. From the Insert menu, select Picture. The Picture dialog box appears.

3. The default picture type is bitmap (.bmp). Click the Files of type box and choose the type of picture files you want to insert. *MicroType 4* allows you to insert pictures saved in bitmap (*.bmp*) or metafile (*.wmf*) format.

4. Locate the picture file you want to insert. Select the filename and click Open. The program inserts the picture at the cursor location.

To change the size of a picture:

1. Select the picture you want to change. A border with handles (small squares) appears around the image.

2. From the Format menu, choose Format Picture.

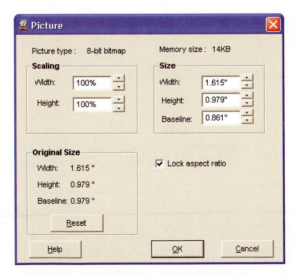

3. Click the Lock aspect ratio checkbox if you want the picture to keep its original proportions (width to height) when you change the size.

4. Set the Scaling or Size to the desired size. Use Scaling to set size as a percent of the original. Use Size to set size at a specific height or width (in inches). Tap the TAB key after you enter a value in percent or inches to change the remaining values automatically.

5. Click OK to apply the picture format changes.

# NEW KEYS: 6 AND 2

## 5A | Conditioning Practice

Key each line twice SS; then key a 1' timed writing on line 3.

| | | |
|---|---|---|
| Alphabet | 1 | Phil J. Valdez was an extremely good quarterback for a year. |
| Figures | 2 | Jane was born on May 30, 1975; Mike was born on May 6, 1984. |
| Easy | 3 | Jane and Dick may both bid on the ivory chair in the chapel. |

GWAM 1' | 1 | 2 | 3 | 4 | 5 | 6 | 7 | 8 | 9 | 10 | 11 | 12 |

## 5B | New Keys: 6 and 2

Key each line twice SS (slowly, then faster); DS between 2-line groups.

### Learn 6

1 j y 6 j y 6 | y6 y6 | j6 j6  Key these numbers:  6, 66, and 666.
2 Maybe you should have added 6 and 66 rather than 66 and 666.

### Learn 2

3 s w 2 s w 2 | w2 w2 | s2 s2  Key these numbers:  2, 22, and 222.
4 We will meet on April 22, May 22, August 22, and October 22.

### Combine 6 and 2

5 Pat changed April 26, 1626, to April 26, 1662, in his notes.
6 Only 26 of the 62 girls can attend the meeting on August 26.
7 At half-time the score was 62 to 26; Ray had made 26 points.
8 The score was 62 to 26; Justin had 26 points and Bart had 6.

## 5C | Figure-Key Mastery

Key each line twice SS (slowly, then faster); DS between 2-line groups.

1 Bonds had 734 homers at the end of 2006; K. Griffey had 563.
2 Franco had 2,566 hits at the end of 2006; Finley had 2,531.
3 L. Nolan Ryan had 5,714 strikeouts in 5,386 innings pitched.
4 H. Aaron had 755 home runs in 12,364 at bats in 3,298 games.

**6** Right index finger

**2** Left ring finger

**Business Letter 2**

1. Key the following information as a business letter to be printed on letterhead paper. (You will actually print on plain paper.) Use block format with mixed punctuation. Use a 12-point font and center the letter vertically.

2. View the letter to verify that the format is correct. Spell-check and proofread carefully. Correct all errors. Save as *U10L7Letter2*.

May 25, 20--

Dr. Fouad A. Shia
212 Seventh Street
Bangor, ME 04401-4447

Dear Dr. Shia:

Thank you for giving a seminar for our staff at Bank Mart last week. Volunteer speakers like you are an important part of our training program.

The results of the evaluations completed by our staff members are enclosed. All participants ranked each of your topics as important to their needs. The topic about retirement planning received the highest score.

Most staff members rated your speaking style and materials as very good or excellent. Most of the staff involved said they hope you will come back for another seminar.

Sincerely,

Ms. Susan L. Delpiore
Training and Development

xx

Enclosure

c Mr. L. James Walter, Vice President of Operations

## 5D  Writing:  Word Choice

Study the spelling and definitions of the words below.  Key the Learn lines, noting the word choices.  Key the Apply lines, selecting the correct words.  Save as *U3L5WordChoice*.

**its** (adjective)  of or relating to itself as the possessor

**it's** (contraction)  it is; it has

Learn 1  **It's** time for the play to begin.

Learn 2  When will you take the dog for **its** shots?

Apply 3  Be sure to feed the cat before (it, it's) time to go.

Apply 4  Please return the car to (it, it's) rightful owner.

---

## 5E │ Skill Transfer:  Straight Copy, Script, and Rough Draft

1.  Key each paragraph once SS; DS between paragraphs.
2.  Key a 1' timed writing on each paragraph; determine *gwam* on each.  Compare the rates.
3.  Key one or two more 1' timings on the two slowest paragraphs to improve skill transfer.

**MicroType**

*Timed Writing*

E

**All letters used**

**Proofreaders' Marks**

| | | |
|---|---|---|
| ∧ | = | insert |
| # | = | add space |
| ∩ | = | transpose |
| ϱ | = | delete |
| ⌒ | = | close up |
| ≡ | = | capitalize |

**Straight Copy**                                                            GWAM 1'

The 2006 Winter Olympics were held in Torino, Italy.     11
The traditional winter sports of figure skating and speed    22
skating were complemented by the newer Olympic events of    33
freestyle skiing and snowboarding.     40

**Script**

Four Americans took medals in the half-pipe snowboarding event.  Shaun     14
White and Daniel Kass took the gold and silver in the men's event while     28
Hanna Tetter and Gretchen Bleiler took the gold and silver in the women's event.     44

**Rough Draft**

The speed skating was another exciting event for the     11
Americans.  In the men's 1,000-meter event Shani Davis skated     22
to the gold.  Chad Hendrick won it in the 5,000-meter men's     34
speed skating event and joey Chek won the godl in the     45
500-meter event.  Americans also won four silver and 1 bronze     57
in men's speed skating events.     63

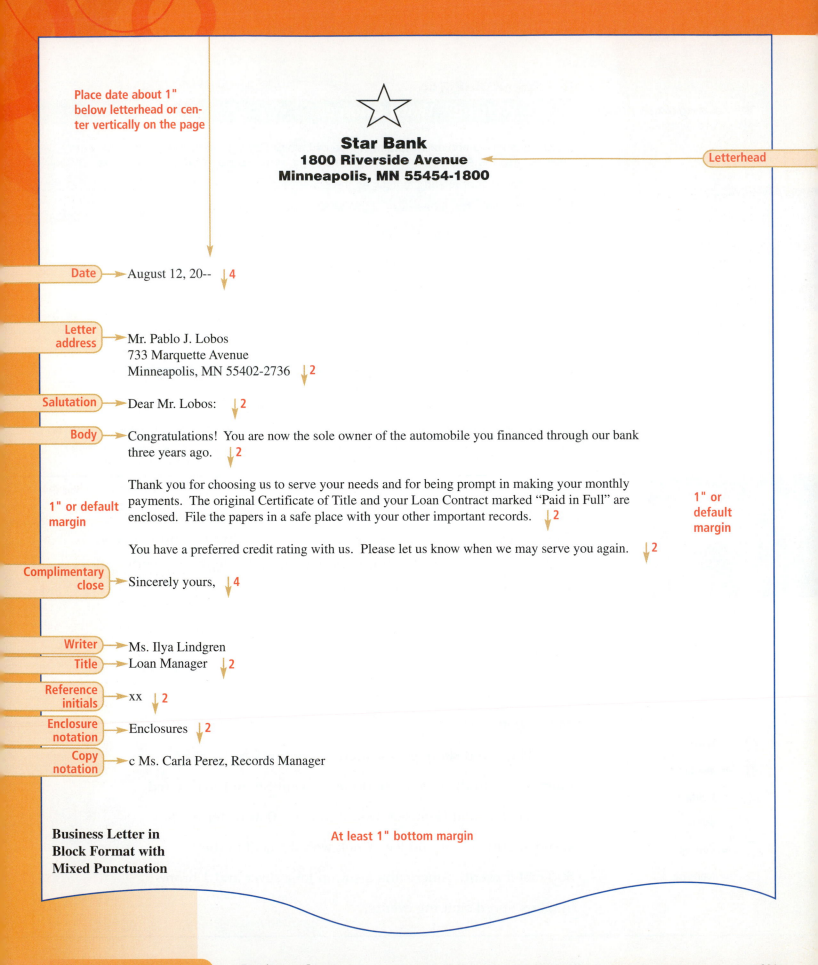

**Place date about 1" below letterhead or center vertically on the page**

⭐

## Star Bank
### 1800 Riverside Avenue
### Minneapolis, MN 55454-1800

**Letterhead**

**Date** → August 12, 20-- ↓4

**Letter address** → Mr. Pablo J. Lobos
733 Marquette Avenue
Minneapolis, MN 55402-2736 ↓2

**Salutation** → Dear Mr. Lobos: ↓2

**Body** → Congratulations!  You are now the sole owner of the automobile you financed through our bank three years ago. ↓2

**1" or default margin**

Thank you for choosing us to serve your needs and for being prompt in making your monthly payments.  The original Certificate of Title and your Loan Contract marked "Paid in Full" are enclosed.  File the papers in a safe place with your other important records. ↓2

**1" or default margin**

You have a preferred credit rating with us.  Please let us know when we may serve you again. ↓2

**Complimentary close** → Sincerely yours, ↓4

**Writer** → Ms. Ilya Lindgren
**Title** → Loan Manager ↓2

**Reference initials** → xx ↓2

**Enclosure notation** → Enclosures ↓2

**Copy notation** → c Ms. Carla Perez, Records Manager

**Business Letter in Block Format with Mixed Punctuation**

**At least 1" bottom margin**

## 5F | Speed Building

1. Key two 1' timed writings on each paragraph.

2. Key a 2' timed writing on paragraphs 1–2 combined.

**MicroType**

*Timed Writing*

A

**All letters used**

|  | GWAM | 1' | 2' |
|---|---|---|---|
| Which of the states has the least number of people? | | 10 | 5 |
| Few people realize that this state ranks first in coal, | | 21 | 11 |
| fifth in natural gas, and seventh in oil production. Quite | | 33 | 17 |
| a significant number of deer, antelope, and buffalo dwell | | 45 | 22 |
| within the boundaries of this exquisite state. A major | | 56 | 28 |
| portion of Yellowstone National Park is located in the | | 66 | 33 |
| state. If you still don't know which state is being | | 77 | 38 |
| described, it is Wyoming. | | 82 | 41 |
| Wyoming is located in the western portion of the | | 92 | 46 |
| United States. The state is bordered by six different | | 102 | 51 |
| states. Plains, mountain ranges, and national parks make | | 114 | 57 |
| up a vast portion of the landscape of the state. Several | | 125 | 63 |
| million people come to the state each year to view the | | 136 | 68 |
| beautiful landscape of this unique state. Visitors and | | 147 | 74 |
| the extraction of natural resources make up a major portion | | 159 | 79 |
| of the economy of the state. | | 164 | 82 |

GWAM 1' | 1 | 2 | 3 | 4 | 5 | 6 | 7 | 8 | 9 | 10 | 11 | 12
2' | 1 | 2 | 3 | 4 | 5 | 6

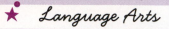
## 6H Writing: Word Choice

Study the spelling and definitions of the following words. Key the Learn line, noting the word choices. Key the Apply lines, selecting the correct words. Save as *U10L6Writing*.

**accept** (verb)  receive willingly; agree to

**except** (preposition)  excluding; but

Learn 1  All will be there to accept a trophy except Paul and Sue.

Apply 2  Please (accept, except) my apology for being late this morning.

Apply 3  I can tutor you any day this week (accept, except) Tuesday.

---

# LESSON
# 7

## OBJECTIVES

1. *To key business letters in block format with mixed punctuation.*
2. *To insert and size a picture.*

 **Tip**

Open or mixed punctuation may be used with the block format. Mixed punctuation uses a colon (:) after the salutation and a comma (,) after the complimentary close.

# BUSINESS LETTERS

## 7A | Conditioning Practice

Key each line twice SS; then key a 1' timed writing on line 3. Find *gwam*.

Alphabet 1  Quinn, zip your jacket and fix her muffler to brave raging winds.

Figures 2  I bought new cars on May 3, 1987, July 6, 2004, and June 5, 2008.

Speed 3  When Ann signs the form, I may pay them to dismantle the cubicle.

**GWAM** 1' | 1 | 2 | 3 | 4 | 5 | 6 | 7 | 8 | 9 | 10 | 11 | 12 | 13 |

## 7B | Business Letter

A business letter is very similar to a personal-business letter. However, a business letter may contain additional parts. A business letter is usually printed on paper with a **letterhead**. A letterhead includes the company name and address. It may also include a business logo, telephone number, or website address. Sometimes the name, title, and e-mail address of an individual are part of the letterhead. A return address is not keyed above the date because it is shown in the letterhead.

A business letter usually contains the sender's **job title**. This title is keyed on the same line as the name or on the next line. Reference initials, enclosure and attachment notations, and copy notations are formatted in letters in the same manner as they are in memos.

### Business Letter 1

1. Key the information on the following page as a business letter in block format with mixed punctuation. (Read the tip at the left about mixed punctuation.)

2. Use a 12-point font. Center the letter vertically on the page. Assume that the letter will be printed on letterhead paper as shown in the illustration. Do not include a return address above the date.

3. View the letter to verify the format is correct. Spell-check and proofread carefully. Correct all errors. Save as *U10L7Letter1*.

**Our World**

### 5G ▪ Forgotten Wonders of the World

Several forgotten wonders of the world are listed below. Use an encyclopedia or the Internet to learn about one of these forgotten wonders. Take notes and be prepared to write a paragraph or two about the forgotten wonder you researched. Note the addresses of the Internet sites you use to learn about the topic.

- Abu Simbel Temple
- The Great Wall
- The Leaning Tower of Pisa
- The Colosseum
- The Parthenon
- Taj Mahal

Your instructor may provide a world map to use with this activity. If directed, indicate the location of the forgotten wonder and label it on the map.

*Social Studies*

For additional practice **MicroType**＋ Numeric Keyboarding＋Lesson 5

---

## LESSON

# 6

### OBJECTIVES

1. *To improve technique of number keys.*
2. *To build straight-copy speed and control.*

## REVIEW NUMBERS

### 6A | Conditioning Practice

Key each line twice SS; then key a 1' timed writing on line 3.

Alphabet 1 Jack Z. Voss will be our equipment manager for the next day.

Figures 2 Will bowled 138, 90, and 145; Janet bowled 157, 143, and 98.

Easy 3 Pamela kept the man busy with all the forms for the auditor.

GWAM 1' | 1 | 2 | 3 | 4 | 5 | 6 | 7 | 8 | 9 | 10 | 11 | 12 |

## 6F | Personal-Business Letter with Envelope

1. Key the following information as a personal-business letter. Use block format with open punctuation. Use a 12-point font. Use a 2" top margin, 1.25" side margins, and 1" bottom margin for the letter. Spell-check and proofread carefully. Correct all errors. Save as *U10L6Letter*.

2. Prepare a large envelope to accompany the letter. Save the envelope as *U10L6Env4*.

8503 Kirby Drive
Houston, TX 77054-8220
May 10, 20--

Ms. Jenna St. John
Personnel Director
Regency Company
219 West Greene Road
Houston, TX 77067-4219

Dear Ms. St. John

Ms. Anne D. Salgado, my teacher, told me about your company's Computer Learn Program. She speaks very highly of your company and the computer program. She thinks I would benefit greatly by taking this course. After learning more about the program, I agree that the course would be helpful to me.

I am in the seventh grade at Eisenhower School. I have completed a computer applications course. I learned to integrate spreadsheets with word processing reports. I have also taken a programming course that served as an introduction to Visual Basic and HTML.
I developed and maintain a website for my baseball team.

I would like to visit with you to talk more about the summer program. Please telephone me at 713-555-0121 or e-mail me at dougr@suresend.com to suggest a meeting date.

I can meet with you any day after school. Thank you.

Sincerely

Douglas H. Ruckert

**Our World**

### 6G ▪ Research Museum Art

Art can help us learn about the cultures of others. The Smithsonian Institute has art museums devoted to:

- African art (The National Museum of African Art)
- Native American art (The National Museum of the American Indian)
- Asian art (The Freer Gallery of Art and the Arthur M. Sackler Gallery)

Find one or more of these museums at the Smithsonian Institute (www.si.edu). View some of the images you find. Write a short paragraph about the impressions you gained of another culture from viewing the art. Save as *U10L6Internet*.

*Social Studies*

**TIP**

Keep eyes on copy as you key numbers.

## 6B | Figure-Key Mastery

1. Key each line twice SS; DS between 2-line groups.

```
1   1 and. 2 and. 3 and. 4 and. 5 and. 6 and. 7 and. 8 and. 9 and
2   10 the 29 the 38 the 47 the 56 the 106 the 729 the 38 the 54
3   67 when 90 when 89 when 23 when 45 when 12 when 567 when 789
4   1 one. 2 two. 3 three. 4 four. 5 five. 6 six 7 seven 8 eight
5   9 nine 10 ten 11 eleven 12 twelve 13 thirteen 14 fourteen 15
```

★ *Language Arts*

## 6C Writing: Word Choice

Study the spelling and definitions of the words below. Key the Learn lines, noting the word choices. Key the Apply lines, selecting the correct words. Save as *U3L6WordChoice*.

**fair** (adjective)  just, equitable, visually beautiful or admirable

**fare** (noun)  a transportation charge

Learn 1   Do you think it is **fair** to charge that much?

Learn 2   She paid the bus **fare** at the depot.

Apply 3   Kyle said he didn't think life was always (fair, fare).

Apply 4   Do you have enough money for the taxi (fair, fare)?

## 6D | Keyboard Reinforcement

1. Key each line twice SS; DS between 2-line groups.
2. Key two 30" timed writings on each line.

```
1   I may cycle to the city and then go to the dock by the lake.
2   The key, Jay, is to name eight goals and then work for them.
3   Jamal may make a map of the ancient city for the title firm.
4   The social for the girls is to be held by the dock at eight.
5   The dog is with the maid and the man by the big city chapel.
6   Their neighbor may dismantle the cycle in the big cornfield.
7   Jane and I may handle the problem with the eighth amendment.
8   He may work with them on the problems with the turn signals.
```

| **GWAM** 30" | 2 | 4 | 6 | 8 | 10 | 12 | 14 | 16 | 18 | 20 | 22 |

## 6D | Print Setup

The Print Setup feature can be used to format envelopes if your printer supports the desired envelope size. Two commonly used envelopes are the Large (No. 10) envelope and the Small (No. 6 3/4) envelope.

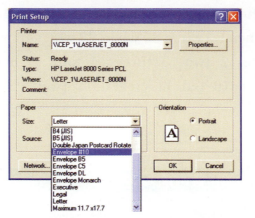

To use Print Setup to choose an envelope size:

1. From the File menu, choose Printer Setup. The Print Setup dialog box appears.

2. Choose an option from the Size drop-down list. Choose Envelope 6 3/4 for a small envelope. Choose Envelope #10 for a large envelope.

3. Choose Landscape orientation.

4. Follow the format guides in **6C** to set margins and tabs as needed to key the address information.

5. Print the envelope.

**Practice What You Have Learned**

1. Open a new document. Access Print Setup and choose the options for a small envelope.

2. Key a small envelope using your address as the return address and the following address as the delivery address.

Mrs. Joyce Forno
6701 Carmel Road, Suite 203
Charlotte, NC 28226-0200

3. Save the document as *U10L6Env1*. Print the envelope.

4. Open a new document. Access Printer Setup and choose the options for a large envelope. Key a large envelope using your address as the return address and the following address as the delivery address.

Miss Arnella Wilson
Electric Products, Inc.
8746 La Jolla Parkway
San Diego, CA 92136-3927

5. Save the document as *U10L6Env2*. Print the envelope.

## 6E | Small Envelope

1. Create and print a small envelope using the two addresses provided.

2. Spell-check the addresses and proofread carefully. Correct all errors. Save as *U10L6Env3*.

**Return Address:**

Mr. Ralph McNash
5270 Center Drive
Charlotte, NC 28226-0705

**Delivery Address:**

Mr. Karl Fernandez
Tudor Publishers
9812 Rockwood Road
Charlotte, NC 28215-8555

## 6E | Speed Building

1. Key two 1' timed writings on each paragraph.
2. Key two 2' timed writings on paragraphs 1–2 combined.

**MicroType**
*Timed Writing*
**A**

**All letters used**

**Quarter-Minute Checkpoints**

| gwam | 1/4' | 1/2' | 3/4' | Time |
|------|------|------|------|------|
| 16 | 4 | 8 | 12 | 16 |
| 20 | 5 | 10 | 15 | 20 |
| 24 | 6 | 12 | 18 | 24 |
| 28 | 7 | 14 | 21 | 28 |
| 32 | 8 | 16 | 24 | 32 |
| 36 | 9 | 18 | 27 | 36 |
| 40 | 10 | 20 | 30 | 40 |

GWAM 2'

As you build your keying power, the number of errors  5
you make is not very important because most of the errors  11
are accidental and incidental.  Realize, however, that  16
documents are expected to be without flaw.  A letter,  22
report, or table that contains flaws is not usable until  27
it is corrected.  So find and correct all errors.  32

The best time to detect and correct errors is  37
immediately after you finish keying the copy.  Therefore,  42
just before you print or close a document, proofread and  48
correct any errors you have made.  Learn to proofread  53
carefully and to correct all errors quickly.  To do the  59
latter, know ways to move the pointer and to select copy.  65

GWAM 2' | 1 | 2 | 3 | 4 | 5 | 6 |

## 6C | Envelope Format

Two commonly used envelopes are the Large (No. 10) envelope and the Small (No. 6 3/4) envelope.

An envelope contains a return address and a delivery address. The return address includes the sender's name, street address, city, state, and ZIP Code. The delivery address includes the recipient's title, name, street address, city, state, and ZIP Code. A company name may also be included in either address.

Study the formatting guides for small and large envelopes. For the return address, use block style and single spacing. Position the return address by setting a .25" top and left margin as shown in the illustration. Key the return address using block style and single spacing.

Position the delivery address about 2" from the top edge of the envelope by tapping ENTER about seven times after keying the last line of the return address—fewer times if the return address is longer. Position the delivery address so it begins approximately 2.5" from the left for a Small (No. 6 3/4) envelope and 4" for a Large (No. 10) envelope. For a Small envelope, set a left tab at 2 ¼ on the Ruler Bar. For a Large envelope, set a left tab at 4 ¼ on the Ruler Bar. Use single spacing and begin each line of the delivery address at the tab setting.

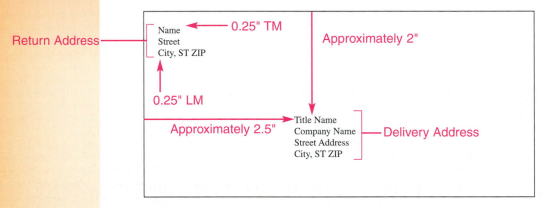

**Small (No. 6 3/4) Envelope**

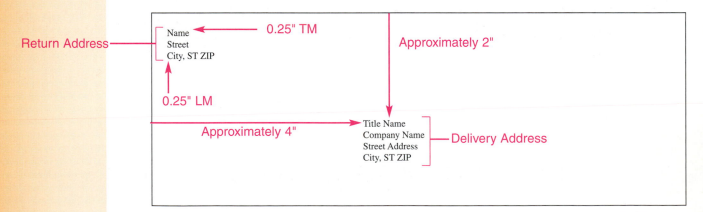

**Large (No. 9 or 10) Envelope**

## Math Activities

**6F** ▪ **Math Challenge 3**

### REWRITE PERCENTS AS FRACTIONS AND DECIMALS

1. Key a paragraph explaining how you rewrite percents as fractions and decimals.

2. Using a pencil and paper, rewrite the following percents as fractions, reduced to their lowest terms. Compare your answers with those provided by your instructor.

   2a. 64%        2b. .7%        2c. .03%
   2d. 3.35%      2e. 30.56%

3. Using a pencil and paper, rewrite the following percents as numbers with decimals, rounded to thousandths if needed. Compare your answers with those provided by your instructor.

   3a. 5%         3b. 76%        3c. 9.456%
   3d. .0935%     3e. 756.68%

4. Save your answers as *U3L6Math*.

### 6G ▪ Career Exploration Portfolio – Activity 3

- You must complete Career Exploration Activities 1 and 2 before completing this activity.

1. Retrieve your completed Career Clusters Interest Survey from your folder.

2. Review the Career Cluster Plans of Study for your top three career clusters. Do this by returning to http://www.careerclusters.org and clicking on the Free Career Cluster – Plans of Study link. This will take you to a screen where you can establish a login address and password (be sure to record your login information in a safe place for future use). Select your top three career clusters. Click your first choice and open and print the file. Click the Back button to return to the career clusters and open and print the second career cluster. Repeat the procedure for the third career cluster.

3. Place your printed files in your folder and file it in the storage area.

**For additional practice** ▶**MicroType**✦ **Numeric Keyboarding**✦**Lesson 6**

## 6B | Margins

Use the Margin feature to change the amount of white space at the top, bottom, right, and left edges of the page. The default margin settings vary on different programs. Default margin settings for MicroType 4 are 1".

To set margins for a document:

1. On the menu bar, click Format. Click Page Settings. The Page Setting dialog box appears.

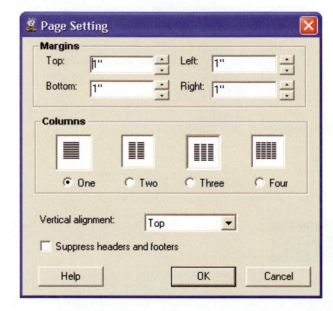

2. Key the desired measurements (in inches) in the Top, Bottom, Left, and Right text boxes. Click OK. The left and right margin settings are indicated on the Ruler by the left and right margin markers.

### Practice What You Have Learned

1. Open the data file *CD-U10L6Margins*.

2. Read the paragraphs. Change the margin settings as directed in the document. Close without saving the document.

**MicroType**

TIP

Drag the margin indicators on the Ruler to change the margins quickly.

Left margin indicator

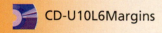

CD-U10L6Margins

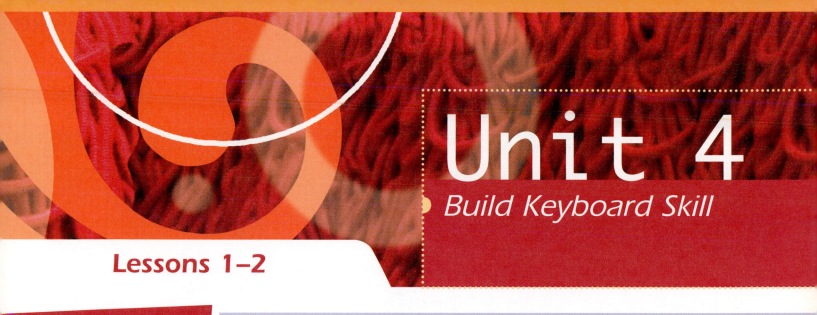

# Unit 4
## Build Keyboard Skill

### Lessons 1–2

### OBJECTIVES

1. *To improve technique on individual letters.*
2. *To improve keying speed on timed writings.*

**Technique Goals**
- curved, upright fingers
- quick-snap keystrokes
- quiet hands and arms

## SKILL DEVELOPMENT 1

### 1A | Conditioning Practice

Key each line twice SS; then key a 1' timed writing on line 3. Determine *gwam*.

| | | |
|---|---|---|
| Alphabet | 1 | Jackie and Zelda's next big purchase may require two favors. |
| Figures | 2 | Jay moved from 1475 Oak Lane to 3068 Hudson Road on July 29. |
| Easy | 3 | Vivian and Diana may sign the audit form for the city audit. |

**GWAM** 1' | 1 | 2 | 3 | 4 | 5 | 6 | 7 | 8 | 9 | 10 | 11 | 12 |

### 1B | Technique Mastery:  Individual Letters

1. Key each line twice SS (slowly, then faster); DS between 2-line groups.
2. Take 30" timed writings on selected lines.

| | | |
|---|---|---|
| A | 1 | Jana Bahr ate the meal, assuming that her taxi had departed. |
| B | 2 | Bob may be too busy to be able to buy me a book before noon. |
| C | 3 | Cecil Cacciola took a raccoon from my clinic on Circle Cove. |
| D | 4 | Donald doubted that Todd could decide on the daily dividend. |
| E | 5 | Ellen and Steven designed evening dresses for several years. |
| F | 6 | Felicia and her friend split their fifer's fees fifty-fifty. |
| G | 7 | Garn Taggart haggled with Dr. Gregg over the geography exam. |
| H | 8 | The highest honors for Heath were highlighted on each sheet. |
| I | 9 | Heidi Kim is an identical twin who idolizes her twin sister. |
| J | 10 | Janet and Jody joined Jay in Jericho in West Jordan in July. |
| K | 11 | Karl kept Kay's knickknack in a knapsack in the khaki kayak. |
| L | 12 | Molly filled the small holes in the little yellow lunch box. |
| M | 13 | Mr. Mark murmured about the minimal number of grammar gains. |

**GWAM** 30" | 2 | 4 | 6 | 8 | 10 | 12 | 14 | 16 | 18 | 20 | 22 |

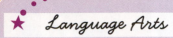

## 5D Writing: Number Expression

Read the following number usage rule. Key the Learn line, noting number choices. Key the Apply lines, making the necessary corrections. Save as *U10L5Writing*.

**Rule 2:** Use figures for numbers above ten and for numbers one through ten when they are used with numbers above ten.

Learn 1   Awards were given to 6 sophomores, 9 juniors, and 15 seniors.

Apply 2   He gave nine C's, twelve B's, and two A's.

Apply 3   She ordered nine apples, twelve bananas, and fifteen pears.

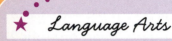

## 5E Reading

 CD-U10L5Read

Open the file *CD-U10L5Read*. Read the document carefully and close the file. Let your instructor know when you are ready to answer questions covering the content of the file.

---

## LESSON

**6**

# PERSONAL-BUSINESS LETTERS AND ENVELOPES

### 6A | Conditioning Practice

Key each line twice SS; then key a 1' timed writing on line 3. Find *gwam*.

Alphabet 1   The quiet crowd was amazed by the five goals Kip and Jaxi scored.

Figures 2   My cash discount (2/10, N/45) on 7 items @ $69.38 will be $9.

Speed 3   The dry oak wood with a small bit of coal may make a giant flame.

GWAM 1' | 1 | 2 | 3 | 4 | 5 | 6 | 7 | 8 | 9 | 10 | 11 | 12 | 13 |

### OBJECTIVES

1. *To change margin settings.*
2. *To format small envelopes.*
3. *To format personal-business letters in block style and open punctuation.*

## 1C | Keyboard Reinforcement

1. Key lines twice SS; DS between 2-line groups.
2. Key a 1' writing on selected lines.

**Easy sentences (Think, say, and key the words at a steady pace.)**

1 Keith may make them turn by the lake by the eight big signs.

2 I may go to the city to work for the six firms on the audit.

3 Jan may make the eight girls pay for the keys to the chapel.

4 Jake and I paid the auto firm to do the work on the big bus.

5 Glen and I may go with the boys to fix the hut for the maid.

6 The city may make the boys turn their key to the old chapel.

7 I paid the man for the work he did in the field by the lake.

8 The eight girls kept us busy with the work on the city dock.

GWAM | 1' | 1 | 2 | 3 | 4 | 5 | 6 | 7 | 8 | 9 | 10 | 11 | 12 |

---

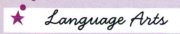

## 1D Writing: Capitalization

Read the capitalization rules below. Study the Learn lines. Note how the rules are applied. Key the Learn lines and the Apply lines, making the necessary corrections. Save as *U4L1Capitalization*.

**Rule 7:** Capitalize names of clubs, schools, companies, and other organizations.

Learn 1  The Boston Pops will perform during the celebration.

Learn 2  Intel and Yahoo presented at the 2007 Technology Symposium.

Apply 3  weber state university has a chapter of phi beta lambda.

Apply 4  a representative from Microsoft spoke at the 2008 technology institute.

**Rule 8:** Capitalize the names of holidays.

Learn 5  Another name for the Fourth of July is Independence Day.

Learn 6  Labor Day started during Grover Cleveland's term.

Apply 7  the first thanksgiving in the U.S. was held in 1621.

Apply 8  memorial day was originally called decoration day.

**Letter 3**

1. Key the following personal-business letter in block format using open punctuation. Use a 12-point font. Center the document vertically on the page.

2. View the letter to check the format. Spell-check the letter and proofread carefully. Correct all errors. Save as *U10L5Letter3*.

14820 Conway Road
Chesterfield, MO 63025-1003
September 10, 20--

Ms. Kelly Mueller
Fundraising Projects, Inc.
15037 Clayton Road
Chesterfield, MO 63107-8734

Dear Ms. Mueller

The Science Club at Milton High School is going to raise funds to help pay **the** medical bills of one of our members who is suffering from a life-threatening ~~sickness~~ **illness**.

Our **tentative** plan is to fundraise during October, November, and December at each of the home varsity football, soccer, and basketball games. There are 20 such events scheduled during that time period. Our Principal has given us permission to ~~set up and~~ staff a table at each event.

We are interested in selling shirts, hats, sweats, etc. that ~~has~~ **have** our school name and mascot, but we need to speak with you about this plan before proceeding further. We need to know the cost of the items, a recommended selling price, and payment arrangements. Our next meeting is scheduled for (Sept) **sp** 20 in Room 210 in the high school at 2:15 p.m. Can you meet with us ~~for about an hour~~ **stet** to tell us how your company can help us in this project?

You can e-mail your response to Seerhoff@stargate.net. I need to know your availability by September 15. Thank you.

Sincerely

Karen Seerhoff
President

## 1E | Handwritten Copy (Script)

Key each quote twice (slowly, then faster); DS between 2-line groups.

1. *"Glory is fleeting, but obscurity is forever."*
2. *"We didn't lose the game, we just ran out of time."*
3. *". . . the harder I work, the more luck I seem to have."*

## 1F | Speed Building

1. Key two 1' guided timed writings on each paragraph; determine *gwam*.
2. Key two 2' timed writings on paragraphs 1–2 combined; determine *gwam*.
3. Key one 3' timed writing on paragraphs 1–2 combined; determine *gwam*.

**MicroType**

*Timed Writing*

**A** ▽

**All letters used**

### Quarter-Minute Checkpoints

| *gwam* | 1/4' | 1/2' | 3/4' | Time |
|---|---|---|---|---|
| 16 | 4 | 8 | 12 | 16 |
| 20 | 5 | 10 | 15 | 20 |
| 24 | 6 | 12 | 18 | 24 |
| 28 | 7 | 14 | 21 | 28 |
| 32 | 8 | 16 | 24 | 32 |
| 36 | 9 | 18 | 27 | 36 |
| 40 | 10 | 20 | 30 | 40 |

| | GWAM | 2' | 3' |
|---|---|---|---|

Who lived a more colorful and interesting — 4 | 3
existence than this President? He was a rancher in — 9 | 6
the west. He participated as a member of the Rough — 14 | 10
Riders. He was an historian. He went on an African — 20 | 13
Safari. He was quite involved in the development of — 25 | 16
the Panama Canal. He was the youngest person ever to — 30 | 20
become President of the United States; however, he was — 35 | 24
not the youngest person that was ever elected to the — 41 | 27
office of President. And these are just a few of his — 46 | 31
accomplishments. — 48 | 32

Theodore Roosevelt was an active and involved — 52 | 35
man. He lived life to the fullest and tried to make — 57 | 38
the world a better place for others. Today, we still — 63 | 42
benefit from some of his many deeds. Some of the — 68 | 45
national forests in the West came about as a result of — 73 | 49
legislation enacted during the time he was President. — 78 | 52
He worked with college leaders to organize the — 83 | 55
National Collegiate Athletic Association. — 87 | 58

GWAM | 2' | 1 | 2 | 3 | 4 | 5 | 6
       | 3' | 1 | 2 | 3 | 4

**Letter 2**

1. Key the following personal-business letter in block format using open punctuation. Refer to the model letter on the previous page as needed. Center the document vertically on the page.

2. View the letter to check the format. Spell-check the letter and proofread carefully. Correct all errors. Save as *U10L5Letter2*.

13811 Seagonville Road
Dallas, TX 75253-1380
October 15, 20--


Ms. Luz Ruiz
3707 S. Peachtree Road
Mesquite, TX 75180-3707

Dear Ms. Ruiz

I am a student at Holton High School. My teacher has asked me to invite you to make a presentation on how my classmates can lessen the risk of having their identity stolen when using the Internet.

A few classmates have already fallen victim to this crime. Mrs. Young, our computer applications instructor, wants all of us to be aware of what we should do to lessen the chance of having our identity stolen. Mrs. Young heard you present on this topic at a teachers' conference last month. She recommended that we invite you since you are an expert in this area.

Our class meets each weekday from 9:20 a.m. to 10:10 a.m. Mrs. Young has indicated you can select a date that is convenient for you. She needs at least one-week notice to make the necessary arrangements.

If you want, you can e-mail me at doyle@gateway.com or call me at 432-555-0135 after 3:30 p.m. to discuss this in greater detail. Thank you.

Sincerely


Ms. Janet Doyle

**Language Arts**

## 1G Composition

Use the notes you took on a forgotten wonder of the world for Unit 3, Lesson 5, on page 97. Prepare a summary of the information in a paragraph or two. Consider informing your reader about what the forgotten wonder is, when it was built, and where it was built, as well as any other unique things you learned from your research.

Save the document as *U4L1Wonder.* When you are finished, print a copy to take home and edit tonight. Bring the edited copy to class tomorrow and turn it in to your instructor.

**For additional practice  MicroType + Keyboarding Skill Builder + Lesson C**

---

## LESSON

# 2

### OBJECTIVES

1. *To improve technique on individual letters.*
2. *To improve keying speed on timed writings.*
3. *To learn to use the Help word processing feature.*

### Technique Goals

- curved, upright fingers
- quick-snap keystrokes
- quiet hands and arms

# SKILL BUILDING

## 2A | Conditioning Practice

Key each line twice SS; then key a 1' timed writing on line 3. Determine *gwam.*

| Alphabet | 1 | Many expect Frank Valdez to quit working on all of the jobs. |
| Figures | 2 | The exam on May 9 over pages 387 to 460 is worth 125 points. |
| Easy | 3 | The big sign down by the civic hall is for Dana's Handiwork. |

**GWAM** 1' | 1 | 2 | 3 | 4 | 5 | 6 | 7 | 8 | 9 | 10 | 11 | 12 |

## 2B | Technique Mastery: Individual Letters

1. Key each line twice SS (slowly, then faster); DS between 2-line groups.

2. Take 30" timed writings on selected lines.

| N | 1 | Nadine knew her aunt made lemonade and sun tea this morning. |
| O | 2 | Owen took the book from the shelf to copy his favorite poem. |
| P | 3 | Pamel added a pinch of pepper and paprika to a pot of soup. |
| Q | 4 | Quent posed quick quiz questions to his quiet croquet squad. |
| R | 5 | Risa used a rubber raft to rescue four girls from the river. |
| S | 6 | Silas said his sister has won six medals in just four meets. |
| T | 7 | Trisha told a tall tale about three little kittens in a tub. |
| U | 8 | Ursula asked the usual questions about four issues you face. |
| V | 9 | Vinny voted for five very vital issues of value to everyone. |
| W | 10 | Wilt wants to walk in the walkathon next week and show well. |
| X | 11 | Xania next expects them to fix the extra fax machine by six. |
| Y | 12 | Yuri said your yellow yacht was the envy of every yachtsman. |
| Z | 13 | Zoella and a zany friend ate a sizzling pizza in the piazza. |

**GWAM** 30" | 2 | 4 | 6 | 8 | 10 | 12 | 14 | 16 | 18 | 20 | 22 |

**Return address** → 91 Kenwood Street
Brookline, MA 02446-2412

**Date** → October 15, 20-- ↓4

**Letter address** → Ms. Brittany Houser
2130 Mt. Pleasant Drive
Bridgeport, CT 06611-2301 ↓2

**Salutation** → Dear Ms. Houser ↓2

**Body** → A **personal-business** letter has several parts. The letter begins with the return address and the date. The letter address comes next. The salutation and the body of the letter follow the address. ↓2

**1" LM or default**

The **return address** contains the street address on one line and the city, state, and ZIP Code on the next line. The **date** (month day, year) is keyed on the line below the return address. The **letter address** is keyed a quadruple space (tap Enter four times) below the date. Use a personal title (Miss, Mr., Ms., Mrs.) or a professional title (Dr., Lt., Senator) before the receiver's name. ↓2

A **salutation** (greeting) is keyed a double space below the letter address. Begin the **body** (message) of the letter a double space below the salutation. Single-space the body with double spacing between the paragraphs. A **complimentary close** (farewell) is keyed a double space below the last line of the body. Quadruple-space after the complimentary close and key the **name of the writer**. ↓2

**1" RM or default**

When all lines of the letter begin at the left margin, the letter is arranged in **block format**. When there is no punctuation after the salutation and complimentary close, **open punctuation** style has been used. Use a **top margin** of 2" or center a one-page letter vertically on the page. Use 1" or default margins for the **side** and **bottom margins**. ↓2

**Complimentary close** → Sincerely ↓4

**Writer** → Robbie Morrison

At least 1" bottom margin

**Personal-Business Letter
in Block Format
with Open Punctuation**

1. Key lines twice SS; DS between 2-line groups.
2. Key the drill again at a faster pace.

**Space Bar and ENTER Key**

1  Joy will be here by noon.
2  Judy took the dog to the lake.
3  Keith will take the exam on Friday.
4  Felipe is the best player on their team.
5  Jordan is planning on going to the game with her.
6  The video games will be released in a week or two.

## Language Arts

## 2D Writing: Word Choice

Study the spelling and definitions of the words below. Key the Learn lines, noting the word choices. Key the Apply lines, selecting the correct words. Save as *U4L2WordChoice*.

**desert** (noun)  a region rendered barren by environmental extremes

**dessert** (noun)  the last course of a lunch or dinner

Learn 1  Tom decided to have **dessert** after all.

Learn 2  Maria drove through the **desert** on her way to California.

Apply 3  I included the cost of the (desert, dessert) in the banquet costs.

Apply 4  Parts of the Mojave (Desert, Dessert) are located in four states.

© CREATAS IMAGES

## OBJECTIVES

1. *To use the Vertical Alignment feature of the word processor.*
2. *To format personal-business letters in block format with open punctuation.*

### 5A | Conditioning Practice

Key each line twice SS; then key a 1' timed writing on line 3. Find *gwam*.

Alphabet 1   Jaye's expensive black racquet is the wrong size for my children.

Figures 2   The store will sell 43 tables, 59 beds, 187 chairs, and 206 rugs.

Speed 3   The six men got paid for the handiwork they did on the city dock.

**GWAM** 1' | 1 | 2 | 3 | 4 | 5 | 6 | 7 | 8 | 9 | 10 | 11 | 12 | 13 |

### 5B | Vertical Alignment

Use the Vertical Alignment feature to center lines of text between the top and bottom margins of the page. This feature places an equal (or nearly equal) amount of white space above and below the text. This feature can also be used to align text at the top margin (the default vertical alignment).

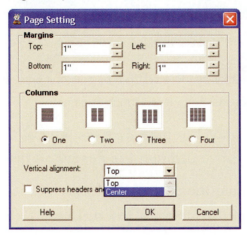

To set the vertical alignment for a document:

1. From the Format menu, select Page Settings.

2. From the drop-down list beside Vertical alignment. select Center or Top.

**Practice What You Have Learned**

1. Open a new document.

2. Click Center alignment on the toolbar to center text horizontally.

3. Key your name and home address on the first three or four lines.

4. Vertically align the text in the center of the page. View the page to verify the text is vertically centered. Save the document as *U10L5Center*.

### 5C | Personal-Business Letters

**Letter 1**

1. Read the model letter on the following page and note the formatting directions. Key the letter in block format with open punctuation. Center the letter vertically on the page.

2. View the letter to check the format. Spell-check the letter and proofread carefully. Correct all errors. Save as *U10L5Letter1*.

The Help feature provides assistance in the form of "how-to" information while the user works with the software.

MicroType

**TIP**

Tap the F1 function key to display the Help dialog box.

CD-U4L2Read

## 2E | Help

### Learn to Use Help

To use the WP Help feature:

1. On the menu bar, click Help. Choose Help Topics. The Help dialog box appears.

2. Click the Index tab. Key the topic you are looking for, such as *print*.

3. Click Display. The information for that topic will display, or you will be able to select from options relating to your topic. For example, when you display *print*, you can select from *Print* or *Printing a Saved Timed Writing*.

4. Click the Print tab if you wish to print the information.

5. On the Help window, click the Close button to close Help.

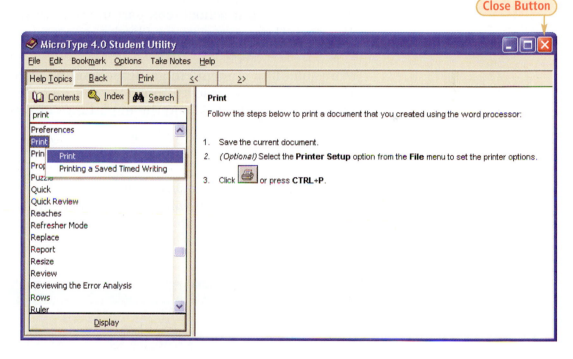

### Practice What You Have Learned

1. Open the file *CD-U4L2Read*.

2. Display and print the Help topic for the Print command. Close the Help window.

3. Place the insertion point in the first paragraph of the document. From the Format menu, choose Paragraph to display the Paragraph dialog box.

4. Tap the F1 function key to display the Help topic related to the Paragraph command.

5. Print the Help topic and close the Help window. Close the document.

**E-mail 2**

1. Key the following e-mail message. If you are not using e-mail software, format the document as a memo using this additional information:

   **Names for MicroType users:** Janet Wilson, Kerry Newberg, Luis Menendez

2. Spell-check the e-mail message and proofread carefully. Correct all errors. Save the message as *U10L4Email2*.

TO:  wilson@mtunion.org
Cc:  newberg@mtunion.org
Bcc:  menendez@ama.org
FROM:  Darrell Unis
DATE:  Current Date
SUBJECT:  JUMP ROPE FOR HEART

In September, our school took part in an event to raise funds for the American Heart Association. Physical education teacher Jackie Ruppert was in charge of the event.

More than fifty students in grades seven and eight were in the program. The students progressed through several rope-jumping activity stations. They also viewed a video on the importance of staying fit.

The students were asked to jump in memory of a loved one. Students collected donations to support their rope jumping. Together, the students collected $4,735 for the Heart Association. For the students' efforts, the Lincoln School received gift certificates for sports and exercise equipment. The school will have the American Jump Team perform at a school assembly in late November.

---

★ *Language Arts*

## 4E Writing: Word Choice

Study the spelling and definitions of the following words. Key the Learn line, noting the word choices. Key the Apply lines, selecting the correct words. Save as *U10L4Writing*.

**principal** (noun/adjective)  head of a school; most important

**principle** (noun)  rule or code of conduct

Learn 1  Our principal asked us to write good conduct principles.

Apply 2  The (principal, principle) will hold a staff meeting.
Apply 3  The (principal, principle) reason was clearly stated.
Apply 4  I always try to follow the (principals, principles) of fair play.

---

★ *Language Arts*

## 4F | Composition: Giving Directions

A person in a wheelchair asks you for directions from your school to the nearest hospital emergency room. Write the directions you would give this person. Include suggestions for parking, entering the hospital, and finding the emergency room. Save the document as *U10L4Directions*.

## 2F | Speed Building

1. Key one 1' unguided timed writing and two 1' guided timed writings on each paragraph.

2. Key two 2' unguided writings on paragraphs 1–2 combined; find *gwam*.

| Quarter-Minute Checkpoints | | | |
|---|---|---|---|
| *gwam* 1/4' | 1/2' | 3/4' | Time |
| 16 | 4 | 8 | 12 | 16 |
| 20 | 5 | 10 | 15 | 20 |
| 24 | 6 | 12 | 18 | 24 |
| 28 | 7 | 14 | 21 | 28 |
| 32 | 8 | 16 | 24 | 32 |
| 36 | 9 | 18 | 27 | 36 |
| 40 | 10 | 20 | 30 | 40 |

GWAM 2'

Each President since George Washington has had a — 4
cabinet. The cabinet is a group of men and women selected — 10
by the President. The senate must approve them. It is the — 16
exception rather than the rule for the President's choice — 22
to be rejected by this branch of the government. In — 27
keeping with tradition, most of the cabinet members belong — 33
to the same political party as the President. — 38

The purpose of the cabinet is to provide advice to the — 43
President on matters pertaining to the job of President. — 49
The person holding the office, of course, may or may not — 55
follow the advice. Some Presidents have frequently — 60
utilized their cabinet. Others have used it little or not — 66
at all. For example, President Wilson held no cabinet — 72
meetings at all during World War I. — 75

GWAM 2' | 1 | 2 | 3 | 4 | 5 | 6 |

## INTERNET

## 2G | Research News

The Internet can be used to learn about current news, weather, and sports from newspapers. Find today's news headlines by looking at an online newspaper.

1. Access the USA Today website at http://www.usatoday.com or a website for one of your state's newspapers.

2. What are some of the headlines for the latest news events reported on the website?

3. Access and read one of the articles that is of particular interest to you.

4. Take a few notes on the article you read, and be prepared to tell the class about the article.

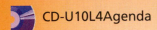
CD-U10L4Agenda

## 4D | E-mail Messages with Special Features

**E-mail 1**

1.  Study the information and format guides contained in the report in **4C**.

    **E-mail users:**

    a.  Key the e-mail message below, using what you have learned.

    b.  Create a group mailing list for the addresses on the TO line. Name the group Committee. Use this group name to insert the addresses.

    c.  Key addresses on the copy and blind copy heading lines.

    d.  Open the data file *CD-U10L4Agenda*. Save the file as *Agenda*. Attach the file Agenda to the e-mail message.

    **MicroType users:**

    Format the message as a memo, using this additional information:

    TO: **Jill Sheck**, **Beatrice Wei**, **Vera Donte**; Cc: **Vivian Harris**; Bcc: **Bob Voltz**

2.  Spell-check the message and proofread carefully. Correct all errors. Save the message as *U10L4Email1*.

TO:  sheck@harris.com; wei77@robust.com; donte@ati.com

Cc:  harris@taft.k12.pa.us

Bcc:  voltz@taft.k12.pa.us

FROM:  Jamie Redstone

DATE:  Current Date

SUBJECT:  SCHOOL SERVICE PROJECT COMMITTEE

ATTACH:  Agenda

Please remember our meeting tomorrow at 3 p.m. in the middle school library. We will meet at the front desk and then go to a conference room the librarian has reserved for us. I created a list of items we need to discuss. See the file Agenda that is attached.

The members of our committee will need to communicate by e-mail frequently over the next several weeks. I recommend that you create a group to include the addresses of all our committee members. You can use the addresses from the To: line of this message.

# Math Activities

**2H** ▪ **Math Challenge 4**

## MENTAL MATH

1. Work with a classmate to determine the answers to the following questions mentally—without using a pencil or calculator. If your answers don't agree, explain to each other how your answer was calculated. Check your answers with those provided by your instructor.

   1a. Rewrite .5 as a percent.

   1b. Rewrite .635 as a percent.

   1c. Rewrite 65% as a decimal.

   1d. Rewrite .7% as a decimal.

   1e. Rewrite 33/50 as a percent.

   1f. Rewrite 77/50 as a percent.

   1g. Rewrite 53.3% as a fraction.

   1h. Rewrite .02% as a fraction.

2. Save your answers as *U4L2Math*.

## Careers ·····················

### 2I ▪ Career Exploration Portfolio – Activity 4

▪ You must complete Career Activities 1–3 before completing this activity.

1. Retrieve your Career folder and find the printed Career Cluster Plan of Study for the career cluster that is your first choice.

2. Review the plan and write a paragraph or two about why you would or would not consider a career in this cluster. Print your file, then save it as *U4L2Career4*, and keep it open.

3. Exchange papers with a classmate. Have the classmate offer suggestions for improving the content and correcting any errors he or she finds in your paragraph(s). Make the changes that you agree with and print a copy to turn in to your instructor. Save it as *U4L2Career4* and close the file.

4. Return your folder to the storage area. When your instructor returns your paper, file it in your Career folder.

**For additional practice** ▶**MicroType** + **Keyboarding Skill Builder** + **Lesson D**

## 4C | Report

1. Review the standard report format in Lesson 3C on pages 207-208. Key the report below in standard format. Use an 11-point font for the report body. Use a bold 14-point font for the report title. Underline the side headings.

2. Create headers to show page numbers properly. Insert hard returns as needed to end the pages properly.

3. Spell-check the report and proofread carefully. View the report to verify that the format is correct. Correct all errors. Save as *U10L4Report*.

### E-MAIL MESSAGES WITH SPECIAL FEATURES

Several features make using e-mail software fast and easy. These features are described in the following sections.

### E-mail Address List

Names and e-mail addresses of persons you send messages to may be kept in an address list. An address can be quickly and accurately entered on the to: line by selecting it from the list.

### E-mail Copies

Copies of an e-mail message can be sent to several people at the same time. To do so, use the copy or blind copy features of e-mail software. You may want the recipient to know that you have sent the message to others. If so, key the e-mail address of the other individuals on the copy line (*Cc:*) in the e-mail heading. At other time, you may **not** want the recipient to know that you have sent the message to others. In this case, key their e-mail addresses on the blind copy line (*Bcc:*) in the e-mail heading.

### Attachments

The attachment feature allows you to send files you have created with your e-mail message. This feature makes it possible to send reports to send reports, tables, spreadsheets, databases, and other documents with an e-mail. The name of this feature varies depending on the software being used. Common names include *Attach* or *Attach File*.

### Forward

The forward feature allows you to send a copy of an e-mail message you received to othe individuals. Do not forward an e-mail unless you are sure the sender would not object.

### Reply

The Reply Feature is used to answer an in coming message. In most programs, you do not have to key the e-mail address when you send a reply. The e-mail programs inserts the address for you. You can choose to send the ~~original~~ message along with your response. This quickly reminds the reader what the message is about. Often, only a brief response is needed.

### E-mail Group List

You may wish to send e-mail to the same several individuals frequently. You can save each person's e-mail adress (and name, if desired) as part of a group. To send a message to all the addresses, enter the group name in the To: box.

# Unit 5
## *Symbol Keyboarding*

### Lessons 1–5

## NEW KEYS:  /, $, %, AND -

### 1A | Conditioning Practice

Key each line twice SS; then key a 1' timed writing on line 3.  Determine *gwam*.

Alphabet 1  Jeff Brock was amazingly quiet during the extensive program.

Figures 2  Trisha bowled 98, 245, and 176 at the tournament on June 30.

Easy 3  Hank may make a big profit if he owns the title to the land.

GWAM  1' |  1  |  2  |  3  |  4  |  5  |  6  |  7  |  8  |  9  |  10  |  11  |  12  |

### 1B | Learn / and $

Key each line twice SS (slowly, then faster); DS between 2-line groups.

#### Learn / (diagonal)

1  ; / ;/ ;/ ;; // /;/ /;/ 1/9 2/8 3/7 4/6 5/6 6/4 7/3 8/2 9/1.

2  Space between a whole number and a fraction:  4 2/3, 16 5/9.

3  Do not space before or after the / in a fraction:  2/3, 7/8.

#### Learn $ (dollar sign)

4  f r $ f r $ ff rr $$ f$ $10 $20 $30 $40 $50 $60 $70 $80 $90.

5  A period separates dollars and cents:  $4.38, $6.25, $19.70.

6  Tom wrote checks for $137.98, $24.50, $106.79 and $1,468.78.

## 3F Speaking: Prepare to Speak

You will attend a meeting of a school club that you joined recently. The members likely will ask you to introduce yourself briefly (in about 1' to 2').

1. Key an outline of the points that you want to include in your introduction. Suggestions follow:
   - State your name and year in school and mention your hobbies.
   - Describe some of your goals related to school, sports, or hobbies.
   - Tell the audience about other things you do or like.

2. Save your outline as *U10L3Speaking*.

---

## LESSON

# 4

### OBJECTIVES

1. *To learn special e-mail features: copy, blind copy, attachments, forward, reply, and group mailing list.*

2. *To practice using proofreaders' marks.*

**Proofreaders' Marks**

lc = set in lowercase

sp = spell out

stet = let it stand

⎯ = underline

⎤ = move right

⎣ = move left

# E-MAIL MESSAGES AND REPORT

### 4A | Conditioning Practice

Key each line twice SS; then key a 1' timed writing on line 3. Find *gwam*.

| | | |
|---|---|---|
| Alphabet | 1 | Paquez will study a few notes just before taking the civics exam. |
| Figure/ Symbols | 2 | The computer costs $485.97 (20% off), and I have saved $361. |
| Speed | 3 | Eight was the divisor for half of the problems she did for Ellen. |

**GWAM** 1' | 1 | 2 | 3 | 4 | 5 | 6 | 7 | 8 | 9 | 10 | 11 | 12 | 13 |

### 4B | Proofreaders' Marks

1. Study the proofreaders' marks given at the left.

2. Key the following rough-draft paragraph using 1.5 spacing and making corrections as you key. Save as *U10L4Marks*.

Seven teams from our middle school had a food drive to help the Valley FOOD PANTRY. Before sending the food to the pantry, each used the food containers they collected to build structures. The structures related to the social studies curriculum. All the teams' structures were then judged by the social studies teachers. Team Tiger was awarded 1st place for creativity. Team Bearcat was awarded 1st place for having the greatest number of packages in their structure.

## 1C | Speed Building: Paragraph

1. Key two 1' timed writings on the paragraph; determine *gwam* on each writing.
2. Key two 2' timed writings on the paragraph; determine *gwam*.

**MicroType**

*Timed Writing*

**A**

**All letters used**

GWAM 2'

|   |   |
|---|---|
| When you key copy that contains both words and | 4 |
| numbers, it is best to key numbers using the top row.  When | 10 |
| the copy consists primarily of figures, however, it may be | 16 |
| faster to use the keypad.  In any event, keying figures | 22 |
| quickly is a major skill to prize.  You can expect to key | 28 |
| figures often in the future, so learn to key them with very | 34 |
| little  peeking. | 36 |

GWAM 2' | 1 | 2 | 3 | 4 | 5 | 6 |

## 1D | Learn % and –

Key each line twice SS (slowly, then faster); DS between 2-line groups.

**Learn % (percent sign)**

1  f r % f r % ff rr %% f% 5%, 10%, 15%, 20%, 25%, 30%, or 35%.

2  Do not space between a number and %:  4%, 76%, 84%, and 97%.

3  Get a 10%, 15%, or 20% discount.  Their markup is about 45%.

**Learn - (hyphen)**

4  ;p- ;p- ;; pp -- ;- ;- Did Mack say 2-ply or 3-ply or 4-ply?

5  Please rate the videos as 1-star, 2-star, 3-star, or 4-star.

6  Did their accident happen in the 50-mile-an-hour speed zone?

## 1E | Speed Building

1. Key two 1' timings on each paragraph of **2F**, page 107 (Unit 4).
2. Key one 2' timing on paragraphs 1–2 combined; determine *gwam*.

**E-mail 2**

1. Key the following e-mail message.

2. Spell-check the message and proofread carefully. Correct all errors. Save the message as *U10L3Email2*.

   **Names for MicroType users:** Che Lu, Janet Unger, and Earl Popelas

TO:  lu@holt.edu, unger@holt.edu, popelas@holt.edu

FROM:  Sandy Dennis

DATE:  February 27, 20--

SUBJECT:  THE STORY OF SCIENCE

Please invite all your students to a showing of "The Story of Science." This award-winning film will be shown at 7 p.m. at the Civic Center. Dates for the film are Thursday, Friday, and Saturday evenings, March 3-5, 20--.

Students will be admitted without charge on Thursday evening. Tell students they will need to present their school ID card at the door.

Students attending on Friday or Saturday evening must pay $7.50 with a valid school ID card. Students without proper ID and adults will be charged $10.

---

★ *Language Arts*

## 3E Writing:  Number Expression

Read the following number usage rule. Key the Learn line, noting number choices. Key the Apply lines, making the necessary corrections. Save as *U10L3Writing*.

**Rule 1:** Spell a number that begins a sentence even when other numbers in the sentence are shown in figures.

Learn 1   Fifteen of the 96 applicants were from New York.

Apply 2   12 of the 25 computers were purchased in 2007.

Apply 3   15 of the 25 players on last year's initial roster were traded.

## 1F Writing: Capitalization

Read the capitalization rules below. Study the Learn lines. Note how the rules are applied. Key the Learn lines and the Apply lines, making the necessary corrections. Save as *U5L1Capitalization*.

**Rule 9:** Capitalize historical periods and events.

Learn 1   The Treaty of Paris culminated the American Revolutionary War.

Learn 2   Lincoln, Lee, and Grant were primary figures of the Civil War.

Apply 3   Many claim that the industrial revolution started in Britain.

Apply 4   The english revolution ended with the execution of Charles I.

**Rule 10:** Capitalize streets, roads, and avenues.

Learn 5   Yankee Stadium is located on E. 161 Street and River Avenue.

Learn 6   The Dwight D. Eisenhower Expressway is part of Interstate 290.

Apply 7   The firm is on the corner of maple street and sierra drive.

Apply 8   The kennedy expressway will merge with the edens expressway.

## 1G | Skill Building: Symbols

Key each line twice SS (slowly, then faster); DS between 2-line groups.

**Combine / and $**

1   Nearly 3/4 of the class has paid $500 for the New York trip.

2   She said only 1/2 of the $500 is refundable after 3/15/2010.

3   Mrs. Rodriguez said the trip will cost $550 after 3/15/2010.

**Combine % and -**

4   Between 50% and 60% take the 2-year or 3-year rental option.

5   Robert paid twenty-two dollars or about 55% of the expenses.

6   Rebecca sent the package by third-class mail at a 9% saving.

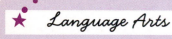

## 1H Reading

 CD-U5L1Read

Open the file *CD-U5L1Read*. Read the document carefully and close the file. Let your instructor know when you are ready to answer questions covering the content of the file.

**For additional practice** ▶ **MicroType** + **Numeric Keyboarding** + **Lessons 7 and 8**

Sometimes more than one person is sent the same message. A comma or semicolon and a space are usually used to separate the addresses in the *To:* box. A subject should be included in the *Subject:* box. Many people delete e-mail messages that do not have a subject line without reading them. Subjects are sometimes keyed in ALL CAPS.

### E-mail Body

The paragraphs in the body of an e-mail message are usually keyed using single spacing and a 12-point font. Double space between paragraphs. Begin all lines at the left margin.

The body may contain special formats such as varying font sizes and colors. Special formatting features should be used sparingly. All e-mail programs do not support format features in the same way.

## 3D | E-mail Messages

### E-mail 1

1. Study the information and format guides contained in the report in **3C**.

2. Key the e-mail message shown in the new message illustration below.

#### E-mail Software Users

If your instructor directs, use her or his e-mail address for the TO line of all e-mail messages. Use your e-mail address for the FROM line in all messages. Do not actually send an e-mail to the address shown in the illustration or problem.

#### MicroType 4 Users

If e-mail software is not available, key all e-mail messages as memos. Use the names given. Use the current date.

3. Spell-check the message and proofread carefully. Correct all errors. Save the message as *U10L3Email1*. Print the e-mail message or memo.

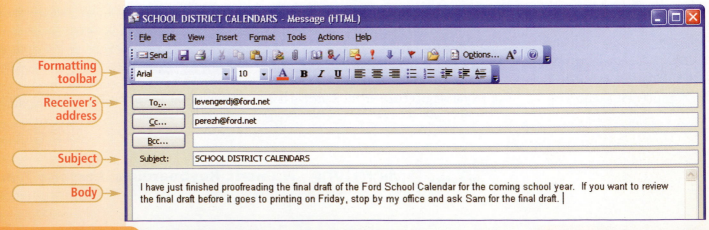

# 2

## OBJECTIVES

1. To learn reach technique for #, &, (, and ).
2. To improve keying speed.

### TIP

- The **#** is the shift of **3** and is keyed with the left middle finger.
- The **&** is the shift of **7** and is keyed with the right index finger.

### TIP

- Do not space between **#** and a figure.
- Space once before and after **&** used to join names.

### 2A | Conditioning Practice

Key each line twice SS; then key a 1' timed writing on line 3. Determine *gwam*.

| | |
|---|---|
| Alphabet 1 | Five kids quickly mixed the prizes, baffling one wise judge. |
| CAPS LOCK 2 | LINCOLN HIGH SCHOOL took first; REGIS HIGH SCHOOL took third. |
| Easy 3 | The big social for the maid was held downtown in the chapel. |

| GWAM | 1' | 1 | 2 | 3 | 4 | 5 | 6 | 7 | 8 | 9 | 10 | 11 | 12 |
|------|----|---|---|---|---|---|---|---|---|---|----|----|----|

### 2B | Learn # and &

Key each line twice SS (slowly, then faster); DS between 2-line groups.

**Learn # (number/pounds)**

1  d e # d e # | d # d # | Martin keyed #384, #275, #417, and #690.

2  Do not space between a number and #:  6# of #532 at $8.90/#.

3  I wrote Check #78 for $25.60 and Check #79 for $4.03 in May.

**Learn & (ampersand)**

4  j u & j u & | j & j & | John & Steve, Maria & Linda, Mike & Joy.

5  Do not space before or after & in initials, e.g., XY&Z, R&R.

6  She works at Hoyle & Rodriguez rather than at Chen & Fenton.

**Combine # and &**

7  Sandy said # stands for number and pounds; & stands for and.

8  He wrote Check #88 to Smith & Jones for a ream of 20# paper.

**Standard Report Format Guides:**

**Top margin:**

Page 1 is 2"; default or 1" on the following pages.

**Side and bottom margins:**

Default or 1".

**Report title:**

Centered in ALL CAPS and followed by a double space. May be keyed in a larger font than the report body.

**Line spacing:**

DS the report body. Indent paragraphs .5".

**Page numbers:**

Right-align the page number in a header.

**MicroType**

**TIP**

Use the Insert, Symbol feature to insert bullets.

## 3C | Standard Report Format

1. Read the formatting guides at the left regarding standard report format.

2. Key the following report using standard report format. Use a 12-point font. Set a 1" top margin for the document. Insert hard returns on page 1 for a 2" top margin on this page. Use a 14-point bold font for the report title. Use a 12-point bold font for the side headings. Use the Insert, Symbol command to insert bullet characters.

3. Use the Zoom feature to view the document and verify that the format is correct. Insert hard page breaks as needed to end the pages properly. Spell-check the report and proofread carefully. Correct all errors. Save as *U10L3Report*.

### E-MAIL MESSAGES

E-mail (electronic mail) use is growing. This growth is due, in part, to the ease of creating and the speed of sending messages. Generally, delivery of an e-mail message takes place within seconds or minutes. The receiver may be in the same building, city, state, or country as the sender.

### E-mail, Memos, and Letters

In many instances, e-mail messages have replaced memos and letters. As you learned earlier, memos are sent from one person to another within the same business.

Business letters are sent from a person within a business to a person outside that business. A letter written by an individual to deal with business of a personal nature is called a personal-business letter. You will format personal-business letters in Lesson 5.

### E-mail Headings

An e-mail message includes heading information and a body. The heading information includes the:

- Address of the person(s) receiving the e-mail
- Address of the person sending the e-mail
- Date the e-mail was sent
- Subject of the e-mail message

Most e-mail programs insert the sender's name and the date automatically. The e-mail address of the person receiving the message should be keyed using uppercase and lowercase letters as given to you.

*(continued)*

**Social Studies**

## 2C | Timed Writings

1. Key one 1' unguided and two 1' guided timed writings on each paragraph, as directed on page 77.

2. Key two 2' unguided writings on the paragraphs; determine *gwam* on each.

**MicroType**

*Timed Writing*

**A** ▼

**All letters used**

| | GWAM 2' |
|---|---|
| The Bill of Rights includes the changes to the | 4 |
| constitution that deal with human rights of all people. | 10 |
| The changes or amendments were to improve and correct the | 16 |
| original document. They were made to assure the quality of | 22 |
| life and to protect the rights of all citizens. | 27 |
| One of the changes provides for the right to religious | 32 |
| choice, free speech, and free press. Another addresses the | 38 |
| right to keep and bear firearms. Another deals with the | 44 |
| rights of the people with regard to unreasonable search and | 50 |
| seizure of person or property. Two others deal with the | 55 |
| right to an immediate and public trial by a jury and the | 61 |
| prevention of excessive bail and fines. | 65 |

GWAM 2' | 1 | 2 | 3 | 4 | 5 | 6 |

## 3B | Zoom

You can increase or decrease the view of your document on the screen. As you increase the Zoom percent, the print becomes larger. The portion of the document displayed on the screen decreases. When you set the Zoom to see the whole page, you can check the format of your document (margins, spacing, etc.) before printing.

To change the view of your document:

1. From the View menu, select Zoom.

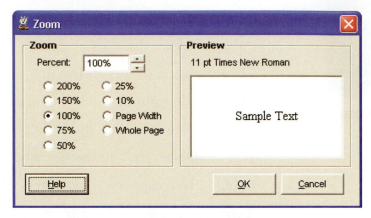

2. Select the percentage you want to zoom. You can either key the exact percentage or click on a radio button to select a preset percent or page width view.

3. Click OK to close the Zoom dialog box.

**Practice What You Have Learned**

1. Open the data file *CD-U10L3View*.

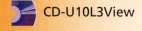 CD-U10L3View

2. Change the Zoom to view the document as a whole page.

3. Change the Zoom to view the document at 75 percent.

4. Change the Zoom to view the document at 80 percent.

5. Change the Zoom to view the document at 200 percent.

6. Close the document without saving.

## 2D | Learn ( and )

Key each line twice SS (slowly, then faster); DS between 2-line groups.

**Learn ( (left parenthesis)**

1   L O   ( L O (|L ( L (|l ( l (|Key (1, (2, (3, (4, (5, (6, (7,

2   (James and Sandy (Ruth and Mick (Ted and Jane (Joe and Laura

**Learn ) (right parenthesis)**

3   : P ) : P )| : ) : )|; ) ; )|a) b) c) d) e) f) g) h) i) j) )

4   Rick and Susan) Felipe and Anna) Jamal and Rhea) Jo and Dave

**Combine ( and )**

5   Thomas Eaton (Colby H. S.) nominated Beth Cox (Osseo H. S.).

6   I said the account (#53-87) has a negative balance (-$3.87).

## 2E | Keyboard Reinforcement

1. Key each line twice SS; DS between 2-line groups.

2. Key a 30" timing on each line.

**Easy sentences (Think, say, and key the words at a steady pace.)**

1   Helen may blame the men for the problem with the city signs.

2   Nancy and I may go downtown to pay for the neighbor's chair.

3   The maid held a social for them in the chapel on the island.

4   The auditor for the firm may sign the forms for Glen and me.

5   Jane owns the land by the lake; she may make a profit on it.

6   Gus and HaI may row to the island for the title to the land.

 **GWAM** 30" | 2 | 4 | 6 | 8 | 10 | 12 | 14 | 16 | 18 | 20 | 22 |

## 2D Writing: Word Choice

Study the spelling and definitions of the following words. Key the Learn lines, noting the word choices. Key the Apply lines, selecting the correct words. Save as *U10L2Writing*.

**cents** (noun)  hundredths of a dollar

**sense** (noun)  soundness of judgment

**since** (adverb)  from then until now; subsequently; because

Learn 1  Since Sue paid with a dollar bill, she expects to receive a few cents in change.

Learn 2  Al made sense when he suggested we save as many cents as we can.

Apply 3  I make more (cents, sense, since) (cents, sense, since) I practiced my speech.

Apply 4  Tom has saved a jar full of (cents, sense, since) (cents, sense, since) May.

*Our World*

## 2E ▪ Research Citizenship

Search for and then complete a citizenship quiz on the Internet. Print one or more pages that reveal your score or the questions if possible. Did you pass the quiz?

Write a paragraph describing the kinds of questions on the quiz. Identify any questions that you missed or were not certain about. *Save as U10L2Internet.*

*Social Studies*

---

## LESSON 3

# STANDARD REPORT AND E-MAIL MESSAGES

### 3A | Conditioning Practice

### OBJECTIVES

1. To learn the Zoom word processing feature.
2. To key and format a standard report.
3. To format e-mail messages.

Key each line twice SS; then key a 1' timed writing on line 3. Find *gwam*.

Alphabet 1  Reba Maja will quickly hire a night supervisor next week for Zed.

Figures 2  Our student club has 18,673 members in 290 chapters in 45 states.

Speed 3  The girl on the bicycle saw eight giant turkeys by the city lake.

GWAM  1' | 1 | 2 | 3 | 4 | 5 | 6 | 7 | 8 | 9 | 10 | 11 | 12 | 13 |

## 2F | Word Choice

Study the spelling and definitions of the words below. Key the Learn lines, noting the word choices. Key the Apply lines, selecting the correct words. Save as *U5L2WordChoice*.

**hour** (noun) the 24th part of a day; a particular time

**our** (adjective) of or relating to ourselves as possessors

Learn 1   It may take longer than an **hour** to finish the test.

Learn 2   Rachel said, "**Our** team is ready for the tournament."

Apply 3   It will take you about one (hour, our) to get to the airport.

Apply 4   You can use (hour, our) computer to finish the job.

**Our World**

## 2G ▪ Natural Wonders of the World

Listed below are a few of the natural wonders of the world. Use an encyclopedia or the Internet to learn about one of them. Take notes and be prepared to share information about the natural wonder you research. Note the addresses of the Internet sites you use to learn about this topic.

**INTERNET**

- The Great Barrier Reef
- Iguassu Falls
- Mount Everest
- Mount Fuji
- Niagara Falls
- Paricutin Volcano

Your instructor may provide a world map to use with Our World activities. If directed, indicate the location of the natural wonder and label it on the map.

*Social Studies*

**For additional practice** ▶ **MicroType** ✦ **Numeric Keyboarding** ✦ **Lessons 9 and 10**

**Memo 2**

1. Key the following information in memo format. Use the Paragraph Spacing feature to insert vertical space between memo parts and paragraphs. Use Arial 12-point font.

2. Spell-check the memo and proofread carefully. Correct all errors. Save as *U10L2Memo2*.

TO:  Olu T. Sangoeyhi, Customer Service | FROM:  Ken M. Zenn, Advertising | DATE:  May 14, 20-- | SUBJECT:  BROCHURE REVIEW

The first draft of the brochure you plan to use to advertise our newest line of cell phones is attached.  Please proofread the copy carefully and make sure the specifications for each are correct.

We are in the process of getting the price for each phone confirmed and will include them on the next draft.  Also, the Marketing staff is determining the distribution area for the brochure.

Please mark your suggested changes and return the brochure to me by next Monday.

xx

Enclosure

c Fred Haus

bc Lois Ford

**Memo 3**

1. Key the following information in memo format. Use the Paragraph Spacing feature to insert vertical space between memo parts and paragraphs. Use Verdana 12-point font.

2. Spell-check the memo and proofread carefully. Correct all errors. Save as *U10L2Memo3*.

TO:  (Insert instructor's name) | FROM:  (Insert your name) | DATE: (Insert current date) | SUBJECT:  CAREER INTEREST

A draft outline describing my participation in the "Presidential Classroom Scholars Program" in Washington, D.C., this past summer is attached. Please review it and give me your feedback within the next few days.

In the meantime, I will begin working on the slides I will use to support my presentation to the school board at the upcoming monthly meeting.

As you suggested, I met with the guidance counselor, Mr. Duncan, to help him make plans to introduce this exciting program to other students.

xx

Attachment

c Mr. Johnson, Principal

## LESSON

# 3

### OBJECTIVES

1. *To learn reach technique for ', ", _, and *.*
2. *To improve keying speed.*

### TIP

- The ' is the key to the right of the ; and is keyed with the right little finger.

- The " is the shift of the ' and is keyed with the right little finger.

- On your screen, apostrophes and quotation marks may look different from those shown in these lines.

### 3A | Conditioning Practice

Key each line twice SS; then key a 1' writing on line 3.  Determine *gwam*.

Alphabet 1   Jake Vogelberg always completed his quizzes and exams first.

Figures 2   Jo's car has 34,729 miles on it; Ben's car has 50,816 miles.

Easy 3   Helen and I may handle all the problems with the city audit.

| GWAM | 1' | 1 | 2 | 3 | 4 | 5 | 6 | 7 | 8 | 9 | 10 | 11 | 12 |

### 3B | New Keys:  ' and "

Key each line twice SS (slowly, then faster); DS between 2-line groups.

**Learn ' (apostrophe)**

1   ;' ;' ;'|;' ;' ;'|You've found David's book, haven't you.

2   I'm sure I've located Jan's car; it's in Jason's new garage.

3   Didn't you find Jill's ring in Michael's locker on Saturday?

**Learn " (quotation mark)**

1   ;" ;" ;"|;" ;" ;"|"Jon," she said, "stop that right now."

2   "George Washington," I said, "was the first U.S. President."

3   "Thomas Jefferson," he said, "was the third U.S. President."

4   "Who," she asked, "was the second President of our country?"

**Tip**

The text at the right indicates a DS before the:

- reference initials
- attachment/enclosure notation
- copy notation
- blind copy notation

---

DS is used when the Paragraph Spacing feature is not used. When keying this memo and others in this lesson, you will use the Paragraph Spacing feature to insert vertical space.

### Memo 1

1. Study the information in the body of the following memo. Review the model memo from Lesson 1.

2. Open a new blank document. Set the line spacing to single, paragraph spacing to 12 points after paragraphs, and the font size to 12.

3. Key the memo. Be careful not to insert extra vertical space between heading parts and paragraphs.

4. Spell-check the report and proofread carefully. Correct all errors. Save as *U10L2Memo1*.

TO:             All Computer Applications Students

FROM:         Mrs. Ronnie Merriman

DATE:         October 15, 20--

SUBJECT:     SPECIAL MEMO PARTS

Sometimes memos need to include special parts. A description and formatting guides for several special parts are given below.

**Attachment or enclosure notation.** An attachment or enclosure notation may appear at the end of a memo. If another document is attached to the memo, the word "Attachment" is keyed at the left margin a double space below the reference initials. (Place the notation below the last line of the body if reference initials are not used.) If a document accompanies the memo but is not attached, key the word "Enclosure." This memo has an attachment notation.

**Copy notation.** If a copy of a memo is being sent to someone other than the person to whom the memo is addressed, include a copy notation. Key a "c" followed by the name of the person(s) who is to receive a copy. The copy notation is keyed a double space below the last line of the body. (Place the copy notation after reference initials or other notations if they are included.) If you do not want the person receiving the memo to know you are sending the memo to others, key "bc" (for blind copy) after the last memo part on all copies but the one being sent to the person named in the TO: heading. This memo has both copy notations keyed in the correct sequence.

xx (Reference initials)

Attachment (Attachment notation)

c Tom Paulson (Copy notation)

bc Mary Trent (Blind copy notation)

## 3C | Speed Check:  Sentences

Key a 30" timing on each line.  If you finish a line before time is called, key the line again.  Your *gwam* is shown below the lines.

1   Will he be here for the dance?

2   Jeffry went snowboarding last week.

3   Mitch went to the mall to buy a sweater.

4   I should be able to go skiing with you today.

5   Jane took her iPod to school with her on Thursday.

6   Several new games are available for the Xbox on Friday.

**GWAM** 30" | 2 | 4 | 6 | 8 | 10 | 12 | 14 | 16 | 18 | 20 |

## 3D | New Keys:  _ and *

Key each line twice SS (slowly, then faster); DS between 2-line groups.

**TIP**

- The _ is the shift of –
  and is keyed with the
  right little finger.

- The * is the shift of **8**
  and is keyed with the
  right middle finger.

**Learn _ (underline)**

1   :_ :_ :_|::_ ::_ ::|-_ -_|I have __ brothers and __ sisters.

2   A _ is used in some Internet locations, i.e., http2_data_2.

3   Ple_se f_ll in ea_h m_ssing let_er t_ com_lete t_e sen_ence.

**Learn * (asterisk)**

4   k i * k i * k i *|* 0 * 5 * 3 * 1 * 9 * 6 * 2 * 8 * 7 * 4 **

5   Use an * (*Jay, *Kate, and *Jon) to designate honor society.

6   Separate the names (*Faye*Felipe*Joan*Dick*) with asterisks.

## 2B | Paragraph Spacing

Paragraph spacing determines the amount of white space above or below a paragraph. In previous activities, hard returns were used to insert additional white space between paragraphs. Now you will learn how to use the Paragraph dialog box to increase the amount of space before paragraphs, after paragraphs, or both.

To change the spacing before and/or after paragraph(s):

1. Position the cursor in the paragraph you want to format. To apply the formatting change to more than one paragraph, select the paragraphs that you want to change.

2. From the Format menu, select Paragraph.

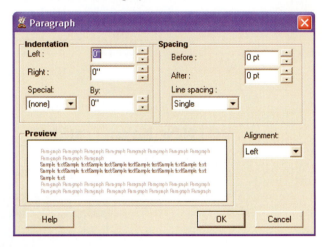

3. Key the number of points (pt) desired in the Spacing box(es). Remember that 72 points equals 1" of vertical space.

To change the spacing before the paragraph is keyed, start with step 2.

**Practice What You Have Learned**

1. Open the data file *CD-U10L2Paragraph*.

2. Select paragraph 1 and set the Spacing After to 36 points.

3. Select paragraph 2 and set the Spacing Before and After to 36 points.

4. Select paragraph 3 and set the Spacing Before to 36 points and the Spacing After to 72 points.

5. Print the document to verify that the spacing between the paragraphs is equal or nearly equal.

6. Save as *U10L2Paragraph*.

CD-U10L2Paragraph

**Right little finger; keep right index finger anchored to j key**

## 3E | Keyboard Reinforcement: BACKSPACE Key

1. Keeping the **j** finger anchored, reach up and tap the BACKSPACE key as you look at the reach. Repeat this reach several times until you can do it without looking.

2. Key the lines below, following the instructions given above each line. Keep the j finger anchored; make the reach to the BACKSPACE key without looking.

   1. Key the following.

      The delete

   2. Use the BACKSPACE key to make the changes shown below.

      The ~~delete~~ backspace

   3. Continue keying the sentence as shown below.

      The backspace key can be

   4. Use the BACKSPACE key to make the change shown below.

      The backspace key ~~can be~~ is

   5. Continue keying the sentence as shown below.

      The backspace key is used to fix

   6. Use the BACKSPACE key to make the change shown below.

      The backspace key is used to ~~fix~~ make

   7. Continue keying the sentence shown below.

      The backspace key is used to make changes.

©CORBIS

## 1C Writing:  Internal Punctuation

Read the following punctuation rules.  Study the Learn lines.  Note how the rules are applied.  Key the Learn lines and the Apply lines, including the necessary punctuation.  Save as *U10L1Writing*.

***Rule 14:*** Use a colon to introduce a question or a quotation.

Learn 1  Who said:  "A date which will live in infamy"?

Learn 2  Dad inquired:  Who broke the window?

Apply 3  Which President said "Four score and seven years ago"?

Apply 4  The teacher asked Will you ever be ready for the exam?

***Rule 15:*** Use a colon between hours and minutes expressed in figures.

Learn 5  Their last performance will start at 7:30 p.m.

Apply 6  We need people to cover the 730 a.m. and 430 p.m. shifts.

Apply 7  The flight left at 545 p.m.; it should arrive in Dallas at 756 p.m.

***Rule 16:*** Use italic to indicate titles of books and names of magazines and newspapers.  (Titles may be keyed in All CAPS or underlined without the italic.)

Learn 8  Both *USA Today* and *U.S. News and World Report* had feature articles.

Apply 9  This week's top book was For One More Day by Mitch Albom.

Apply 10  Did  you  renew  your  subscription  to  Sports  Illustrated?

★ *Language Arts*

## 1D | Composition

Compose and key a paragraph explaining how you set tabs by using the Tab Type button on the Ruler and the Tabs dialog box.  Save your composition as *U10L1Composition*.

---

## LESSON 2

# INTEROFFICE MEMOS

## 2A | Conditioning Practice

### OBJECTIVES

1. *To learn to change the spacing before and after a paragraph.*
2. *To learn to format memos with special parts.*

Key each line twice SS; then key a 1' timed writing on line 3.  Find *gwam*.

Alphabet 1  Pavi will ask six judges to quickly analyze the five board games.

Figure/Symbols 2  T&G Co. issued P.O. #7086-5 to buy 125 desks (#342-64) @ $79 each.

Speed 3  Rosie is the chair of the sorority social to be held at the mall.

GWAM  1' | 1 | 2 | 3 | 4 | 5 | 6 | 7 | 8 | 9 | 10 | 11 | 12 | 13 |

### 3F | Timed Writings

1. Key one 1' unguided and two 1' guided timed writings on each paragraph, as directed on page 77.

2. Key two 2' unguided writings on the paragraphs; determine *gwam* on each.

| | GWAM | 2' | 3' |
|---|---|---|---|
| A business is in business to make a profit. They do | | 11 | 5 |
| this by employing individuals who help the organization | | 22 | 11 |
| achieve its goals. In the past, various styles of | | 32 | 16 |
| leadership were used. Today, however, one of the most | | 42 | 21 |
| common styles used is the democratic style. This is where | | 54 | 27 |
| decisions are made by a team of individuals rather than | | 65 | 33 |
| by just one person. | | 69 | 34 |
| Because more and more companies are operating as a | | 79 | 40 |
| team, it is important for you to learn to participate as | | 90 | 45 |
| part of a team. This requires an effort on your part. | | 101 | 51 |
| Good team members listen to the opinions of other individuals | | 113 | 57 |
| on the team. Good team members are considerate of others. | | 125 | 62 |
| Good team members respect the rights of others. Good team | | 136 | 68 |
| members are excellent communicators. | | 144 | 72 |

GWAM 1' | 1 | 2 | 3 | 4 | 5 | 6 | 7 | 8 | 9 | 10 | 11 | 12
2' | 1 | 2 | 3 | 4 | 5 | 6

**For additional practice** ▶ **MicroType** ✦ **Numeric Keyboarding** ✦ **Lessons 11 and 12**

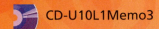
CD-U10L1Memo3

**Memo 3**

1. Open the data file *CD-U10L1Memo3*. Key the following information before the text in the file. Format the memo correctly using a 12-point Verdana font; add reference initials.

2. Spell-check the memo and proofread carefully. Correct all errors. Save as *U10L1Memo3*.

TO: All Student Workers | FROM: Marilyn Hopper, Principal | DATE: May 5, 20-- | SUBJECT: ANSWERING THE SCHOOL OFFICE TELEPHONE

The telephone is a popular means of communicating in our school. Knowing how to use the telephone effectively is important.

Answer all incoming calls promptly. Identify yourself and the school office immediately. Speak in a tone that is relaxed and low-pitched. Keep a writing pad near the phone to record important parts of the call. Thank the caller at the end of the conversation.

**Memo 4**

1. Key the following information in memo format, using 12-point Arial font. Add reference initials.

2. Spell-check the memo and proofread carefully. Correct all errors. Save as *U10L1Memo4*.

TO: Vera L. Bowden, Math Teacher | FROM: Amelia Carter, Business Teacher | DATE: August 12, 20-- | SUBJECT: DONATION RECEIVED

What a pleasant surprise it was to find your $50 donation to FBLA in my mail this morning. Thank you for helping the students in our local FBLA chapter serve those who are less fortunate.

Your contribution will be used to purchase food and clothing for young children as part of Community Day. As you know, it has been a long-standing tradition of FBLA to conduct a fall drive to support this event. The students are working very hard to meet their goals. Your donation will certainly help!

## LESSON

# 4

### OBJECTIVES

1. *To learn reach technique for @, +, !, and \.*
2. *To improve keying speed.*

---

**TIP**

- The **@** is the shift of **2** and is keyed with the left ring finger.
- The **+** is to the right of the hyphen. Press the left shift and tap the **+** with the right little finger.

---

### 4A | Conditioning Practice

Key each line twice SS; then key a 1' timed writing on line 3. Determine *gwam*.

Alphabet 1   Greg and Jazmine quickly gave examples of two helping verbs.

Figures 2   Margaret's ZIP Code is 54720, and Keith's ZIP Code is 61839.

Easy 3   Make a right turn by the lake signs to go to the big chapel.

GWAM   1' | 1 | 2 | 3 | 4 | 5 | 6 | 7 | 8 | 9 | 10 | 11 | 12 |

### 4B | Learn @ and +

Key each line twice SS (slowly, then faster); DS between 2-line groups.

**Learn @ ("at" sign)**

4   s w @ s w @ | s@ s@ | 1@ $20; 13 @ $4; 5 @ $6; 17 @ $8; 9 @ $10.

5   Change the e-mail from smithjp@aol.com to smithjp@yahoo.com.

6   Keith owns 50 shares of BBY @ $49.19 and 50 of JPM @ $48.30.

**Learn + ("plus" sign)**

7   ; + ;+ ;+ | +;+ +;+ | 5 + 4 + 8, x + y + z; a + b + d, 154 + 234

8   When you add 3 + 7 + 2 + 4 + 8 + 5, you get 29 for an answer.

9   When you add 5 + 8 + 1 + 6 + 9 + 7, you get 36 for an answer.

### 4C | Speed Check: Sentences

Key a 30" timing on each line. If you finish a line before time is called, key the line again. Your *gwam* is shown below the lines.

1   Jane will call her on Tuesday.

2   Theo will give his speech tomorrow.

3   Kristen drove home in a crazy snowstorm.

4   Derek decided not to play baseball this year.

5   Rafael took first at regional and second at state.

6   Trenton decided not to apply for the job in California.

GWAM   30" | 2 | 4 | 6 | 8 | 10 | 12 | 14 | 16 | 18 | 20 |

TO: **Tab** **Tab** All Computer Applications Students ↓**2**

FROM: **Tab** Mrs. Ronnie Merriman ↓**2**

DATE:**Tab** **Tab**October 5, 20-- ↓**2**

SUBJECT:**Tab** INTEROFFICE MEMORANDUMS ↓**2**

Interoffice memorandums (memos) are written messages used by people within an organization to communicate with one another. ↓**2**

**Memo margins.** The top margin of the first page of a memo is 2". If the memo is more than one page, use the default top margin or a 1" top margin on the following pages. Use 1" or the default margins for the left and right margins. ↓**2**

**Memo headings.** Memos have a heading that includes who the memo is being sent to (TO:). Who the memo is from (FROM:) is listed next. The date the memo is being sent (DATE:) and what the memo is about (SUBJECT:) follow. All lines of the memo heading begin at the left margin. The heading lines are double-spaced. Tab once or twice as needed to align the information following the heading words about 1" from the left margin. ↓**2**

**Memo body.** The paragraphs of the memo all begin at the left margin. The paragraphs are single-spaced with a double space between paragraphs. Paragraph headings are optional. When used, paragraph headings begin at the left margin. Capitalize the first letter of the first word, underline or bold the heading, and follow the heading with a period. ↓**2**

**Reference initials.** If someone other than the person named in the FROM: heading keyed the memo, the initials of the person keying the memo are keyed in lowercase letters at the left margin a double space below the last line of the memo body, as illustrated by the xx in the line below. ↓**2**

xx

## 4D | Learn ! and \

Key each line twice SS (slowly, then faster); DS between 2-line groups.

### Learn ! (exclamation point)

1  A q ! a q ! | a! a! a! | b! c! d! e! f! g! h! i! j! k! l! m! !n!

2  We won!  Do your job!  No more excuses!  Stop it!  Sit down!

3  Have fun!  Be home before midnight!  Nice shot!  Run faster!

### Learn \ (backslash)

4  ; \ ;\ ;\ | \;\ \;\ | ;\ ;\  You do not need to shift for the \.

5  Use the \ key to map the drive to access \\sps25\deptdir556.

6  Map the drive to \\global128\coxjg$, not \\globa1l27\coxjg$.

## 4E | Speed Building

1. Key the lines once SS; DS between 2-line groups.

2. Key a 1' writing on lines 5–8.

**Key easy sentences (Key the words at a brisk, steady pace.)**

1  The maids may make a profit if they handle their work right.

2  Jake may make a bid for the antique bottle for the neighbor.

3  Helen and Ross may make a map of the city for the eight men.

4  The city auditor held a formal social for six men and women.

5  Shane and Orlando may work with the men on the turn signals.

6  The dog and Pamela slept downtown in a cubicle in city hall.

7  Keith and Diana may cycle to the city dock by the big lake.

8  Half of us may be kept busy with the work on the big chapel.

**GWAM**  1' |  1  |  2  |  3  |  4  |  5  |  6  |  7  |  8  |  9  |  10  |  11  |  12  |

# Unit 10
## Prepare Correspondence

### Lessons 1–9

## INTEROFFICE MEMORANDUMS

### Memo Format Guides

- **Top margin: 2" on page 1; 1" or default on all others.**
- **Side & bottom margins: default or 1".**
- **DS between heading lines.**
- **SS paragraphs in body; DS between paragraphs.**
- **Body: Begin all lines at the left margin.**
- **Heading information: Key heading words in ALL CAPS. Tab once or twice as needed to align the information following the heading words at 1" from the left margin. You may need to tab only once if a small font is used or more times if a larger font is used.**

### 1A | Conditioning Practice

Key each line twice SS; then key a 1' timed writing on line 3. Find *gwam*.

Alphabet 1  Zev quickly ruined the waxed floor as the big, open jam jar fell.

Figures 2  The combinations on the two locks I have are 20-46-7 and 19-35-8.

Speed 3  Their visit was to end the problem so the firm may make a profit.

**GWAM** 1' | 1 | 2 | 3 | 4 | 5 | 6 | 7 | 8 | 9 | 10 | 11 | 12 | 13 |

### 1B | Interoffice Memos

**Memo 1**

1. Study the information in the body of the memo and the formatting guides on the following page. Read the Memo Format Guides at the left.

2. Key the memo in correct format using the default font. Key your initials for the reference initials instead of xx. Spell-check the memo and proofread carefully. Correct all errors. Save as *U10L1Memo1*.

**Memo 2**

1. Key the following information in memo format. Use reference initials to show you keyed the memo.

2. Change the font size to 12 point. Spell-check the memo and proofread carefully. Correct all errors. Save as *U10L1Memo2*.

TO:          Betsy Jamison

FROM:        Cindy Grossman

DATE:  September 23, 20--

SUBJECT:     TRANSFER OF FUNDS

Please notify Mrs. Christine Molinaro that she can now transfer funds from her existing account to the new account.

Have her complete the Authorization to Transfer Securities or Money form to make the initial transfer from Account 3257-2136 to Account 6467-7124.

We will link her checking account to her new account within the next 10 days so future transfers can be done electronically.

## 4F | Timed Writings

1. Key a 1' timed writing on paragraph 1, then on paragraph 2.
2. Key a 2' timed writing on paragraphs 1–2 combined.
3. Key a 3' timed writing on paragraphs 1–2 combined.

|  | GWAM | 2' | 3' |
|---|---|---|---|
| Whether you are an intense lover of music or simply | | 5 | 3 |
| enjoy hearing good music, you are more than likely aware of | | 11 | 7 |
| the work completed by Beethoven, the German composer. He | | 17 | 11 |
| is generally recognized as one of the greatest composers to | | 23 | 15 |
| ever live.  Much of his early work was influenced by those | | 28 | 19 |
| who wrote music in Austria, Haydn and Mozart. | | 33 | 22 |
| It can be argued whether Beethoven was a classical or | | 38 | 25 |
| romantic composer.  This depends upon which period of time | | 44 | 29 |
| in his life the music was written.  His exquisite music has | | 50 | 33 |
| elements of both.  It has been said that his early works | | 56 | 37 |
| brought to a conclusion the classical age.  It has also | | 62 | 41 |
| been stated that Beethoven's later work started the | | 67 | 44 |
| romantic age of music. | | 69 | 46 |

GWAM   2'   1    2    3    4    5    6
       3'     1       2       3       4

New Keys:  @, +, !, and \

## Math Activities

**3H ▪ Math Challenge 9**

### FIND THE PERCENT OF MARKUP

1. Key a sentence to explain how you find the percent of markup between two prices in problems like this: *What is the % of markup based on cost if the cost is $30 and the selling price is $36?*

2. Solve the following problems and key your answers in sentence form. Round answers to tenths if needed. For example, an appropriate sentence for the answer to the problem stated above is: *The percent of markup based on cost is 20% when an item costing $30 is sold for $36.*

   2a. cost is $46; selling price is $57.50; markup is based on cost

   2b. cost 1,056.45; selling price $1,580.99; markup is based on cost

   2c. cost is .66; selling price is .99; markup is based on selling price

   2d. A store manager bought shirts for $22 each and sold them for $27.50. What is the markup based on cost? What is the markup based on selling price?

3. Save your answers as *U9L3Math*.

---

## Careers ····················

### 3I ▪ Career Exploration Portfolio – Activity 9

▪ You must complete Career Activities 1–3 before completing this activity.

1. Retrieve your Career folder and the information in it that relates to the career cluster that is your third choice.

2. Reflect on the skills and knowledge you have gained in the courses you have taken and the extracurricular activities in which you are involved that will be beneficial in the career you selected as your third choice. Then compose a paragraph or two describing the connection between what you have learned and/or your activities and this career. Print your file and then save it as *U9L3Career9* and keep it open.

3. Exchange papers with a classmate and have the classmate offer suggestions for improving the content and correcting any errors he or she finds in your paragraph(s). Make the changes that you agree with and print a copy to turn in to your instructor. Save it as *U9L3Career9* and close the file.

4. Return your folder to the storage area. When your instructor returns your paper, file it in your Career folder.

## 4G  Writing:  Capitalization

Read the capitalization rules below.  Study the Learn lines.  Note how the rules are applied.  Key the Learn lines and the Apply lines, making the necessary corrections.  Save as *U5L4Capitalization*.

**Rule 11:**  Capitalize an official title when it precedes a name and elsewhere if it is a title of high distinction.

Learn 1  Was  King  Henry  VIII  the  King  that  had  six  wives?
Learn 2  Mark Van Noy, our student body president, met the President.

Apply 3  The  prime  minister  is  the  head  of  the  UK  Government.
Apply 4  One  of  the  presenters  will  be  lieutenant  governor  Schultz.

**Rule 12:**  Capitalize initials; also, letters in abbreviations if the letters would be capitalized when the words are spelled out.

Learn 5  Does the University of Texas offer both an Ed.D. and a Ph.D.?
Learn 6  J. B. Rodriguez is an active member of DECA this year.

Apply 7  When  usc  plays  ucla,  it  is  very  difficult  to  get  a  ticket.
Apply 8  Do  you  think  s. a. barns  will  make  the  u.s. olympic  team?

**Rule 13:**  Capitalize nouns preceding numbers (except page and line).

Learn 9  After  you  read  Chapter 4,  answer  Question 12  on  p. 157.
Learn 10  Please  deliver  the  package  to  Room  33,  Suite  A.

Apply 11  He  assigned  chapter 2  for  Monday  and  Chapter 3  for Wednesday.
Apply 12  Yes, you have room 112 of suite 10 reserved for the meeting.

---

## 4H  Speaking

Use the notes you took on a natural wonder of the world for **2G**, page 115.  Prepare a summary of the information to present to three of your classmates.  Your presentation will be one to two minutes in length.  Consider informing your classmates about what the natural wonder is, where it is located, and a little history about it that you learned from your research.  Print your summary and take it home to practice your speech.  Your instructor may choose several students to give their speech to the entire class.

**For additional practice** ▶ **MicroType** + **Numeric Keyboarding** + **Lessons 13 and 14**

## 3F Writing: Internal Punctuation

Read the following punctuation rules. Study the Learn lines. Note how the rules are applied. Key the Learn lines and the Apply lines, including the necessary punctuation. Save as *U9L3Writing*.

**Rule 11:** Use a colon to introduce an enumeration or a listing.

Learn 1  These players made the team: R. Sanchez, B. James, and J. Cox.

Apply 2  These days are holidays April 15, May 27, and July 4.

Apply 3  Cancel these classes Math 101, Math 246 and Math 250.

**Rule 12:** Use a semicolon to separate a series of phrases or clauses (especially if they contain commas) that are introduced by a colon.

Learn 4  The dates are as follows: May 1, 2007; May 6, 2008; and May 9, 2009.

Learn 5  The cities included: Casper, WY; Denver, CO; and Ogden, UT.

Apply 6  The fastest runners are: Smith, 20:15 Alou, 20:39 and Cey 20:43.

Apply 7  You are scheduled for: Monday, May 1 Tuesday, May 2 and Friday May 5.

**Rule 13:** Place a semicolon outside a closing quotation mark. (A period or a comma is placed inside a closing quotation mark.)

Learn 8  Mark said, "I vote no"; Sandra said, "I agree."

Apply 9  Todd presented the "Pros" Jane presented the "Cons"

Apply 10  David responded, "1948" Jason responded, "1949"

**Our World**

## 3G ▪ Democratic Society

Nelson Mandela was the first democratically elected state president of South Africa. Read the following quote from Mr. Mandela. Select one of the questions below the quote. Key a paragraph or two with your response. Save the document as *U9L3World*.

*"I have fought against white domination, and I have fought against black domination. I have cherished the ideal of a democratic and free society in which all persons live together in harmony and with equal opportunities. It is an ideal which I hope to live for and to achieve. But if needs be, it is an ideal for which I am prepared to die." Nelson Mandela*

1. What do you think is the meaning of Mr. Mandela's quote?

2. Mr. Mandela refers to a democratic and free society. Do you believe your country is a democratic and free society with equal opportunities?

3. What is Mr. Mandela's background? (You may need to research your answer using an encyclopedia or the Internet.)

*Social Studies*

## NEW KEYS: =, [, ], >, AND <

### OBJECTIVES

1. *To learn reach technique for ".*
2. *To improve keying speed.*

### 5A | Conditioning Practice

Key each line twice SS; then key a 1' writing on line 3. Determine *gwam*.

Alphabet 1  Jack Pabich gave Zelda six of the math equations right away.
Figures 2  Mary was born on May 24, 1987; Jon was born on May 30, 1956.
Easy 3  Diane and Vivian may make the goals if they work with vigor.

**GWAM** 1' | 1 | 2 | 3 | 4 | 5 | 6 | 7 | 8 | 9 | 10 | 11 | 12 |

### 5B | Learn =, [, and ]

Key each line twice SS (slowly, then faster); DS between 2-line groups.

**Learn = (equals sign)**

1  ; = ;= ;=|;= ;= =;= =;=| What does Z = if X = 10 and Y = 12?
2  A = B + C.  A = 12 and B = 8.  Is C = to 4?  What if A = 20?

**Learn [ (left bracket)**

3  ;[ ;[ ;[|[;[ [;[|[1 [0 [2 [9 [3 [8 [4 [7 [5 [6 [12 [357 [489
4  [a [B [c [D [e [F [g [H [i [J [k [L [m [N [o [P [q [R [s [T.

**Learn ] (right bracket)**

5  ; ] ;] ;]|];] ];]|9] 1] 2] 0] 6] 7] 5] 8] 3] 4] 39] 570] 46]
6  z] Y] x] W] v] U] t] S] r] Q] p] O] n] M] l] K] j] I] h] G].

**Combine =, [, and ]**

7  Brackets ([]) are used in algebra:  x = [6(a+b)] − [5(x-z)].
8  Solve the following:  [4a = 16], [2b = 7], and [5x = 9 + 6].

### 5C | Speed Check:  Sentences

1. Key a 30" timing on each line; determine *gwam* on each timing.  If you finish a line before time is called, key the line again.

2. Key another 30" timing on lines 3–6.  Try to increase your keying speed.

1  The state capital of Indiana is Indianapolis.
2  The state capital of Connecticut is Hartford.

3  The capital of the state of Vermont is Montpelier.
4  The capital of the state of Washington is Olympia.

5  The capital of the state of Rhode Island is Providence.
6  The capital of the state of Missouri is Jefferson City.

**GWAM** 30" | 2 | 4 | 6 | 8 | 10 | 12 | 14 | 16 | 18 | 20 |

## 3D | Speed Building

1. Key one 1' writing on paragraph 1; determine *gwam*.

2. Add 2–4 *gwam* to the rate from step 1. Note the quarter-minute checkpoints from the table at the left.

3. Take two 1' guided writings on paragraph 1 to increase speed.

4. Practice paragraphs 2 and 3 in the same way.

5. Take two 3' writings on paragraphs 1–3 combined; determine *gwam* and find errors.

---

**MicroType**
*Timed Writing*
**A**

**All letters used**

| Quarter-Minute Checkpoints | | | |
|---|---|---|---|
| *gwam* | 1/4' | 1/2' | 3/4' | Time |
| 16 | 4 | 8 | 12 | 16 |
| 20 | 5 | 10 | 15 | 20 |
| 24 | 6 | 12 | 18 | 24 |
| 28 | 7 | 14 | 21 | 28 |
| 32 | 8 | 16 | 24 | 32 |
| 36 | 9 | 18 | 27 | 36 |
| 40 | 10 | 20 | 30 | 40 |

| | GWAM | 3' | 5' |
|---|---|---|---|
| It is often said that we live and work in an information age | 4 | 2 | 39 |
| where expert technology skills are important.  Your teachers have | 8 | 5 | 42 |
| likely told you that as you moved through the grades.  Your school | 13 | 8 | 45 |
| has included this course in your studies so you can learn important | 17 | 10 | 47 |
| computer skills that will help you at work, home, and play. | 21 | 13 | 50 |
| When it comes to work, most employers need workers who | 25 | 15 | 52 |
| have a strong work ethic in addition to good computer skills.  Without | 30 | 18 | 55 |
| a strong work ethic, productivity may not reach the required level to | 34 | 21 | 58 |
| justify staying in business.  Therefore, most employers try to | 39 | 23 | 60 |
| carefully analyze this trait when each person is interviewed. | 43 | 26 | 63 |
| Having a strong work ethic is very important for people who | 47 | 28 | 65 |
| work without direct supervision.  This includes workers who work at | 51 | 31 | 68 |
| home or travel where they must set their own schedule and manage | 56 | 33 | 70 |
| their own resources.  It also includes workers who must adapt to | 60 | 36 | 73 |
| changes in the workplace. | 62 | 37 | 74 |

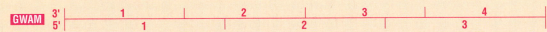

GWAM  3' | 1 | 2 | 3 | 4 |
5' | 1 | 2 | 3 |

---

★ *Language Arts*

## 3E Listening:  Telephone Message

CD-U9L3Listening.wav

1. You answered a telephone call from Georgia Steward, your father's business associate. Ms. Steward asked you to take a message for your father.  Play the sound file *CD-U9L3Listening.wav*.  Take notes as you listen to Ms. Steward's message.

2. Close the sound file.

3. Using your notes, key the message in complete sentences.

4. Check the accuracy of your work with the instructor.

5. Save the message as *U9L3Listening*.

Key each line twice SS (slowly, then faster); DS between 2-line groups.

### TIP

- The **<** is the shift of **,** and is keyed with the right middle finger.
- The **>** is the shift of **.** and is keyed with the right ring finger.

### Learn < ("less than" sign)

1  K< K< K<|k< k< k<|a < b < c < d < e < f < g < h < i < j < k.

2  Use the < for less than.  I said 10 < 12, 20 < 33, 406 < 407.

### Learn > ("greater than" sign)

3  L> L> L>|l> l> l>|l > m > n > o > p > q > r > s > t > u > w.

4  Use the > for more than.  I said 50 > 60, 45 > 44, 791 > 782.

### Combine < and >

5  Kendrick said that 7x > 5y but 7z is < 5y, is X or Y larger?

6  Jennifer used < when she should have used > in the equation.

## 5E | Keyboard Reinforcement

1. Key lines once SS; DS between 2-line groups.
2. Key the lines again at a faster pace.
3. Key a 1' writing on selected lines.

### Easy sentences (Think, say, and key the words at a steady pace.)

1  The giant signs are downtown by the city chapel by the lake.

2  Orlando may make the men visit the big chapel on the island.

3  Their ivory box with the ducks is by the door of the chapel.

4  Kay may go with them when they go to the city for the cycle.

5  A small cornfield is to the right of the dismal city chapel.

6  Jake may go with Diana to pay the neighbor for the ornament.

7  The box with the bugle is on the big mantle by the fishbowl.

8  Janel and Pamela paid the man for the eight bushels of corn.

GWAM  1' |  1  |  2  |  3  |  4  |  5  |  6  |  7  |  8  |  9  |  10  |  11  |  12  |

# LESSON

# 3

## OBJECTIVES

1. *To improve keying techniques.*
2. *To improve keying speed and control.*

### 3A | Conditioning Practice

Key each line twice SS; then key a 1' writing on line 3. Determine *gwam*.

| Alphabet | 1 | Jake, Walter, and Zeb quickly solved the complex algebra formula. |
|---|---|---|
| Figures | 2 | After waiting 75 minutes, Flight 9836 was by Gate 24 at 1:05 p.m. |
| Speed | 3 | The six busy girls may want the shamrock ornament for the chapel. |

GWAM 1' | 1 | 2 | 3 | 4 | 5 | 6 | 7 | 8 | 9 | 10 | 11 | 12 | 13 |

### 3B | Keying Skill: Speed

1. Key lines 1–6 twice.
2. Take two 30" timings on lines 7–9. If you complete the line, key it again.

**Balanced-hand words of 2–5 letters**

1  or me go am do if so an us by to he it is big the six and but for
2  box did end due for may pay man own make also city with they when
3  them such than city they hand paid sign then form work both their
4  of it | it is | of such | paid them | such as | they work | go to | such a name
5  paid for | go to | pay for | big man | the forms | own them | and then | may go
6  is to go | make it for | pay for it | end to end | by the man | down by the
7  She may wish to go to the city to hand them the work form for us.
8  The city is to pay for the field work both of the men did for us.
9  The man may hand them the six forms when he pays for the big box.

GWAM 1' | 1 | 2 | 3 | 4 | 5 | 6 | 7 | 8 | 9 | 10 | 11 | 12 | 13 |

### 3C | Speed Forcing Drill

1. Key each line once at top speed.
2. Key two 20" timings on each line.

**Emphasis: high-frequency balanced-hand words**                       GWAM 15"

| | | |
|---|---|---|
| 1 | Allene is to pay for the six pens for the auditor. | 40 |
| 2 | Henry is to go with us to the lake to fix the bus. | 40 |
| 3 | If the pay is right, Jan may make eight gowns for them. | 44 |
| 4 | They may be paid to fix the six signs down by the lake. | 44 |
| 5 | Enrique works with vigor to make the gowns for a big profit. | 48 |
| 6 | Pamela may hang the signs by the antique door of the chapel. | 48 |
| 7 | Dick and the busy man may work with vigor to fix the eight signs. | 52 |
| 8 | Did the girl bid for the right to the land downtown by city hall? | 52 |

GWAM 15" | 4 | 8 | 12 | 16 | 20 | 24 | 28 | 32 | 36 | 40 | 44 | 48 | 52 |

## 5F | Speed Check: Paragraphs

1. Key a 1' timed writing on paragraph 1 and then on paragraph 2; determine *gwam* on each.
2. Key a 2' timed writing on paragraphs 1–2 combined; determine *gwam* and count errors.
3. Key a 3' timed writing on paragraphs 1–2 combined; determine *gwam* and count errors.

*Social Studies*

**MicroType**

*Timed Writing*

A

**All letters used**

| | GWAM | 2' | 3' |
|---|---|---|---|

The City of Philadelphia is where the roots of — 5 | 3

this nation were founded. Independence Hall, which — 10 | 7

is located in the center of the city, is often — 14 | 10

referred to as the place where the nation was born. — 20 | 13

It was here that they met to discuss and agree upon — 25 | 16

the Declaration of Independence and the United — 30 | 20

States Constitution. It was here that Ben Franklin — 35 | 23

said, "If we don't hang together, we shall assuredly — 40 | 27

hang separately!" — 41 | 27

An easily recognized symbol of our freedom, the — 46 | 31

Liberty Bell, can also be seen in the city which is — 51 | 34

often called "The City of Brotherly Love." Another — 56 | 37

distinction of the city is that it was the first — 61 | 41

capital of our new nation. The building where the — 66 | 44

Senate and the House met is located right next to — 71 | 47

Independence Hall. People can enjoy these and other — 76 | 51

exquisite landmarks by spending time in the city. — 81 | 54

GWAM 2' | 1 | 2 | 3 | 4 | 5 | 6 |
GWAM 3' | 1 | 2 | 3 | 4 |

## 2D | Speed Building

1. Key one 1' unguided and two 1' guided timed writings on each paragraph.
2. Key two 3' unguided writings on paragraphs 1–2 combined; find *gwam*.

**Quarter-Minute Checkpoints**

| gwam | 1/4' | 1/2' | 3/4' | Time |
|------|------|------|------|------|
| 16 | 4 | 8 | 12 | 16 |
| 20 | 5 | 10 | 15 | 20 |
| 24 | 6 | 12 | 18 | 24 |
| 28 | 7 | 14 | 21 | 28 |
| 32 | 8 | 16 | 24 | 32 |
| 36 | 9 | 18 | 27 | 36 |
| 40 | 10 | 20 | 30 | 40 |

| | GWAM | 3' | 5' |
|---|---|---|---|

Securing a job is not as easy as sending a resume or showing   `4  2  36`
up for an interview on time.  Without a doubt, realizing that the   `8  5  39`
employment interview is one of the most important parts of a   `12  7  41`
person's job search is crucial.  Interviewers are often surprised   `17  10  44`
at the number of applicants who appear for the interview without   `21  13  47`
being prepared.  Job seekers can prevent a bad interview by making   `26  15  49`
some advance preparations.   `27  16  50`

A necessary part of preparing for an interview is to know the   `32  19  53`
company.  You can achieve this by doing some research.  If the   `36  21  55`
company has a website, use it to learn about its history, mission,   `40  24  58`
products, and services.  Questions should be developed before the   `44  27  60`
interview.  Experts say it's good to take questions with you to the   `49  29  63`
interview to impress those who meet with you.  Asking questions is   `53  32  66`
an easy way to convey interest in the firm.   `56  34  68`

GWAM  3' | 1 | 2 | 3 | 4 |
      5' | 1 | 2 | 3 |

---

★ *Language Arts*

## 2E Writing:  Word Choice

Study the spelling and definitions of the following words.  Key the Learn lines, noting the word choices.  Key the Apply lines, selecting the correct words.  Save as *U9L2WordChoice*.

**new** (adjective)  not old or familiar

**knew** (verb)  understood

Learn 1  Rebecca has a **new** notebook computer.

Learn 2  The referee **knew** the rules very well.

Apply 3  The (knew, new) basketball coach (knew, new) it was a good play.

Apply 4  Tim (knew, new) he needed to save to buy the (knew, new) skateboard.

# Math Activities

### 5G ▪ Math Challenge 5

## FIND THE PART OF A WHOLE

1. Key a sentence to explain how you find the part of a whole in problems like this: *What is 20% of 50?*

2. Solve the following problems and key your answers in sentence form. Round answers to hundredths if needed. For example, an appropriate sentence for the answer to the problem stated above is: *Ten is 20% of 50.*

   2a. What is 30% of 240?

   2b. What is 150% of 120?

   2c. What is .4% of 8?

   2d. What is 66% of 350?

   2e. Mary is now earning $8.60 per hour and Jane is earning 80% of what Mary earns. How much does Jane earn per hour?

3. Save your answers as *U5L5Math*.

---

### Careers ·······················

### 5H ▪ Career Exploration Portfolio – Activity 5

▪ You must complete Career Exploration Activities 1–3 before completing this activity.

1. Retrieve your Career folder and find the printed Career Cluster Plan of Study for the career cluster that is your second choice.

2. Review the plan and write a paragraph or two about why you would or would not consider a career in this cluster. Print your file, save it as *U5L5Career5*, and keep it open.

3. Exchange papers with a classmate. Have the classmate offer suggestions for improving the content and correcting any errors he or she finds in your paragraph(s). Make the changes that you agree with and print a copy to turn in to your instructor. Save it as *U5L5Career5* and close the file.

4. Return your folder to the storage area. When your instructor returns your paper, file it in your Career folder.

**For additional practice** ▶ **MicroType** + **Keyboarding Skill Builder** + **Lessons 15 and 16**

## 2B | Technique Mastery: Letter Keys

1. Key lines 1–6 below twice.
2. Take three 30" timings on line 7 and then 8. If you complete the line, key it again.

**One-hand words of 2–5 letters**

1 no you was in we my be him are up as on get you only set see rate
2 few area no free you best date far tax case act fact water act on
3 card upon you few ever only fact after act state great as get see

4 you were | set rate | we are | at no | on you | at my best | get set | you were
5 as few | you set a date | my card | water tax | act on a | tax date | in case
6 my only date | water rate | my tax case | tax fact | my best date | my card

7 Get him my only extra database after you set up exact test dates.
8 You set my area tax rate after a great state case on a water tax.

GWAM 1' | 1 | 2 | 3 | 4 | 5 | 6 | 7 | 8 | 9 | 10 | 11 | 12 | 13 |

## 2C | Speed Forcing Drill

1. Key each line once at top speed.
2. Key two 20" timings on each line. If you finish a line before time is called, start over.

**Emphasis: high-frequency balanced-hand words**  GWAM 15"

| | | |
|---|---|---|
| 1 | The man paid the girl to fix the auto turn signal. | 40 |
| 2 | Ellen bid for the antique chair and antique rifle. | 40 |
| 3 | Diana may make the title forms for big and small firms. | 44 |
| 4 | When did the auditor sign the audit forms for the city? | 44 |
| 5 | They kept the girls busy with the work down by the big lake. | 48 |
| 6 | Helen may go with us to the city to pay them for their work. | 48 |
| 7 | The man and I may dismantle the ancient ricksha in the big field. | 52 |
| 8 | Jay may suspend the men as a penalty for their work on the docks. | 52 |

GWAM 15" | 4 | 8 | 12 | 16 | 20 | 24 | 28 | 32 | 36 | 40 | 44 | 48 | 52 |

# Unit 6
## Build Keyboarding Skill

**Lessons 1–2**

## OBJECTIVES

1. *To improve technique on individual letters.*
2. *To improve keying speed on 1' and 2' timed writings.*

## SKILL DEVELOPMENT

### 1A | Conditioning Practice

Key each line twice SS; then key a 1' timed writing on line 3. Determine *gwam*.

Alphabet 1   Ozzie James quickly explored two of the big caves on Friday.
Figures 2   On July 15 the rate was 7.64 percent; it was 8.92 on May 30.
Easy 3   Jay and Jan may do the work on the dock for the haughty man.
GWAM 1' | 1 | 2 | 3 | 4 | 5 | 6 | 7 | 8 | 9 | 10 | 11 | 12 |

### 1B | Speed Building

1. Key the lines once DS.
2. Key a 1' timing on lines 5–8; determine *gwam* on each timing.

**Key easy sentences (Key the words at a brisk, steady pace.)**

1   Half of them may be kept busy with all the work on the dock.
2   Six of the eight title firms may handle the work for Vivian.

3   Pamela and I may make a map of the city for the eight girls.
4   Helen and Pamela may make a profit off the land by the lake.

5   The neighbor may work with the men on the city turn signals.
6   Ruth and the dog slept in a chair in the hall of the chapel.

7   Susie and Dianna may cycle to the city dock by the big lake.
8   Nancy held a formal social at the lake for six of the girls.
GWAM 1' | 1 | 2 | 3 | 4 | 5 | 6 | 7 | 8 | 9 | 10 | 11 | 12 |

## 1C | Outline

1. Key the following outline. Center the title. Double-space the outline.
2. Set a decimal tab at 0.2" to align the roman numerals. Set left tabs at 0.375", 0.625", and 0.875" to indent the levels of the outline.
3. Spell-check and proofread the outline. Correct all errors. Save as *U9L1Outline*.

Earth's Nearest Neighbor in Space

I. Introduction

    A. The moon's size

    B. The moon's reflection

    C. The moon's atmosphere

II. The Moon's Surface

    A. Lowlands (called maria) and highlands

    B. Craters

        1. Ray craters

        2. Secondary craters

III. The Moon's Composition

    A. Soil

        1. Dark gray to brownish gray color

        2. Consists of ground-up rock and bits of glass

        3. Depth of soil varies

    B. Rocks

        1. Minerals in the rock

        2. Basalt and breccia rocks

---

## LESSON

# 2

### OBJECTIVES

1. *To improve keying techniques.*
2. *To improve keying speed and control.*

## SKILL BUILDING

## 2A | Conditioning Practice

Key each line twice SS; then key a 1' writing on line 3. Determine *gwam*.

| | | |
|---|---|---|
| Alphabet | 1 | Mary Nix thought the five jigsaw puzzles could be solved quickly. |
| Figures/Symbols | 2 | The final payment on my car loan (#32769-5) was paid on 5/14/08. |
| Speed | 3 | Di may go with the busy girls to see the ritual for the sorority. |

GWAM 1' | 1 | 2 | 3 | 4 | 5 | 6 | 7 | 8 | 9 | 10 | 11 | 12 | 13 |

$\equiv$ = capitalize
$\wedge$ = insert
$\cup$ = transpose
# = insert space
lc = lowercase
$\frown$ = close up
$\mathcal{y}$ = delete

## 1C | Rough-Draft Copy

Key each line twice (slowly, then faster); DS between 2-line groups.

1  the first word of a line should be capitalized.

2  Laborday is a holiday; therefore, it should be capitalized.

3  Tim was marked down fornot capitalizing the W on wednesday

4  You should have Capitalized the countries, cities, and states.

5  always capitalize a name ofa river or name of an ocean.

6  misouri river and atlantic ocean would be examples of this.

7  Capitalize may and june because they are months.

8  your school, jeffersons middle school, shouldbe capitalized.

9  Capitalize a titel such as mr., ms., Dr., and miss.

10  If intel is the name of a compnany it should be Capitalized.

## 1D | Speed Forcing Drill

Key each line once at top speed. Then try to complete each sentence on the 15", 12", or 10" call, as directed by your instructor. Force speed to higher levels as you move from line to line.

| | GWAM | 15" | 12" | 10" |
|---|---|---|---|---|
| 1 | Please return the coat to the store for John. | 36 | 45 | 54 |
| 2 | When do you think you will be able to finish? | 36 | 45 | 54 |
| 3 | Glen will finish the house plans by next Saturday. | 40 | 50 | 60 |
| 4 | I can meet her at the library after I finish work. | 40 | 50 | 60 |
| 5 | Jane will try out for the Olympic team in April or May. | 44 | 55 | 66 |
| 6 | The next assignment should be turned in before Tuesday. | 44 | 55 | 66 |
| 7 | Jason's plane was delayed because of the terrible snowstorm. | 48 | 60 | 72 |
| 8 | Are we still planning on going snowboarding later this week? | 48 | 60 | 72 |

*E-mail Etiquette*

When writing an e-mail message, you should key words and sentences with initial caps and lowercase letters--just as you do when writing a school report. Use all caps only to draw the reader's attention to one or ~~several~~ *a few* words. Those who use proper *lc* Netiquette interpret an e-mail message that is keyed in ALL CAPS as "shouting."

Spamming is another practice you want to avoid because it wastes other peoples' time. Spamming is

> . . . the posting of unsolicited posts (usually advertising posts) to a large number of mailing lists . . . without regard for topical relevance. Essentially, spams are widely posted junk mail. . . . Spamming is extremely bad netiquette and will provoke the indignation of the online community. (http://www.albion.com/netiquette/netiquiz.html)

Another "rule of the road" applies to private e-mail messages. Messages that contain personal information should not be sent to others without the writer's okay. Common courtesy requires making sure the writer does not mind sharing the message before you send it to others.

Chat Rooms

Always become familiar with a chat room (or any other part of cyberspace) before you take part in a discussion. You need to do this to learn the basic rules and the kinds of topics discussed in the chat room. If the chat room topics cannot be openly discussed with your friends or parents, you should stay out of the chat room.

Summary

You may use the computer to "talk" with others often. Remember that the people you are "talking" with are real people with feelings. Think of them as you would your friends and family. Be sensitive to their feelings when you give your opinions or state your message (http://www.albion.com/netiquette/corerules.html).

Works Cited

Agency for Instructional Technology. *Communication 2000 2E: Communication and Ethics.* Cincinnati: South-Western Educational and Professional Publishing, 2002.

"The Core Rules of Netiquette." Albion.com. http://www.albion.com/netiquette/corerules.html (accessed December 27, 2006).

"The Netiquette Quiz." Albion.com. http://www.albion.com/netiquette/netiquiz.html (accessed December 27, 2006).

## Social Studies

### 1E | Speed Building: Guided Writing

1. Key one 1' unguided and two 1' guided timed writings on each paragraph; determine *gwam*.

2. Key two 2' unguided writings on paragraphs 1–2 combined; determine *gwam*.

**MicroType**
*Timed Writing*
A

**All letters used**

**Quarter-Minute Checkpoints**

| gwam | 1/4' | 1/2' | 3/4' | Time |
|------|------|------|------|------|
| 16 | 4 | 8 | 12 | 16 |
| 20 | 5 | 10 | 15 | 20 |
| 24 | 6 | 12 | 18 | 24 |
| 28 | 7 | 14 | 21 | 28 |
| 32 | 8 | 16 | 24 | 32 |
| 36 | 9 | 18 | 27 | 36 |
| 40 | 10 | 20 | 30 | 40 |

GWAM 2'

One of the best-known inaugural addresses ever given by — 6
a President was given by John Kennedy. The exact words of — 11
this president are permanently imprinted into the minds — 16
of numerous Americans. If you were to say, "Ask not what — 21
your country can do for you but what you can do for your — 27
country," quite a few Americans would know the individual — 33
you were quoting. — 34

These words alone make an impression. However, the — 40
way President Kennedy delivered them with such zealousness — 46
made them have an even greater impact. What do you think — 51
he meant by these words? Do you think it is more or less — 57
important for Americans to try and live by these words — 62
today than when Kennedy delivered them in his inaugural — 67
address? — 68

GWAM 2' | 1 | 2 | 3 | 4 | 5 | 6 |

## Language Arts

### 1F Writing: Word Choice

Study the spelling and definitions of the words below. Key the Learn lines, noting the word choices. Key the Apply lines, selecting the correct words. Save the file as *U6L1WordChoice*.

**no** (adverb/adjective/noun) not in any respect or degree; not so; indicates denial or refusal

**know** (verb) to be aware of the truth of; to have understanding of

Learn 1 Will you vote yes or **no** on the amendment?

Learn 2 I do not **know** how I plan to vote.

Apply 3 There are (no, know) seats available in that section.

Apply 4 Do you (no, know) what the final score was?

# Unit 9
## Assess MLA Reports and Build Skill

**Lessons 1–3**

---

## MLA REPORT FORMATTING SKILLS

### 1A | Conditioning Practice

Key each line twice SS; then key a 1' writing on line 3.  Determine *gwam*.

Alphabet 1  Zen caught two very quiet lambs just before they exited the park.

Figures 2  Order 43-598 for a Star 607 computer was delivered on August 12.

Speed 3  The six ivory mementos and oak ornaments are by the enamel board.

**GWAM** 1' | 1 | 2 | 3 | 4 | 5 | 6 | 7 | 8 | 9 | 10 | 11 | 12 | 13 |

### 1B | MLA Report

1. Key the report below and on pages 190–191 in MLA report style.  Insert an appropriate header using your name as the writer.  Use *Mr. Hector Nuevos* as the instructor, *Computer Applications* as the course name, and the current date in the report identification lines.

2. Use bold and a 16-point font for the report title and the *Works Cited* title.  Use bold and a 12-point font for the side headings.  Italicize *netiquette* wherever it appears in the body of the report.  (Do not apply italic in Internet addresses or the Works Cited list.)

3. Insert hard page breaks as needed to end pages properly.  Format the Works Cited page properly.

4. Spell-check and proofread the report carefully.  Correct all errors.  Save the report as *U9L1Internet.*

*Internet Etiquette*

What kind of Internet user are you? Are you the same kind of person on the Internet as you are when you meet face-to-face with a friend? Do you have respect for other people's time? Do you respect their privacy? Do you abuse the power the Internet gives you (Communication 2000 50)? Several informal "rules of the road" are being created as more and more people communicate with one another on the Internet.  The rules are called "Netiquette." Netiquette covers the dos and don'ts of online communication.  It includes the guidelines we should follow to be courteous to others.  By using the rules, you will help yourself look good and avoid wasting other people's time and energy.

*(continued)*

## 1G | Research Information about Prominent People

The Internet can be used to gather information. Perhaps you are interested in a sports figure, a musician, or a political figure. You can learn more about this person by using a search engine to locate sites containing information about him or her.

1. Access a search engine of your choice or as your teacher directs.

2. Perform a search using the name of the person you are interested in learning more about.

3. Generally, several sites will come up relating to the search term. Scroll down and read the information given about the sites.

4. Click on the site that appears to have the information you want. Read the information on the site.

5. After you are done reading the site, use Back to return to the listing of sites. If time permits, select additional sites to review.

6. Be prepared to tell the class something you have learned about the person you researched.

**For additional practice** MicroType + **Keyboarding Skill Builder + Lesson E**

---

# LESSON

# 2

### OBJECTIVES

1. *To improve technique on individual letters.*
2. *To improve keying speed on 1' and 2' writings.*

# SKILL BUILDING

## 2A | Conditioning Practice

Key each line twice SS; then key a 1' timed writing on line 3. Determine *gwam*.

Alphabet 1   Jung Ramirez expects five banks to do the few deals quickly.

Figures 2   Their address is 1536 Stagecoach Rd., Eugene, OR 97402-0827.

Easy 3   Jana may work with them to make a big profit for their firm.

GWAM 1' | 1 | 2 | 3 | 4 | 5 | 6 | 7 | 8 | 9 | 10 | 11 | 12 |

**7G** ▪ **Research a Favorite Pet**

Go online and research information about your pet or a pet you would like to have. Look for background information on the specific breed of a pet. Learn about its physical characteristics, temperament, health, and behavior. List five facts about the pet that you learned. Save the document as *U8L7Internet*.

*Social Studies*

# Math Activities

## 7G ▪ Math Challenge 8

### FIND THE PERCENT OF CHANGE

1. Key a sentence to explain how you find the percent of change between two numbers in problems like this: *What is the percent of change if 30 changes to 45?*

2. Solve the following problems to determine the percent of change. Key your answers in sentence form. Round answers to thousandths if needed. For example, an appropriate sentence for the answer to the problem stated above is: *When 30 changes to 45, the percent of increase is 50%.*

2a. 50 changes to 80    2b. 65 changes to 195

2c. 100 changes to 55    2d. .02 changes to 0.06

2e. Kelly bought a share of stock for $50 and one year later sold it for $47. What was the percent of change? Was it a positive or negative change?

3. Save your answers as *U8L7Math*.

---

## Careers

### 7I ▪ Career Exploration Portfolio – Activity 8

▪ You must complete Career Activities 1–3 before completing this activity.

1. Retrieve your Career folder and the information in it that relates to the career cluster that is your second choice.

2. Reflect on the skills and knowledge you have gained in the courses you have taken and the extracurricular activities in which you are involved that will be beneficial in the career you selected as your second choice. Then compose a paragraph or two describing the connection between what you have learned and/or your activities and this career. Print your file and then save it as *U8L7Career8* and keep the file open.

3. Exchange papers with a classmate and have the classmate offer suggestions for improving the content and correcting any errors he or she finds in your paragraph(s). Make the changes that you agree with, and print a copy to turn in to your instructor. Save it as *U8L7Career8* and close the file.

4. Return your folder to the storage area. When your instructor returns your paper, file it in your Career folder.

Technique Goals
• curved, upright fingers
• quick-snap keystrokes
• quiet hands and arms

## 2B | Technique: Response Patterns

1. Key each line twice SS (slowly, then faster); DS between line groups.

2. Key a 1' timed writing on lines 3, 6, 9, and 12.

3. If time permits, key additional writings on lines 3, 6, 9, and 12.

**Letter response**

1  at no in we up be my are pin tar lip car him sad joy set gas

2  were you | at my | red kiln | as you see | you are | fat man | fast bear

3  My dreaded cat darted up a tree as we sat in Reese's garage.

**Word response**

4  it do am me so men did and lap fit ham pan got hen own signs

5  When they | to us | by the | it is | to go | she may | for me | to fix the

6  Orlando may fix the dock if I do the work for the eight men.

**Combination response**

7  is be he as is my to in is no am we by on it up do at or cat

8  we may | to be | is up | to my | or up | is at | go in | do we | if we go up

9  John and Jill may be there at noon; we may see both of them.

**Letter response**

10  Jimmy averaged my fastest rates.  I deserved a better grade.

**Combination response**

11  Edward was the man they saw down at the lake in the red bus.

**Word response**

12  Rodney may go to the lake with the neighbor to fix the door.

GWAM  1' | 1 | 2 | 3 | 4 | 5 | 6 | 7 | 8 | 9 | 10 | 11 | 12 |

**Tip**

**Combination response:** Most copy requires word response for some words and letter response for others.  In such copy (lines 7–9), use top speed for easy words, lower speed for words that are harder to key.

## 2C | Speed Forcing Drill

Key each line once at top speed.  Then try to complete each sentence on the 15", 12", or 10" call, as directed by your teacher.  Force speed to higher levels as you move from line to line.

| Emphasis:  high-frequency balanced-hand words | GWAM | 15" | 12" | 10" |
|---|---|---|---|---|
| 1  The girls may go to the big chapel with them. | | 36 | 45 | 54 |
| 2  She may make the maid go to the city with us. | | 36 | 45 | 54 |
| 3  Orlando may go to the city to sign the work forms. | | 40 | 50 | 60 |
| 4  Henry owns both of the antique signs on the shelf. | | 40 | 50 | 60 |
| 5  The neighbor may fix the turn signal on their big auto. | | 44 | 55 | 66 |
| 6  Diane may make the men go downtown on the big city bus. | | 44 | 55 | 66 |
| 7  Mr. Dock may pay for the work on the big signs for the city. | | 48 | 60 | 72 |
| 8  Sue may go with me to the cornfield by the dock to buy corn. | | 48 | 60 | 72 |

## 7E | MLA Report

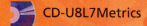
CD-U8L7Metrics

1. Open the data file *CD-U8L7Metrics*.

2. Key the following information as the last paragraph before the *Metrics Basics* side heading. Format the report in MLA style. Create a header with your last name and a page number. Since the report will have a title page, begin page 1 with the title.

3. Set tabs at 2" and 3.5" for the listing in the *Common Equivalents* section, and underline the column headings *English Unit* and *Metric Unit*. Bold the side headings and use 12-point font. Use 14-point bold font for the report title and the *Works Cited* title.

4. Spell-check and proofread the report carefully. Correct all errors. Insert hard page breaks as needed to end pages properly.

5. Save the report as *U8L7Metrics*.

6. Prepare a title page for the report. Use your name as the writer, **Ms. Francine Requa** as the teacher, **Mathematics** as the course name, and the current date. Save the report as *U8L7MetricsTP*.

Today metrics are everywhere in our country! Track and field distances, heights, and weights are now measured in metrics. Car engines and and soft drink container sizes are stated in metrics. the size of film and the nutrition information listed on food packages are given in metric units. The size of the nuts, bolts, and screws that hold our are products together are other examples of common items that are measured in metric unit. there are many other examples as well.

---

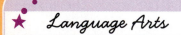
*Language Arts*

## 7F Writing: Word Choice

Study the spelling and definitions of the following words. Key the Learn lines, noting the word choices. Key the Apply lines, selecting the correct words. Save as *U8L7WordChoice*.

**cite** (verb)  to quote

**site** (noun)  a place occupied or to be occupied by a building

**sight** (noun)  something seen or worth seeing; a view or glimpse

Learn 1  Tom will **cite** the description of the historical **site** in his research paper.

Learn 2  The **sight** was spectacular from the **site** of their house.

Apply 3  The men will work at the (cite, site, sight) that has a beautiful (cite, site, sight).

Apply 4  I will (cite, site, sight) the building code when they approve the (cite, site, sight).

## 2D | Speed Building

1. Key one 1' unguided and two 1' guided timed writings on each paragraph.
2. Key two 2' unguided writings on paragraphs 1–2 combined; determine *gwam*.

**MicroType**

*Timed Writing*

**A**

**All letters used**

### Quarter-Minute Checkpoints

| gwam | 1/4' | 1/2' | 3/4' | Time |
|------|------|------|------|------|
| 16 | 4 | 8 | 12 | 16 |
| 20 | 5 | 10 | 15 | 20 |
| 24 | 6 | 12 | 18 | 24 |
| 28 | 7 | 14 | 21 | 28 |
| 32 | 8 | 16 | 24 | 32 |
| 36 | 9 | 18 | 27 | 36 |
| 40 | 10 | 20 | 30 | 40 |

One of the great statesmen of our nation was Benjamin    5
Franklin.  Among other things, the man is quite well known    11
for his work as an author, as a philosopher, as a scientist,    17
and as a diplomat and representative of our country.  Recog-    23
nized as one of the excellent leaders of the Revolution, he    29
is considered a founding father of the United States.  His    35
name can be seen on the Declaration of Independence as well    41
as the United States Constitution.    44

Some of the things that Franklin is given the credit    49
for include the Franklin stove, the lightning rod, bifocals,    55
and many, many witty quotes in his almanac.  Franklin once    61
said, "If you would not be forgotten as soon as you are    67
dead, either write something worth reading or do things worth    73
the writing."  Because of his many personal accomplishments    79
and the written documents that his signature appears on,    85
Mr. Franklin will not likely be forgotten very soon!  He is    91
a role model that all Americans should try to model their    97
life after.    98

GWAM 2' | 1 | 2 | 3 | 4 | 5 | 6 |

## 7C | Show and Hide Codes

Code marks that show the use of the TAB key, Space Bar, and ENTER key are inserted in the document when these keys are pressed. Viewing these codes can be helpful when formatting documents. The codes are: → for TAB; • for Space Bar; ¶ for ENTER.

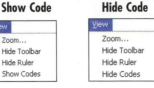

**Show Code**    **Hide Code**

To show codes:

1. On the menu bar, click View.

2. Click Show Codes. Codes appear in the document when TAB, ENTER, and Space Bar are tapped.

To hide codes:

1. On the menu bar, click View.

2. Click Hide Codes.

### Practice What You Have Learned

1. Key the following text, inserting tabs and hard returns as directed.

   <TAB> <TAB>This line is indented two tab stops from the margin.<Hard Return>

   This line is not indented from the left margin.<Hard Return>

   <TAB> <TAB> <TAB>This text is indented three tab stops.<Hard Return>

2. Show the codes and verify that the TAB, Space Bar, and ENTER codes appear in the document.

3. Hide the codes.

---

★ *Language Arts*

### 7D Proofreading: Rough Draft

**Proofreaders' Marks**

≡ = capitalize

⌒ = close up

ℐ = delete

∧ = insert

∩ = transpose

⁋ = paragraph

1. Study the proofreaders' marks given at the left.

2. Key the following rough-draft paragraphs using DS and 0.5" first-line indentations. Make corrections as you key.

3. Save as *U8L7RoughDraft*.

just how well do you adjust to <sup>big</sup> changes in your life.?

You should recognize that change is sa certain as life and death and taxes. You can <sup>not</sup> avoid chagne, but your can adjust to it. How quickly you can do this is a <sup>good</sup> index of the success you are likley to have in the future years. Can you think of changes that have affected your in the past year? Were you able to adjust too them?

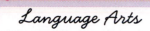

## Language Arts

### 2E  Writing:  Terminal Punctuation

Read the punctuation rules below.  Study the Learn lines.  Note how the rules are applied. Key the Learn lines and the Apply lines, including the necessary punctuation.  Save as *U6L2Punctuation*.

**Rule 1:**  Use a period at the end of a declarative sentence (a sentence that is not regarded as a question or exclamation).

Learn 1   I will be in town on Wednesday.

Learn 2   The new digital cameras are very nice.

Apply 3   I will have the exams corrected by Friday

Apply 4   Jason got an iPod for his birthday

**Rule 2:**  Use a period at the end of a polite request stated in the form of a question but not intended as one.

Learn 5   Class, will you please be quiet now.

Learn 6   Jared, will you please be early.

Apply 7   Justin, will you please let the dog out

Apply 8   Mary, will you please empty the garbage

## Language Arts

### 2F  Listening

CD-U6L2Listening.wav

1. Play the sound file *CD-U6L2Listening.wav*, which contains directions for driving to Mansfield Soccer Field.

2. Take notes as you listen to the directions.

3. Close the file.

4. Using your notes, key the directions in sentence form.

5. Check the accuracy of your work with your teacher.

6. Save the directions as *U6L2Listening*.

**6H Reading: Television Show**

Open the file *CD-U8L6Read*. Read the document carefully; then close the file. Let your teacher know when you are ready to answer questions covering the content of the file.

## LESSON 7

### OBJECTIVES

1. *To learn and practice these word processing features: Cut, Copy, Paste, and Show/Hide Codes.*

2. *To learn proofreaders' marks.*

3. *To format a report using MLA format.*

**MicroType**

**TIP**

Access the Cut, Copy, and Paste commands quickly by clicking buttons on the toolbar.

**Cut  Copy Paste**

# MLA REPORTS WITH PROOFREADERS' MARKS

## 7A | Conditioning Practice

Key each line twice SS; then key a 1' writing on line 3. Determine *gwam*.

Alphabet 1  I quickly explained to all how Zev lost his major fight with Job.

Figures 2  Rooms 1398 and 2076 were used for the 7:45 p.m. parents' meeting.

Speed 3  Leo paid the men for the work they did on the shanty by the lake.

**GWAM** 1' | 1 | 2 | 3 | 4 | 5 | 6 | 7 | 8 | 9 | 10 |

## 7B | Cut, Copy, and Paste

The Cut command removes selected text from the document. The Paste command places text that has been cut or copied into the document. The Copy command copies the selected text so it can be pasted to another location, leaving the original text unchanged.

To cut or copy text:

1. Select the text to be cut or copied.

2. On the menu bar, click Edit. Click Cut or Copy.

To paste text that has been cut or copied:

1. Move the insertion point to the desired location.

2. On the menu bar, click Edit. Click Paste.

**Practice What You Have Learned**

1. Open a new document. Key the following lines.
   Get a haircut on Thursday at Rubino's Hair Care.
   Go to the soccer game on Monday evening at Becker Field.
   Visit Uncle Ron and Aunt Mary on Sunday at Chet's Diner.
   Pick up Kim and go to a social at King School on Friday evening.
   Get tickets on Wednesday to go to see City Rockers at Renzie Lake.
   Get new shoes on Tuesday at the Footwear Factory.
   Meet Brett at the Roadhouse on Saturday.

2. Bold all names of days, italicize all names of people, and underline names of places.

3. Use Cut and Paste to arrange lines in order by day, starting with Monday.

4. Use Copy and Paste to make two additional copies of the lines. Place each copy a double space below the preceding one.

5. Save the document as *U8L7Paste*.

## Math Activities

**2G** ▪ **Math Challenge 6**

### FIND WHAT PERCENT ONE NUMBER IS OF ANOTHER

1. Key a sentence to explain how you find what percent one number is of another in problems like this: *What percent of 50 is 30?*

2. Solve the following problems and key your answer in sentence form. For example, an appropriate sentence for the answer to the problem stated above is: *Thirty is 60% of 50.*

   2a. What percent is 30 of 240?

   2b. What percent of 200 is 33?

   2c. What percent is .4 of 10?

   2d. What percent of 80 is 160?

   2e. Together Tim and George raised $460. If Tim raised $253, what percent did George raise?

3. Save your answers as *U6L2Math*.

## Careers ................

**2H** ▪ **Career Exploration Portfolio – Activity 6**

▪ You must complete Career Exploration Activities 1–3 before completing this activity.

1. Retrieve your Career folder and find the printed Career Cluster Plan of Study for the career cluster that is your *third* choice.

2. Review the plan and write a paragraph or two about why you would or would not consider a career in this cluster. Print your file, save it as *U6L2Career6*, and keep it open.

3. After composing a paragraph or two, print a copy of your response and exchange papers with a classmate. Have the classmate offer suggestions for improving the content and correcting any errors he or she finds in your paragraph(s). Make the changes that you agree with and print a copy to turn in to your instructor. Save your file as *U6L2Career6* and close it.

4. Return your folder to the storage area. When your instructor returns your paper, file it in your Career folder.

**For additional practice** ▸ **MicroType** ✦ **Keyboarding Skill Builder** ✦ **Lesson F**

Tips for Success in Math

Here are some tips for reducing math anxiety. If you follow them, you will improve your performance in math classes. Several of them are taken from Professor Ellen Freedman's list of "Ten Ways to Reduce Math Anxiety":

1. Be positive; not negative--tell yourself you can do math.

2. Ask questions--don't wait until tomorrow's class to ask about something you don't understand today. Write down questions while doing your homework to ask in the next class.

3. Practice math--do your homework every day. Do problem examples in the textbook for more practice.

4. Take notes--make note cards on how to solve problems. Copy all information that your teacher puts on the board. Prepare a glossary of terms for each chapter.

5. Read your math textbook--preview the major topics in the chapter; preview the end-of-chapter problems. When reading the chapter, study the example problems. Review the chapter's main points before doing end-of-chapter problems. Solve problems for understanding, not just for the right answer.

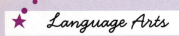

## 6G Writing: Internal Punctuation

Read the following punctuation rules. Study the Learn lines. Note how the rules are applied. Key the Learn lines and the Apply lines, including the necessary punctuation. Save as *U8L6Writing*.

**Rule 9:** Use a semicolon to separate independent clauses in a compound sentence when the conjunction is omitted.

Learn 1  George W. Bush was the 43d President; his father was the 41st.

Learn 2  Sandra is an excellent dancer; she practices every day.

Apply 3  World War I started in 1914 World War II started in 1939.

Apply 4  Lance is a very good student he spends hours and hours studying.

**Rule 10:** Use a semicolon to separate independent clauses when they are joined by a conjunctive adverb (*however*, *therefore*, *consequently*, and so on).

Learn 5  We stood in line for two hours; however, it was worth it.

Learn 6  We worked on math for two hours; consequently, we were late.

Apply 7  I had to work late however, I still saw part of the game.

Apply 8  He has no formal training however, he is a fast learner.

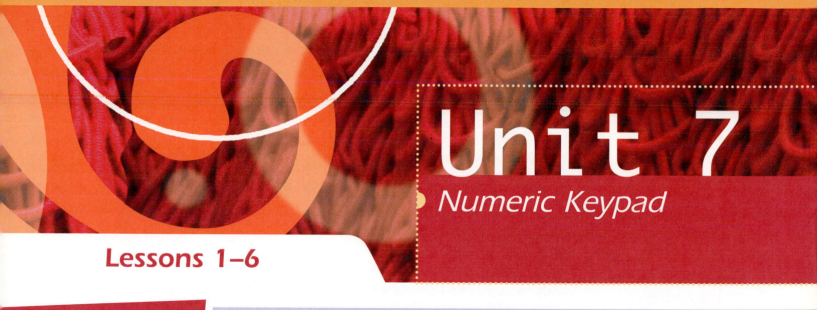

# Unit 7
## *Numeric Keypad*

## Lessons 1–6

**NUMERIC KEYPAD KEYS: 4, 5, 6, AND 0**

### OBJECTIVE

*To learn keying techniques for 4, 5, 6, and 0 on the numeric keypad.*

### 1A | Home-Key Position

Position yourself in front of the keyboard with the book at the right—body erect, both feet on floor.

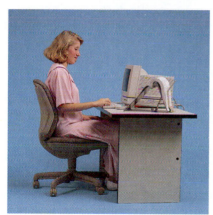

**Proper position at keyboard**

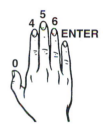

Place your fingers on the numeric keypad with the

- index finger on 4
- middle finger on 5
- ring finger on 6
- thumb on 0

### 1B | Access the Calculator

Follow the instructions given below to access the calculator on your computer.

1. Click Start.
2. Click All Programs.
3. Click Accessories.
4. Click Calculator.
5. Activate the NUM (number) LOCK located above the **7** on the numeric keypad.

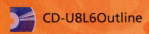

CD-U8L6Outline

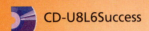

CD-U8L6Success

## 6E | Outline

1. Open the data file *CD-U8L6Outline*.

2. Set a decimal tab at 0.2" to align the roman numerals. Set left tabs at 0.375", 0.625", and 0.875" to indent the levels of the outline. Change the line spacing to DS. Remove spaces and insert tabs as needed to format the outline properly.

3. Save as *U8L6EOutline*.

## 6F | MLA Report

1. Open the data file *CD-U8L6Success*. Key the report identification title and the first two paragraphs that follow at the beginning of the report. Key the *Tips for Success in Math* section following the *Math Myths* section and before the *Works Cited* section.

2. Format the report in MLA style; insert an appropriate header. Set tabs at 0.5" and 0.75" to key the numbered lists.

3. Bold the side headings using a 14-point font. Use bold and an 18-point font for the report title and Works Cited title.

4. Format the Works Cited page. Spell-check and proofread the report carefully. Correct all errors. Insert hard page breaks as needed to end pages properly.

5. Save the report as *U8L6Success*.

Jessica Youngwood
Ms. Patricia Troutman
English
16 May 20--

Success in Math

Math anxiety affects all of us at some time, but it is a barrier we can overcome (*Coping with Math Anxiety*). Math anxiety is having feelings of tension that interfere with your ability to use numbers and solve math problems. Math anxiety affects people of all ages. It is not limited only to our feelings in math classrooms. For example, people may suffer math anxiety when asked to divide a restaurant check into equal parts. A similar feeling may be present when we must compute the price of an item that is on sale. A need to determine quickly the batting averages of players on their teams may cause anxiety in coaches. Unfortunately, students who think they have math anxiety are likely to take as few math classes as they can. These same students may avoid taking more than the required science courses. Students who make these choices will severely limit their academic and career choices.

On the positive side, researchers such as Cruikshank and Sheffield (24) believe that teachers can help students reduce their level of math anxiety. When they do, these students will enjoy the same advantages as those who easily use numbers and solve math problems in school and at work.

*(continued)*

**Numeric Keypad Home Keys**

### 1C | New Keys: 4, 5, 6, and 0 (Home Keys)

Use the calculator accessory on your computer to complete the following drills. To use the numeric keypad on your computer keyboard, the NUM LOCK must be turned on.

1. Key each number and enter it by tapping the + key with the little finger of the right hand.

2. After keying each number in the column, verify your answer with the answer shown below the column.

3. Tap the ESC key on the main keyboard to clear the calculator; then key numbers in the next column.

4. Repeat steps 1–3 for Drills 1–6 to increase your input rate.

**TIP**

Tap each key with a quick, sharp stroke with the *tip* of the finger; release the key quickly. Keep the fingers curved and upright.

Tap the **0** with the side of the right thumb, similar to the way you tap the Space Bar.

**Drill 1**

| A | B | C | D | E | F |
|---|---|---|---|---|---|
| 4 | 5 | 6 | 4 | 5 | 4 |
| +4 | +5 | +6 | +6 | +6 | +5 |
| 8 | 10 | 12 | 10 | 11 | 9 |

**Drill 2**

| A | B | C | D | E | F |
|---|---|---|---|---|---|
| 44 | 55 | 66 | 45 | 65 | 46 |
| +44 | +55 | +66 | +56 | +54 | +54 |
| 88 | 110 | 132 | 101 | 119 | 100 |

**Drill 3**

| A | B | C | D | E | F |
|---|---|---|---|---|---|
| 44 | 55 | 64 | 46 | 64 | 54 |
| 55 | 44 | 56 | 55 | 65 | 55 |
| +66 | +66 | +45 | +64 | +66 | +56 |
| 165 | 165 | 165 | 165 | 195 | 165 |

**Drill 4**

| A | B | C | D | E | F |
|---|---|---|---|---|---|
| 40 | 404 | 650 | 400 | 540 | 500 |
| 50 | 506 | 605 | 500 | 506 | 506 |
| +60 | +650 | +450 | +600 | +600 | +405 |
| 150 | 1560 | 1705 | 1,500 | 1,646 | 1,411 |

**Drill 5**

| A | B | C | D | E | F |
|---|---|---|---|---|---|
| 44 | 405 | 406 | 604 | 540 | 450 |
| 55 | 650 | 605 | 506 | 604 | 604 |
| +66 | +406 | +405 | +504 | +650 | +560 |
| 165 | 1,461 | 1,416 | 1,614 | 1,794 | 1,514 |

**Drill 6**

| A | B | C | D | E | F |
|---|---|---|---|---|---|
| 55 | 460 | 564 | 404 | 400 | 1,605 |
| 64 | 505 | 450 | 550 | 505 | 2,640 |
| +46 | +406 | +504 | +640 | +660 | +650 |
| 165 | 1,371 | 1,518 | 1,594 | 1,565 | 4,895 |

1. Study the Tip and the model outline below.

2. Key the outline. Double-space the outline. Center the title. Set a decimal tab at 0.2" to align the roman numerals. Set left tabs at 0.375", 0.625", and 0.875" to indent the levels of the outline.

3. Spell-check and proofread the outline. Correct all errors. Save as *U8L6DOutline*.

**1" Top Margin**

Computer Graphics

**1" side margins**

  I.  Introduction

     A.  What is a computer graphics program?

     B.  Why and when should you use one?

**DS outline body**

 II.  Graphics Programs

     A.  Those that come with a software program

     B.  Those that are stand-alone programs

**Indent each outline level**

III.  Computer Graphs

     A.  Bar graphs

        1.  Vertical bar

        2.  Horizontal bar

     B.  Circle graphs

        1.  Whole circle

        2.  Exploded circle

        3.  Segmented circle

     C.  Line graphs

        1.  Without shaded areas

        2.  With shaded areas

## 1D | Math Calculations

Use the numeric keypad to solve the math problems below.

1. In January 4,650 copies of the book were sold. The sales for February and March were 4,604 and 6,540. How many copies of the book were sold during the first three months of the year?

2. Mr. Jackson was paid $6,505 in January, $5,640 in February, and $6,400 in March. What were his total earnings during the first quarter of the year?

3. The daily sales for last week were: Monday – $56,400; Tuesday – $65,645; Wednesday – $46,005; Thursday – $55,064; Friday – $46,500; and Saturday – $55,600. What was the total amount of sales for the week?

4. If Mr. Alou drove 5,560 miles in January, 4,060 in February, 6,005 in March, 5,664 in April, 6,005 in May, and 5,660 miles in June, how many miles did he drive during the first half of the year?

---

★ *Language Arts*

## 1E Writing: Terminal Punctuation

Read the punctuation rules below. Study the Learn lines. Note how the rules are applied. Key the Learn lines and the Apply lines, including the necessary punctuation. Save as *U7L1Punctuation*.

**Rule 3:** Use a question mark at the end of a sentence intended as a question.

Learn 1  Jerry, did you take the English exam on Friday?

Learn 2  What was the final score of the Phoenix Suns game?

Apply 3  What time is your appointment with Mr. Sanchez

Apply 4  Does your new computer have Windows Vista

**Rule 4:** Use an exclamation point after emphatic (forceful) exclamations.

Learn 5  I told you before, the answer is no!

Learn 6  That is a fantastic idea!

Apply 7  You have to be kidding

Apply 8  You really have to go see that movie; it is unbelievable

## Practice What You Have Learned

1. Open a new document. Set a left tab at 1", a center tab at 2.5", a decimal tab at 3.75", and a right tab at 5.25". Key the following text using the tabs just set.

| Red Team | Jim Barrymore | $107.58 | First Place |
| Blue Team | Mary Guerra | $98.65 | Second Place |
| White Team | Sandy Harrison | $87.53 | Third Place |

2. Save the document as *U8L6Tabs*.

## 6C | Clear Tabs

Tabs you set can be cleared (removed) individually or all at once.

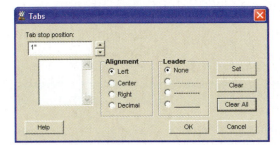

To clear a tab(s) you have set:

1. Select the paragraph(s) for which you want to clear (delete) tabs.

2. On the menu bar, click Format. Click Tabs. In the Tabs dialog box, click Clear All to clear all the tabs you have set.

3. To clear a single tab, select the tab position in the Tabs dialog box and click Clear.

4. Click OK to close the dialog box.

## Practice What You Have Learned

1. Open a new document. Set a left tab at 1", center tabs at 2.75" and 4.5", and a right tab at 6". Key the following text in bold using the tabs just set:

| **Team** | **Name** | **Amount** | **Place** |

2. Place the insertion point on the line below the keyed text. Clear the center tab at 4.5" by dragging it from the Ruler.

3. Set a decimal tab at 4.5". Key the following three lines of text using the four tabs.

| Red | Jim Barrymore | $107.58 | First |
| Blue | Mary Guerra | $98.65 | Second |
| White | Sandy Harrison | $87.53 | Third |

4. Save the document as *U8L6SetTabs*. Leave the document open.

5. Select all the lines and use the Tabs dialog box to clear all the tabs.

6. Save the document as *U8L6Clear*.

1. Key a 30" timed writing on each paragraph; determine *gwam* on each writing.

2. Using your better *gwam* as a base rate, add two words a minute to the base rate and key two 30" timings on each paragraph trying to attain the new rate.

3. Key two 1' timings on paragraphs 1–2.

**MicroType**

*Timed Writing*

**E**

**All letters used**

| | GWAM 2' |
|---|---|
| •    2   •    4   •    6   •    8   • | |
| Are you one of the people who often look from | 4 |
|  10   •    12   •    14   •    16   •    18   • | |
| the copy to the screen and down at your hands? If | 9 |
| 20   •    22   •    24   •    26   •    28   • | |
| you are, you can be sure that you will not build a | 14 |
| 30   •    32   •    34   •    36   •    38   • | |
| speed to prize. Make eyes on copy your next goal. | 19 |
|    •    2   •    4   •    6   •    8   • | |
| When you move the eyes from the copy to check | 24 |
|  10   •    12   •    14   •    16   •    18   • | |
| the screen, you may lose your place and waste time | 29 |
| 20   •    22   •    24   •    26   •    28   • | |
| trying to find it. Lost time can lower your speed | 34 |
| 30   •    32   •    34   •    36   •    38   • | |
| quickly and in a major way, so do not look away. | 39 |

GWAM 2' | 1 | 2 | 3 | 4 | 5 |

For additional practice **MicroType** + **Numeric Keypad** + **Lesson 1**

**LESSON**

# 2

**OBJECTIVE**

*To learn keying techniques for 7, 8, and 9 on the numeric keypad.*

## NUMERIC KEYPAD KEYS: 7, 8, AND 9

**2A** | **Home-Key Review**

1. Review the home keys by calculating the totals for the problems shown below.

2. Check your answers with the problem totals shown in blue.

| A | B | C | D | E | F |
|---|---|---|---|---|---|
| 45 | 504 | 645 | 604 | 400 | 650 |
| 50 | 650 | 540 | 405 | 500 | 450 |
| +64 | +645 | +600 | +560 | +654 | +564 |
| 159 | 1,799 | 1,785 | 1,569 | 1,554 | 1,664 |

## 5F ▪ Aerial Maps

Use the Internet to find an aerial and/or topographical map. Look for a map of your town, school, home, or other favorite location. (Use Internet sites such as http://terraserver.homeadvisor.msn.com or http://www.terraserver.com/home.asp or http://maps.google.com.) Print the map or picture you found. Identify the location or building. Write a paragraph describing the search process you used to find the location. Save as *U8L5World*.

*Social Studies*

---

## LESSON
# 6

### OBJECTIVES

1. *To learn and practice setting and clearing tabs.*
2. *To create an outline.*
3. *To format an MLA report.*

### MicroType
**TIP**

To set a left, right, or center tab using the Ruler, click the Tab Style button on the toolbar as many times as needed to select the desired tab style. Then click the Ruler at the position where the new tab is to be placed.

| L | ┛ | ┴ |
|---|---|---|
| **Left** | **Right** | **Center** |

# MLA REPORTS AND OUTLINES

## 6A | Conditioning Practice

Key each line twice SS; then key a 1' writing on line 3. Determine *gwam*.

| | | |
|---|---|---|
| Alphabet | 1 | Holly, Jakim, and Vega expected a new quest for an African zebra. |
| Figures/Symbols | 2 | The computer costs $485.97 (20% off), and I have saved have $361. |
| Speed | 3 | The girls laid the world maps and rifle by the end of the mantle. |

**GWAM** 1' | 1 | 2 | 3 | 4 | 5 | 6 | 7 | 8 | 9 | 10 |

## 6B | Set Tabs

Tabs are set locations at which text can be placed. By default, left tabs are set at half-inch (0.5") intervals from the left margin. These default tabs do not have tab markers on the Ruler. Left, center, right, and decimal tabs may be set anywhere on the Ruler. Left tabs align text at the left. Right tabs align text at the right. Center tabs center text on the tab position. Decimal tabs center text at the decimal point.

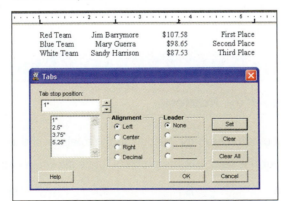

**To set tabs in a document:**

1. On the menu bar, click Format. Click Tabs. The Tabs dialog box appears.

2. Key a number in the Tab stop position box. Click an Alignment option (Left, Center, Right, Decimal). Click Set. Repeat for all tabs you wish to set.

3. Click OK to close the dialog box. A tab marker appears on the Ruler for each tab you set. (Default tabs to the left of any set tab are deleted automatically.)

## 2B | New Keys: 7, 8, and 9

### Learn Reach to 7

1. Locate **7** (above **4**) on the numeric keypad.

2. Watch your index finger move up to **7** and back to **4** a few times without tapping keys.

3. Practice tapping **7** and then **4** a few times as you watch the finger.

4. With eyes on copy, key the data in Drill 1. Key the number and enter it by tapping the **+** key with the little finger of the right hand. Do not worry about correct totals.

**Drill 1**

| A | B | C | D | E | F |
|---|---|---|---|---|---|
| 747 | 747 | 757 | 707 | 750 | 704 |
| 477 | 477 | 676 | 675 | 747 | 657 |
| +774 | +774 | +704 | +477 | +670 | +607 |
| 1,998 | 1,998 | 2,137 | 1,859 | 2,167 | 1,968 |

### Learn Reach to 8

1. Learn the middle-finger reach to **8** (above **5**) as directed in steps 1–3 above.

2. With eyes on copy, key the data in Drill 2. Key the number and enter it by tapping the **+** key with the little finger of the right hand. Do not worry about correct totals.

**Drill 2**

| A | B | C | D | E | F |
|---|---|---|---|---|---|
| 588 | 585 | 800 | 808 | 680 | 787 |
| 858 | 885 | 786 | 478 | 785 | 800 |
| +885 | +588 | +884 | +685 | +804 | +468 |
| 2,331 | 2,058 | 2,470 | 1,971 | 2,269 | 2,055 |

### Learn Reach to 9

1. Learn the ring-finger reach to **9** (above **6**) as directed above.

2. With eyes on copy, key the data in Drill 3. Key the number and enter it by tapping the **+** key with the little finger of the right hand. Do not worry about correct totals.

**Drill 3**

| A | B | C | D | E | F |
|---|---|---|---|---|---|
| 699 | 709 | 968 | 409 | 569 | 869 |
| 966 | 789 | 987 | 659 | 908 | 794 |
| +996 | +969 | +909 | +879 | +990 | +689 |
| 2,661 | 2,467 | 2,864 | 1,947 | 2,467 | 2,352 |

Algebra is one of the cornerstones of today's technology boom. Without algebra there would not exist a single TV, radio, telephone, microwave oven, or other gadget that makes modern life so comfortable and interesting. Once you learn to use algebra, you will have the opportunity to help design and create the next generation of technology. (*Cord Algebra 1 ix*)

Geometry

Geometry deals with shapes ([http://simple.wikipedia.org/wiki/Geometry](http://simple.wikipedia.org/wiki/Geometry)) such as solids, surfaces, lines, and angles. It is used when we build or measure things. Architects, astronomers, engineers, and surveyors are just a few people who use geometry. Most students will study geometry in high school.

Trigonometry and Calculus

Trigonometry and calculus can also be taken in high school. Trigonometry can be used to find the unknown sides or angles in a triangle. It is used by engineers, surveyors, and scientists. Early explorers used this type of math to help them navigate to the new world. Calculus deals with rates of change. It has many uses in engineering, physics, and other areas of science. Calculus is the math we need to know to understand how the wind blows, water flows, sun shines, and planets move.

Works Cited

Center for Occupational Research and Development. *Cord Algebra 1, Mathematics in Context*. Cincinnati: South-Western Educational Publishing, 1998.

Center for Occupational Research and Development. *Cord Applied Mathematics, Unit 19 Working with Statistics*. Cincinnati: South-Western Educational Publishing, 1989.

Simple English Wikipedia. "Geometry." 23 December 2006. [http://simple.wikipedia.org/wiki/Geometry](http://simple.wikipedia.org/wiki/Geometry).

---

★ *Language Arts*

## 5E Writing: Word Choice

Study the spelling and definitions of the following words. Key the Learn line, noting the word choices. Key the Apply lines, selecting the correct words. Save as *U8L5WordChoice*.

**one** (adjective) being a single thing

**won** (verb) gain victory in a contest

Learn 1 Sarah scored more than **one** goal in each game we **won**.

Apply 2 The basketball team (one, won) three games by (one, won) point.

Apply 3 Betty scored only (one, won) point, but we still (one, won).

## 2C | Practice All Reaches

1. Key and enter the numbers for Drills 4 and 5. Check your answers with the problem totals shown in blue.

2. Repeat Drills 1 and 2 to increase your input speed.

**Drill 4**

| A | B | C | D | E | F |
|---|---|---|---|---|---|
| 748 | 576 | 486 | 890 | 490 | 407 |
| 507 | 809 | 895 | 449 | 867 | 965 |
| 689 | 405 | 907 | 780 | 758 | 609 |
| +768 | +679 | +756 | +645 | +906 | +487 |
| 2,712 | 2,469 | 3,044 | 2,764 | 3,021 | 2,468 |

**Drill 5**

| A | B | C | D | E | F |
|---|---|---|---|---|---|
| 70 | 864 | 594 | 8 | 978 | 706 |
| 769 | 590 | 45 | 556 | 59 | 467 |
| 5 | 708 | 606 | 76 | 50 | 805 |
| +59 | +7 | +479 | +940 | +706 | +489 |
| 903 | 2,169 | 1,724 | 1,580 | 1,793 | 2,467 |

## 2D | Math Calculations

Use the numeric keypad to solve the math problems below.

1. The daily gallons of gas sold this week were: Monday – 5,964; Tuesday – 9,057; Wednesday – 4,789; Thursday – 5,540; Friday – 6,945; and Saturday – 8,788. What was the total number of gallons of gas sold during this week?

2. Rebecca read 67 pages on Monday, 49 pages on Tuesday, 48 pages on Wednesday, and 50 pages on Thursday. What was the total number of pages she read during these four days?

3. What is the sum of 4,807, 6,459, 7,064, and 7,854?

4. Five hundred people attend the play on Monday, 487 on Tuesday, and 609 on Wednesday. How many people attended the play during these three days?

★ *Language Arts*

## 2E Writing: Word Choice

Study the spelling and definitions of the words below. Key the Learn lines, noting the word choices. Key the Apply lines, selecting the correct words. Save as *U7L2WordChoice*.

**complement** (noun) something that completes or makes up a whole

**compliment** (noun) an expression of praise or congratulation

Learn 1 The rugs you bought will **complement** the other furnishings.

Learn 2 Dr. Chan gave Mary a **compliment** on her term paper.

Apply 3 Who gave Raul the (complement, compliment) on his work?

Apply 4 The color of the wood will (complement, compliment) the wall color.

CD-U8L5Math

1. Open the data file *CD-U8L5Math*. Insert a header using your last name and a page number. **Note:** Since a title page will be attached to this MLA report, the student, teacher, course, and date information is omitted from page 1; only the title information is repeated, and it is keyed 1" from the top edge of the paper.

2. Key the report title and report sections below. Place them at the beginning of the document before the *Probability and Statistics* side heading. Key the Works Cited page at the end of the document.

3. Format the report in MLA style.

4. Use bold and a 14-point font for the side headings. Use bold and a 16-point font for the report title and the Works Cited page title. Use 22-point font size for all the symbols and special characters.

5. Spell-check and proofread the report carefully. Correct all errors.

6. Insert hard page breaks as needed to end and begin pages properly.

7. Save the report as *U8L5Math*.

8. Prepare a title page for the report. Use *Mathematics* as the report title, your name as the writer, your teacher's name, *Math* as the course, and today's date.

9. Save the title page as *U8L5MathTP*.

Mathematics

Mathematics (math) is an important area of study for students. All students will take several different kinds of math courses before they finish high school.

Arithmetic

Arithmetic is an area of math that is studied in the early grades by everyone. As you know, it deals with the study of numbers. When you use arithmetic, you will:

1. Add
2. Subtract
3. Multiply
4. Divide

Arithmetic is the type of math that you use almost every day. It serves as the basis for many other kinds of mathematics.

Algebra

This type of math is used widely in business, industry, and science to solve problems. Algebra uses symbols to solve problems for unknown numbers or values. Some common symbols are:

$$( ) \{ \} f < > = * + - / \; x \; y \; z$$

Most students begin to learn algebra in the middle or junior high school grades. Others will begin their study of algebra in the early high school years. The power of algebra is that it lets us create, write, and rewrite formulas that are used to solve problems.

*(continued)*

## 2F | Timed Writings

1. Key a 1' timed writing on each paragraph; determine *gwam* on each writing.

2. Add 2–4 *gwam* to your best rate in step 1 for a new goal.

3. Key two 1' guided writings on each paragraph at new goal rate. (See page 77 for procedures for setting goals.)

| MicroType | | GWAM 1' |
|---|---|---|
| *Timed Writing* | Government is the structure by which public laws are | 10 |
| LA | made for a group of people. One type of structure is where | 22 |
| | the populace has the right to elect citizens to govern for | 34 |
| **All letters used** | them and make the laws. A representative government would | 46 |
| | be an example of this way of making the laws and policies. | 57 |

The democracy or the republic forms of government are 10
two names that are quite often used to refer to this type 22
of governance by the people. This type of a structure is 34
in direct contrast to a dictatorship where all the 44
decisions are made by just one person. 51

GWAM 1' | 1 | 2 | 3 | 4 | 5 | 6 | 7 | 8 | 9 | 10 | 11 | 12 |

For additional practice  MicroType + Numeric Keypad + Lesson 2

## LESSON 3

### NUMERIC KEYPAD KEYS: 1, 2, AND 3

#### 3A | Keypad Review

**OBJECTIVE**

*To learn keying techniques for 1, 2, and 3 on the numeric keypad.*

1. Review the keypad by calculating the totals for the problems shown below.

2. Check your answers with the problem totals shown in blue.

| A | B | C | D | E | F | G |
|---|---|---|---|---|---|---|
| 45 | 77 | 470 | 679 | 864 | 705 | 488 |
| 67 | 88 | 580 | 584 | 579 | 804 | 757 |
| +89 | +99 | +960 | +507 | +705 | +956 | +690 |
| 201 | 264 | 2,010 | 1,770 | 2,148 | 2,465 | 1,935 |

## 5C | Title Page

1. Study the title page format guides below.

2. Key the title page shown below.

3. Spell-check and proofread the document. Correct all errors. Save the title page as *U8L5Title*.

The Way to Happiness

**Title Centered, one-third down page (Approx. 3.5")**

by

Harold McKibben

**Name Centered, begin one-half down page (Approx. 5.5" line)**

Ms. Sandy Forde

Unified Arts

15 September 20--

**Instructor, Course, Date, begin at about 8.5" line to leave at least a 1" bottom margin**

### 3B | New Keys: 1, 2, and 3

**Learn Reach to 1**

1. Locate **1** (below **4**) on the numeric keypad.

2. Watch your index finger move down to **1** and back to **4** a few times without tapping keys.

3. Practice tapping **1** and then **4** a few times as you watch the finger.

4. With eyes on copy, key the data in Drill 1. Key the number and enter it by tapping the + key with the little finger of the right hand. Do not worry about correct totals.

**Drill 1**

| A | B | C | D | E | F | G |
|---|---|---|---|---|---|---|
| 441 | 411 | 101 | 110 | 168 | 415 | 110 |
| 411 | 141 | 415 | 819 | 710 | 716 | 910 |
| +114 | +114 | +617 | +510 | +514 | +819 | +615 |
| 966 | 666 | 1,133 | 1,439 | 1,392 | 1,950 | 1,635 |

**Learn Reach to 2**

1. Learn the middle-finger reach to **2** (below **5**) as directed in steps 1–3 above.

2. With eyes on copy, key the data in Drill 2. Key the number and enter it by tapping the + key with the little finger of the right hand. Do not worry about correct totals.

**Drill 2**

| A | B | C | D | E | F | G |
|---|---|---|---|---|---|---|
| 522 | 252 | 254 | 202 | 426 | 728 | 269 |
| 452 | 522 | 267 | 725 | 912 | 622 | 720 |
| +252 | +225 | +289 | +802 | +279 | +102 | +822 |
| 1,226 | 999 | 810 | 1,729 | 1,617 | 1,452 | 1,811 |

**Learn Reach to 3**

1. Learn the ring-finger reach to **3** (below **6**) as directed above.

2. With eyes on copy, enter the data in Drill 3. Key the number and enter it by tapping the + key with the little finger of the right hand. Do not worry about correct totals.

**Drill 3**

| A | B | C | D | E | F | G |
|---|---|---|---|---|---|---|
| 633 | 363 | 639 | 630 | 935 | 394 | 536 |
| 336 | 336 | 538 | 378 | 463 | 833 | 303 |
| +636 | +362 | +437 | +935 | +803 | +730 | +738 |
| 1,605 | 1,061 | 1,614 | 1,943 | 2,201 | 1,957 | 1,577 |

Double-click a symbol or character in the Symbol dialog box to insert it quickly; then close the dialog box.

## 5B | Symbols and Special Characters

Symbols and special characters can be inserted into your document. These characters can be made larger or smaller. To size a symbol, select it and change its size in the Font dialog box or the Font Size drop-down list.

To insert a symbol or special character:

1. Position the cursor at the location where you want to insert the symbol or character.

2. Select Symbol from the Insert menu.

3. Select the Symbols tab or the Special characters tab. When the Symbols tab is selected, make sure that (*normal text*) is selected in the Font list. *All Characters* should be selected in the Subset list.

4. Click the symbol or character you want to insert. Click Insert to insert the symbol or special character. Then click Done to close the dialog box.

To size symbols and special characters:

1. Select the symbol or special character.

2. Select Font from the Format menu.

3. Select or key the desired font size in the Size box and click OK.

### Practice What You Have Learned

1. Open a new document. Change the font size to 16. Key the following line, inserting the copyright symbol as shown. (This symbol is available on both the Symbols tab and the Special Characters tab.)

   Copyright 2008 © by South-Western, a part of Cengage Learning.

2. Change the font size to 12. Key the following line, inserting the trademark symbol as shown. Do not space between the trademark symbol and the word that comes before the symbol.

   Century 21™ is a trademark used in this textbook.

3. Key the following text in 11-point font and insert the symbols shown. Change the size of the symbols to 20 points.

   ☐Yes, I will attend.

   ☐No, I cannot attend.

4. Save the document as *U8L5Symbols*.

## 3C | Practice All Reaches

1. Key and enter the numbers for the problems below. Check your answers with the problem totals shown in blue.

2. Repeat the drill to increase your input speed.

**Drill 4**

| A | B | C | D | E | F | G |
|---|---|---|---|---|---|---|
| 192 | 698 | 217 | 102 | 708 | 465 | 133 |
| 378 | 75 | 35 | 360 | 18 | 709 | 404 |
| +54 | +346 | +698 | +549 | +273 | +280 | +605 |
| 624 | 1,119 | 950 | 1,011 | 999 | 1,454 | 1,142 |

**Drill 5**

| A | B | C | D | E | F | G |
|---|---|---|---|---|---|---|
| 279 | 527 | 879 | 208 | 645 | 105 | 481 |
| 805 | 52 | 546 | 194 | 879 | 963 | 554 |
| +36 | +687 | +820 | +753 | +233 | +159 | +788 |
| 1,120 | 1,266 | 2,245 | 1,155 | 1,757 | 1,227 | 1,823 |

*Language Arts*

## 3D Writing: Commas

Read the punctuation rules below. Study the Learn lines. Note how the rules are applied. Key the Learn lines and the Apply lines, including the necessary punctuation. Save as *U7L3Punctuation*.

**Rule 1:** Use a comma after introductory phrases or clauses.

Learn 1  When you have decided on a school, please let us know.

Learn 2  If you retake the exam, you should be able to improve your score.

Apply 3  If you go to New York be sure to go to a play on Broadway.

Apply 4  When you are in Green Bay visit the Packer Hall of Fame.

**Rule 2:** Use a comma after words in a series.

Learn 5  New York, San Diego, and Chicago are possible convention sites.

Learn 6  I have seen the Mets, Cubs, and Braves play this year.

Apply 7  She owns Disney Intel McDonalds and U.S. Bank stock.

Apply 8  He took classes in biology history and math this semester.

## 4F Writing: Internal Punctuation

Read the following punctuation rules. Study the Learn lines. Note how the rules are applied. Key the Learn lines and the Apply lines, inserting punctuation as needed. Save as *U8L4Writing*.

**Rule 7:** Use a comma to separate two or more parallel adjectives (adjectives that could be separated by the word and instead of a comma).

Learn 1   The jubilant, enthusiastic players joined in the celebration.

Learn 2   The big black box contained the props for the play.

Apply 3   Abraham Lincoln was an industrious dedicated leader.

Apply 4   The old stone fence had stood for many years.

**Rule 8:** Use a comma to set off nonrestrictive clauses (not necessary to the meaning of the sentence); however, do not use commas to set off restrictive clauses (necessary to the meaning of the sentence).

Learn 5   The manuscript, which Stan prepared, has been published.

Learn 6   The report that presents the financial statements is ready.

Apply 7   The student with the highest GPA will be honored.

Apply 8   The game which was played in the rain was very exciting.

---

## LESSON

# 5

### OBJECTIVES

1. *To learn and practice inserting and sizing symbols.*
2. *To format an MLA report with title page.*

# MLA REPORTS AND TITLE PAGE

## 5A | Conditioning Practice

Key each line twice SS; then key a 1' writing on line 3. Determine *gwam*.

Alphabet 1   The major duck exhibit used the dozen plaques given by Fred Webb.

Figures 2   Our student club has 18,673 members in 290 chapters in 45 states.

Speed 3   Eighty firms bid on the six authentic maps of the ancient island.

GWAM   1' |   1   |   2   |   3   |   4   |   5   |   6   |   7   |   8   |   9   |   10   |

### 3E | Math Calculations

Use the numeric keypad to solve the math problems below.

1. Jana had 98, 88, and 93 on her three tests; she had 25, 22, and 24 on her quizzes. How many total points has she accumulated so far?

2. Last week Jerome had scores of 189, 176, and 198 for his three games of bowling. What were his total pins for the three games?

3. The Carson family estimated their rent and utility expenses for next month as follows: rent, $575; electric, $87; water, $45; and gas, $133. What is the total amount they will need to cover these expenses?

4. Rene made deposit of $406 on March 1, $463 on March 15, $358 on April 1, and $392 on April 15. What is the total amount of these four deposits?

### 3F | Timed Writings

1. Key one 1' unguided and two 1' guided timed writings on each paragraph; determine *gwam*.

2. Key two 2' unguided writings on paragraphs 1–2 combined; determine *gwam*.

**MicroType**
*Timed Writing*
LA

**All letters used**

|  | GWAM | 2' | 3' |
|---|---|---|---|
| Laura Ingalls Wilder is a beloved writer of books for | | 5 | 3 |
| children. Most of her books are based on her own | | 10 | 6 |
| experiences as a youth. Her first book was about her life | | 16 | 10 |
| in Wisconsin. From just reading such a book, children are | | 22 | 14 |
| able to fantasize about what it would have been like to | | 27 | 18 |
| live with the pioneers during this time period of our | | 33 | 22 |
| nation. | | 33 | 22 |
| Besides writing about her own life and the life of her | | 39 | 26 |
| own family, she also wrote about the life of her husband, | | 45 | 30 |
| Almanzo, and his family. Her second book was about the | | 50 | 33 |
| early years of his life growing up on a farm near the | | 56 | 37 |
| Canadian border in the state of New York. Through these | | 61 | 41 |
| exquisite books, this period of time in our history is | | 67 | 44 |
| preserved forever. | | 69 | 46 |

GWAM 2' | 1 | 2 | 3 | 4 | 5 | 6 |

Interests are best described as activities you like or subjects that appeal to you. By listing and analyzing your interests, you should be able to identify a desirable work setting. For example, your list may reveal that you like to work with things more than with people.

Perhaps you like to work alone most of the time and work with others only once in a while. You may like to work outdoors rather than indoors.

### Works Cited

Fulton-Calkins, Patsy and Joanna D. Hanks. *Procedures & Theory for Administrative Professionals.* 5th ed. Cincinnati: South-Western, 2004.

United States Department of Labor. The Bureau of Labor Statistics. *Occupational Outlook Handbook,* 2006–07 Edition. http://stats.bls.gov/oco/ (accessed December 23, 2006).

University of Waterloo. Career Services. "Step 1: Self-Assessment." Career Development eManual. http://www.cdm.uwaterloo.ca/step1.asp (accessed December 23, 2006).

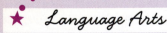

*Language Arts*

## 4E Speaking: Preparing to Speak

You are running for treasurer of your school's Future Business Leaders Association chapter. You must make a 1' to 2' speech to the voting members. Follow the steps below. Save the document as *U8L4Speaking*.

1. Key a list of the major points you want to make about yourself and why you would make a good treasurer. Include experiences that show you to be capable, reliable, responsible, and dependable, especially in managing money. Examples follow:

   - Business and accounting courses you have completed or are taking

   - Leadership positions you hold/held in other organizations

   - Jobs you hold/held

   - Banking, budgeting, fundraising, etc. experiences you have had

2. If time and resources permit, follow your teacher's instructions to record your speech in a sound file.

3. Submit your list (and sound file, if made) to your instructor.

# NUMERIC KEYPAD KEYS:  .  (DECIMAL)

## LESSON 4

### OBJECTIVES

1. *To learn reachstrokes for the decimal on the numeric keypad.*
2. *To reinforce all numeric keypad numbers.*

## 4A | Keypad Review

1. Review the keypad by calculating the totals for the problems shown below.
2. Check your answers with the problem totals shown in blue.

| A | B | C | D | E | F | G |
|---|---|---|---|---|---|---|
| 24 | 35 | 742 | 126 | 984 | 157 | 455 |
| 76 | 90 | 853 | 459 | 651 | 268 | 833 |
| +81 | +84 | +961 | +783 | +327 | +349 | +177 |
| 181 | 209 | 2,556 | 1,368 | 1,962 | 774 | 1,465 |

## 4B | Learn Reach to . (decimal)

1. Learn the ring-finger reach to the . **(decimal)** located below the **3**.
2. With eyes on copy, calculate the totals for each problem below.
3. Repeat the drills to increase your input speed.

**Drill 1**

| A | B | C | D | E | F | G |
|---|---|---|---|---|---|---|
| 3.36 | 3.87 | 73.91 | 18.97 | 67.14 | 64.18 | 81.97 |
| +4.07 | +3.56 | +24.67 | +2.67 | +3.81 | +81.64 | +2.45 |
| 7.43 | 7.43 | 98.58 | 21.64 | 70.95 | 145.82 | 84.42 |

**Drill 2**

| A | B | C | D | E | F |
|---|---|---|---|---|---|
| 3.7 | 21.8 | 21.46 | 28.01 | 17.09 | 12.6 |
| 5.7 | 61.9 | 73.58 | 16.79 | 26.05 | 35.7 |
| +9.4 | +8.7 | +9.04 | +3.54 | +5.55 | +4.8 |
| 18.8 | 92.4 | 104.08 | 48.34 | 48.69 | 53.1 |

1. Study the Tips related to formatting long quotations ellipsis points.

2. Key the text as an MLA report with a Works Cited page. Use a 14-point font for the report title and *Work Cited* title. Use bold for the side headings.

3. Spell-check and proofread the report carefully. Correct all errors. Save the report as *U8L4WorksCited*.

Connor 1

Derek Connor
Ms. Melanie Kyle
Unified Arts
15 March 20--

Career Planning

Career planning is an important, ongoing process. You can never begin planning too early for your career. The career you eventually choose will affect the quality of your life. One important step in career planning is to learn about various jobs. You can learn about jobs from many sources.

*The Occupational Outlook Handbook*

One very good resource for you to learn about jobs is the *Occupational Outlook Handbook*. This United States Department of Labor publication is:

> . . . a nationally recognized source of career information, designed to provide valuable assistance to individuals making decisions about their future work lives. The *Handbook* is revised every two years. The *Occupational Outlook Handbook* tells you the training and education needed, earnings, expected job prospects, what workers do on the job (http://stats.bls.gov/oco/).

This resource will tell you about thousands of jobs. Some of the jobs described include rock star, athlete, zookeeper, police officer, and reporter. In addition, the *Handbook* will tell you where to look to get more information about a career.

Self-Assessment

Another useful step in career planning is to complete a self-assessment. This process will reveal your values and interests. Making the right plans for your future during these changing times can be difficult. The self-assessment process will give you more choices and broaden your options. Then you can feel sure that you are on the right career path (http://www.cdm.uwaterloo.ca/step1.asp).

Values and Interests

Even though you may not give it much thought, you have developed a set of values. These values help you set your priorities in life. Values affect the importance you place on family, security, and wealth (Fulton-Calkins and Hanks 37). You should identify your values early in life. Then you can consider those values when you choose a career.

*(continued)*

## 4C | Practice All Reaches

1. Key and enter the numbers for the problems below. Check your answers with the problem totals shown in blue.

2. Repeat the drills to increase your input speed.

**Drill 3**

| A | B | C | D | E | F | G |
|---|---|---|---|---|---|---|
| 95.1 | 577 | 948 | 711 | 787 | 202 | 944 |
| 84.7 | 602 | 87 | 655 | 54 | 400 | 522 |
| +62.3 | +468 | +881 | +992 | +357 | +971 | +333 |
| 242.1 | 1,647 | 1,916 | 2,358 | 1,198 | 1,573 | 1,799 |

**Drill 4**

| A | B | C | D | E | F | G |
|---|---|---|---|---|---|---|
| 505.5 | 244 | 178 | 120 | 121 | 124 | 252 |
| 311.2 | 37 | 46 | 721 | 67 | 945 | 874 |
| +88.4 | +590 | +688 | +322 | +282 | +755 | +363 |
| 905.1 | 871 | 912 | 1,163 | 470 | 1,824 | 1,489 |

**Drill 5**

| A | B | C | D | E | F | G |
|---|---|---|---|---|---|---|
| 29.1 | 481 | 287 | 512 | 780 | 460 | 114 |
| 61.7 | 95 | 26 | 466 | 57 | 701 | 527 |
| +2.6 | +375 | +630 | +255 | +384 | +280 | +605 |
| 93.4 | 951 | 943 | 1,233 | 1,221 | 1,441 | 1,246 |

★ *Language Arts*

## 4D Writing:  Word Choice

Study the spelling and definitions of the words below.  Key the Learn lines, noting the word choices.  Key the Apply lines, selecting the correct words.  Save as *U7L4WordChoice*.

**hear** (verb)  to gain knowledge of by the ear

**here** (adverb)  in or at this place; at this point; in this case; on this point

Learn 1  Did you **hear** him give his speech?

Learn 2  Will you be **here** for the presentation?

Apply 3  He said he will be (hear, here) at noon.

Apply 4  Did you (hear, here) all those sirens last night?

# MicroType

Click the Bold and/or Italic buttons on the toolbar to set format options quickly.

**B**      **I**

**Bold**    **Italic**

## 4C | Font Styles

Use formatting commands to create *italic text*, **bold (dark) text**, and ***bold italic text***.

To change font styles before keying text:

1. On the menu bar, click Format. Click Font. The Font dialog box appears.

2. Click the desired formatting for Font style. Click OK.

3. Key the text. To resume keying with regular character style, access the Font dialog box. Choose Regular for Font style.

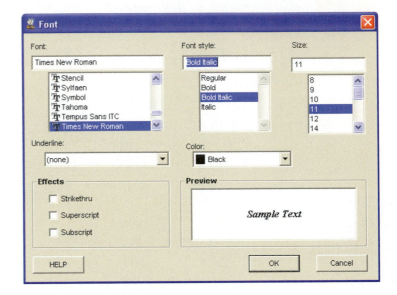

To change font styles for text you have already keyed, select the text and follow the steps above.

**Practice What You Have Learned**

1. Bold, italicize, and underline text as shown as you key the following copy.

   Tim used the **bold** feature to see the **main points** in his notes.

   Shakespeare wrote *Hamlet* and *Much Ado About Nothing*.

   Do you know the difference between ***principal*** and ***principle***?

   *Italic* or <u>underline</u> is acceptable for book titles.

   This sentence has **bold**, *italic*, and <u>underlined</u> letters.

   Use ***<u>bold</u>***, ***<u>italic</u>***, and ***<u>underlining</u>*** on the same word sparingly.

2. Save the document as *U8L4Fonts*.

## 4E | Math Calculations

Use the numeric keypad to solve the math problems below.

1. Alexandra ran 3.7 miles on Monday, 4.2 miles on Tuesday, 2.9 miles on Wednesday, 5.2 miles on Thursday, and 2.75 miles on Friday. How many miles did she run this week?

2. Martin made $76.43 for Week 1, $72.38 for Week 2, 68.96 for Week 3, and 80.06 for Week 4. What is the total amount he made for the four weeks?

3. Melissa is taking a bus from New York City to San Francisco. The fare is $76.77 from New York to Chicago, $58.69 from Chicago to Denver, and $66.87 from Denver to San Francisco. What is Melissa's total cost to travel from New York City to San Francisco?

4. Matt ordered tickets to four different Timberwolves games. The cost of the tickets was $16.00, $60.00, $24.00, and $16.00. There is also a $5.00 processing fee. How much did the tickets cost?

## 4F | Timed Writings

1. Key one 1' timed writing on each paragraph.
2. Key two 2' timed writings on paragraphs 1–2 combined.

**MicroType**

*Timed Writing*

**A**

**All letters used**

GWAM 2'

As you build your keying power, the number of errors — 5

you make is not very important because most of the errors — 11

are accidental and incidental. Realize, however, that — 16

documents are expected to be without flaw. A letter, — 22

report, or table that contains flaws is not usable until — 27

it is corrected. So find and correct all errors. — 32

The best time to find and correct errors is — 37

immediately after you finish keying the copy. Therefore, — 43

just before you print or close a document, proofread and — 48

correct any errors you have made. Learn to proofread — 54

carefully and to correct all errors quickly. To do the — 59

latter, know ways to move the pointer and to select copy. — 65

GWAM 2' | 1 | 2 | 3 | 4 | 5 | 6 |

**For additional practice** MicroType + Numeric Keypad + Lesson 4

# 4

## OBJECTIVES

1. *To learn and practice these word processing features: Paragraph Indentations, Bold, and Italic.*

2. *To format a report using MLA format.*

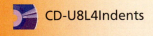
CD-U8L4Indents

# MLA REPORTS WITH LONG QUOTATIONS

## 4A | Conditioning Practice

Key each line twice SS; then key a 1' writing on line 3. Determine *gwam*.

| | | |
|---|---|---|
| Alphabet | 1 | Hazel and Gwen fixed seven jumper cables very quickly for Terrel. |
| Figures/Symbols | 2 | My cash discount (2/10, N/45) on 7 items @ $69.38 will be $9.71. |
| Speed | 3 | Claudia may focus on the work if she is apt to make a big profit. |

GWAM 1' | 1 | 2 | 3 | 4 | 5 | 6 | 7 | 8 | 9 | 10 |

## 4B | Paragraph Indentation

The Paragraph Indentation command is used to indent all the lines of a paragraph the same number of spaces from the left or right margins.

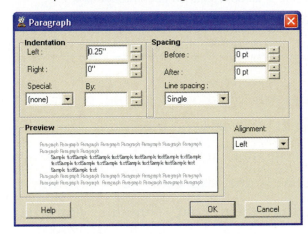

To change paragraph indentation after text has been keyed:

1. Position the cursor in the paragraph you want to indent. (To apply the same indent to more than one paragraph, select the paragraphs that you want to change.)

2. Select Paragraph from the Format menu. The Paragraph dialog box appears as shown below.

3. Key (or select) the desired size of the indentation in the Left and/or Right Indentation boxes.

4. Click OK to apply the paragraph changes.

**Practice What You Have Learned**

1. Open the data file *CD-U8L4Indents*.

2. Indent the second paragraph 1.0" from the left margin.

3. Indent the third paragraph 1.25" from the left and right margins.

4. Indent the fourth paragraph 1.5" from the left margin. Then indent the first line of the paragraph an additional 0.5".

5. Save the document as *U8L4Indents*.

## OBJECTIVES

1. *To learn subtraction using the numeric keypad.*
2. *To learn multiplication using the numeric keypad.*

## TIP

For a long subtraction problem or a mixed addition and subtraction problem:

- Key the first number.
- Tap – (minus) or + (plus) as shown in front of the next number; then key the number.
- After the last number, tap ENTER.

### 5A | Keypad Review

1. Review the keypad by calculating the totals for the problems shown below.

2. Check your answers with the problem totals shown in blue.

| A | B | C | D | E | F |
|---|---|---|---|---|---|
| 15 | 29 | 491 | 208 | 561 | 408 |
| +62 | +80 | +780 | +610 | +268 | +248 |
| +73 | +43 | +553 | +306 | +609 | +357 |
| 150 | 152 | 1,824 | 1,124 | 1,438 | 1,013 |

### 5B | Subtraction

**Learn Reach to – (minus key)**

1. Locate – (minus key) on the numeric keypad above the + (plus key).

2. Watch your little finger move up to the – (minus) and back to the + (plus) a few times without tapping keys.

3. Practice tapping – (minus) a few times as you watch the finger.

4. With eyes on copy, key and enter the data in Drills 1–3. Key the first number and tap – (minus). Key the second number and tap ENTER with the right little finger.

5. Check your answers with the problem answers shown in blue.

6. Tap the ESC key on the main keyboard to clear the calculator; then key the numbers in the next column.

**Drill 1**

| A | B | C | D | E | F |
|---|---|---|---|---|---|
| 58 | 92 | 709 | 758 | 427 | 961 |
| −35 | −46 | −312 | −403 | −218 | −354 |
| 23 | 46 | 397 | 355 | 209 | 607 |

**Drill 2**

| A | B | C | D | E | F |
|---|---|---|---|---|---|
| 89 | 79 | 798 | 768 | 518 | 68.1 |
| −35 | −58 | −645 | −358 | −204 | −29.4 |
| 54 | 21 | 153 | 410 | 314 | 38.7 |

**Drill 3**

| A | B | C | D | E | F |
|---|---|---|---|---|---|
| 89 | 90 | 794 | 817 | 928 | 71.9 |
| −10 | −18 | −132 | −208 | −124 | + 39.2 |
| −27 | −5 | − 45 | −64 | +209 | −7.0 |
| −41 | −34 | −67 | −104 | +190 | −32.1 |
| −5 | −27 | −120 | −52 | − 101 | +49.0 |
| 6 | 6 | 430 | 389 | 1,102 | 121.0 |

**1" Top Margin**

**Page Title** →     Works Cited

**DS**

**Hanging Indent Format** →

Hoggatt, Jack P. and Jon A. Shank. *Century 21 Computer Applications and Keyboarding*, 8th ed.

Cincinnati:  Thomson South-Western, 2006.

**DS**

**1" Margin**     Anson, Chris M. and Robert A. Schwegler. *The Longman Handbook for Writers and Readers*, 3d ed.     **1" Margin**

New York:  Addison-Wesley Educational Publishers, Inc., 2003.

**At Least 1" Bottom Margin**

---

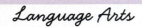 **Language Arts**

## 3F  Writing:  Word Choice

Study the spelling and definitions of the following words.  Key the Learn line, noting the word choices.  Key the Apply lines, selecting the correct words.  Save as *U8L3WordChoice*.

**weak** (adjective)  lacking strength or vigor

**week** (noun)  seven successive days

Learn 1   The soccer team played a **weak** game last **week**.

Apply 2   Andy grew (weak, week) in the past (weak, week).

Apply 3   Bill and Sally were the (weak, week) links this (weak, week).

---

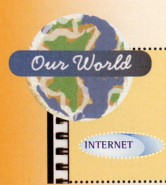 *Our World*

**INTERNET**

### 3G ▪ Research a City

Identify a city you would like to visit.  Then go online to learn about attractions you would visit and a place you would stay while in the city.  Assume you will be in the city for three days.  Write a paragraph or two identifying the city, where you would stay, and what you would do and see while in the city.  Save the document as *U8L3Internet*.

 *Social Studies*

---

## 5C | Multiplication

### Learn Reach to * (multiplication key)

1. Locate the * (multiplication key) on the numeric keypad.

2. Watch your ring finger move up to the * (multiplication) and back to the **6** key a few times without tapping keys.

3. Practice tapping * (multiplication) a few times as you watch the finger.

4. With eyes on copy, key and enter the data in Drills 1–3. Key the first number, tap * (multiplication), key the next number, and tap ENTER.

5. Check your answers with the problem answers shown in blue.

**Tip**

For a mixed operation problem:

- Key the first number.

- Tap * (multiplication), – (minus), or + (plus) as shown in front of the next number; then key the number.

- After the last number, tap ENTER.

**Drill 1**

| A | B | C | D | E |
|---|---|---|---|---|
| 38 | 42 | 56 | 312 | 31.8 |
| x12 | x19 | x17 | x124 | x12.9 |
| 456 | 798 | 952 | 38,688 | 410.22 |

**Drill 2**

| A | B | C | D | E |
|---|---|---|---|---|
| 413 | 209 | 648 | 387 | 240 |
| x19 | x54 | x41 | x46 | x20 |
| 7,847 | 11,286 | 26,568 | 17,802 | 4,800 |

**Drill 3**

**A**  3 x 3 x 6 = 54

**B**  6 x 7 x 2 = 84

**C**  4 x 6 x 4 = 96

**F**  5 x 79 – 14 = 381

**D**  6 x 10 x 3 = 180

**E**  51 x 10 + 58 = 568

**F**  5 x 79 – 14 = 381

1. Study the formatting guides in the report below and the model copy on the next page.

2. Key the report and the Works Cited page using MLA format. Use bold, 14-point font for the main title and *Works Cited* title. Use bold, 12-point font for the side headings.

3. Spell-check and proofread the report carefully. Correct all errors. Save the report as *U8L3WorksCited*.

Jenkins 1

Gwen Jenkins
Mr. Hopkins
English
20 February 20--

MLA Reports with In-Text Citations and Side Headings

Textual citations can be used to give credit for quoted or paraphrased material. This report explains how to include in-text citations in a MLA report. A separate works cited page is also discussed.

### In-Text Citations

In-text citations are keyed in parentheses in the report body. Citations for references written by one or more authors include the name(s) of the author(s) and page number(s) of the material. Quotations of up to three keyed lines are enclosed in quotation marks. Long quotations (four or more keyed lines) are left indented. Paraphrased material is not enclosed in quotation marks (Hoggatt and Shank 64).

### Works Cited

All references in a MLA-style report are listed on a separate page at the end of the report (Anson and Schwegler 627). This page should have the same margins and header as the report body. The page number should continue in sequence from the last page of your paper.

Center *Works Cited* at the top margin, using the same font size as the report title. A double space below the title, list the works cited. Place the works in alphabetical order by authors' last names, if known. Double-space the list and use hanging indent.

### Side Headings

Side headings are used to guide the reader through the major sections of your report. Double-space before and after each side heading. The side headings may be keyed using a font size slightly larger than that used for the body, but the size selected should be smaller than the font size used for the title. The side headings may be bolded or underlined, but generally not both. All side headings at the same level of organization should be formatted the same.

## 5D Writing: Commas

Read the punctuation rules below. Study the Learn lines. Note how the rules are applied. Key the Learn lines and the Apply lines, including the necessary punctuation. Save as *U7L5Punctuation*.

**Rule 3:** Use a comma before short direct quotations.

Learn 1  Dr. Alvarez said, "I'll be out of the office on Monday."

Learn 2  Sara asked, "Have you read the latest book by John Grisham?"

Apply 3  Mary replied "I'll meet you there a little after 6 p.m."

Apply 4  Coach Johnson remarked "I think we can play better than that."

**Rule 4:** Use a comma before and after a word or words in apposition (words that come together and refer to the same person or thing).

Learn 5  Ashley Logan, the president, called the meeting to order.

Learn 6  The principal, Jan Sabo, dismissed school because of the storm.

Apply 7  John F. Kennedy the 35th President graduated from Harvard.

Apply 8  Mary Jones the freshman played the part of Juliet.

## 5E | Math Calculations

Use the numeric keypad to solve the math problems below.

1. Sandra opened a checking account with $250. She wrote checks for $23.88, $62.51, $47.98, and $6.87. She made one deposit of $52.76 and had a service charge of $2.75. What is her current balance?

2. Felipe makes $6.50 an hour. He worked 3½ hours on Monday, 4 hours on Tuesday, 6 hours on Wednesday, 2 hours on Thursday, and 7½ hours on Friday. How much did he make for these five days?

3. Emilee purchased eight tickets for the Boston Celtics basketball game. Four of the tickets cost $35.50 each; the other four cost $74.00 each. There was a service charge of $1.50 for each ticket. How much did Emilee pay for the eight tickets?

4. Trevor's dad's car gets 19.5 miles to the gallon. How many miles can he go on 15 gallons of gas driving his dad's car? If he gets 28.6 miles to the gallon with his own car, how many *more* miles can he go if he drives his car rather than his dad's car?

5. Maria and her three friends went to a movie. Each ticket cost $8.50. Maria spent $4.25 on refreshments. Mike spent $4.75 on refreshments, and Betty and Jana each spent $5.00 on refreshments. How much did the four spend altogether?

### 3C | Hard Page Breaks

Two types of page breaks (*soft* and *hard*) are used to signal the end of a page. Soft page breaks are inserted automatically when the current page is full. A soft page break moves automatically when additional text is keyed before the soft page break. Hard page breaks are inserted manually when you want to end a page before it is full.

To insert a hard page break:

1. Place the insertion point where you want the page to end and a new page to begin.

2. On the menu bar, click Insert. Click Break. The Break dialog box appears.

3. Click the radio button beside Page break if it is not already selected. Click OK.

To delete a hard page break:

1. Place the insertion point at the beginning of the page after the hard page break.

2. Tap the BACKSPACE key.

#### Practice What You Have Learned

1. Key the following three lines, inserting a return and a hard page break at the end of each line.
   This text is the first line on Page 1.
   This text is the first line on Page 2.
   This text is the first line on Page 3.

2. The page indicator should read *Page 4 of 4*. Revise the text on page 3 to read: **This text is also on Page 2**.

3. Delete the second hard page break. (Place the insertion point at the beginning of page 3 and tap the BACKSPACE key.)

4. Confirm that the last two lines of text appear together on the second page.

5. Save the document as *U8L3PageBreaks*.

### 3D | Insert Underline

The Underline feature can be used to insert a single, double, or dotted line below text. This feature can be used prior to keying the text or after the text has been keyed.

To underline text before keying:

1. On the menu bar, click Format. Click Font. The Font dialog box appears as shown below.

2. Select the Underline style you wish to use from the Underline drop-down list. Click OK.

To underline text you have already keyed, select the text before following the steps above.

#### Practice What You Have Learned

1. Open the data file *CD-U8L3Lines*.

2. Underline *discretion* in line 1.

3. Insert a double line below the final four words in line 1.

4. Insert a dotted line below *Do not* and *personal information* in line 2.

5. Save the document as *U8L3Lines*.

## 5F | Timed Writings

1. Key one 1' unguided and two 1' guided timed writings on each paragraph; determine *gwam*.

2. Key two 2' unguided timed writings on paragraphs 1–2 combined; determine *gwam*.

**MicroType**

*Timed Writing*

**A**

**All letters used**

### Quarter-Minute Checkpoints

| gwam | 1/4' | 1/2' | 3/4' | Time |
|------|------|------|------|------|
| 16 | 4 | 8 | 12 | 16 |
| 20 | 5 | 10 | 15 | 20 |
| 24 | 6 | 12 | 18 | 24 |
| 28 | 7 | 14 | 21 | 28 |
| 32 | 8 | 16 | 24 | 32 |
| 36 | 9 | 18 | 27 | 36 |
| 40 | 10 | 20 | 30 | 40 |

GWAM 2'

Atlanta, the capital of Georgia, is a gem of the — 4
South. It is the largest city in the state and exists — 10
because of railroads. The original site was selected as — 16
the end of the line for the railroad to be built — 21
northward. Eight years later the area became known as — 26
Atlanta. Because of the railroad, Atlanta was the key — 32
supply center for the Confederacy and was virtually — 37
destroyed during the Civil War. — 40

One of the more famous Atlanta citizens was Margaret — 45
Mitchell. The book she wrote exquisitely portrays the area — 51
during the Civil War period. During the war, much of the — 57
city was destroyed. However, a few of the elegant southern — 63
homes of this time period have been restored and are open — 68
for the public to see. Today, Atlanta is recognized as a — 74
modern city that gives those who visit as well as the — 80
residents of the city a variety of cultural and sporting — 85
events for their enjoyment. — 88

GWAM 2' | 1 | 2 | 3 | 4 | 5 | 6 |

For additional practice **MicroType** + **Numeric Keypad** + **Lesson 5–6**

# MLA REPORTS WITH WORKS CITED

## OBJECTIVES

1. To learn and practice these word processing features: Special Paragraph Indentations, Page Break, and Underline.

2. To format MLA reports that have references and a Works Cited page.

**MicroType**

**TIP**

Move just the top part of the left margin marker to create a first-line indent for a paragraph.

Move just the bottom part of the left margin marker to create a hanging indent.

## 3A | Conditioning Practice

Key each line twice SS; then key a 1' writing on line 3. Determine *gwam*.

Alphabet 1   Vic and Hap just want a bear, zebra, quail, monkey, dog, and fox.

Figures 2   His score was 87 percent; he missed items 3, 16, 29, 46, and 50.

Speed 3   The widow may visit downtown mall to see the robot fix six jeeps.

**GWAM**   1' |  1  |  2  |  3  |  4  |  5  |  6  |  7  |  8  |  9  |  10  |

## 3B | Special Paragraph Indentations

The Paragraph dialog box and the margin markers on the Ruler can be used to set special paragraphs indentations. You can indent the first line of paragraph(s) or all lines except the first. Both settings can be useful when keying reports.

**First Line Indent.** This paragraph has a first-line indent of 0.5". This special indent is appropriate for paragraphs in a report that is double-spaced.

**Hanging Indent.** This paragraph has a hanging indent of 0.5". This special indent is appropriate for reference items.

To set a special paragraph indentation:

1. Select the paragraph(s) you wish to indent. On the menu bar, click Format. Click Paragraph. The Paragraph dialog box appears.

2. Click the down arrow for the Special indentation drop-down list. Click First Line or Hanging. Key a number (in inches) in the By box to indicate the amount of the indent.

3. Click OK to close the dialog box.

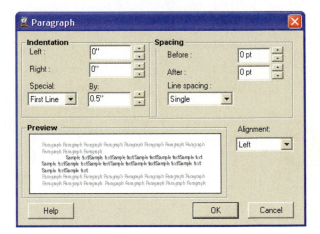

### Practice What You Have Learned

1. Open the file *CD-U8L3Indents*.

2. For paragraphs 1 and 2, indent the first line 0.5".

3. For paragraphs 3 and 4, indent the first line 1.0".

4. For paragraph 5, set a 0.5" hanging indent; for paragraph 6, set a 1.0" hanging indent.

5. Below paragraph 6, key the following two paragraphs.

> Kauchak, Donald and Paul Eggen. *Introduction to Teaching*, 2nd edition. Upper Saddle River, NJ: Pearson Merrill Prentice Hall, 2005.
>
> "Major Natural Lakes of the World." *The World Almanac and Book of Facts*. Mahwah, NJ: World Almanac Books, 2004.

6. Set a 0.5" hanging indent for paragraphs 7 and 8.

7. Save the document as *U8L3Indents*.

## NUMERIC KEYPAD: DIVISION AND MATH CALCULATIONS

### 6A | Keypad Review

1. Review the keypad by calculating the totals for the problems shown below.
2. Check your answers with the problem totals shown in blue.

| A | B | C | D | E | F |
|---|---|---|---|---|---|
| 20 | 58 | 605 | 715 | | |
| +51 | −20 | −324 | +605 | 206 | 618.4 |
| +85 | +48 | +26 | −509 | x4.5 | x3.75 |
| 156 | 86 | 307 | 811 | 927 | 2,319 |

### 6B | Division

**Learn Reach to / (division key)**

1. Locate **/** (division key) on the numeric keypad.

2. Watch your middle finger move up to the **/** (division key) and back to the **5** key a few times without tapping keys.

3. Practice tapping **/** (division key) and then **5** a few times as you watch the finger.

4. With eyes on copy, key the data in Drills 1–3. Key the dividend, tap **/** (division key), key the divisor, and tap ENTER.

5. Check your answer with the answer shown in blue. Answers are rounded to two decimal places.

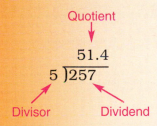

Quotient

51.4
5 )257

Divisor    Dividend

**Drill 1**

| A | B | C | D | E |
|---|---|---|---|---|
| 90 | 16 | 44 | 145 | 132.86 |
| 4)360 | 25)400 | 19)836 | 5)725 | 7)930 |

**Drill 2**

| A | B | C | D | E |
|---|---|---|---|---|
| 24.73 | 78.4 | 412.59 | 154.48 | 198.47 |
| 15)371 | 75)5,880 | 17)7,014 | 52)8,033 | 45)8,931 |

**Drill 3**

| A | B | C | D | E |
|---|---|---|---|---|
| 69.58 | 14.55 | 979.74 | 263.18 | 128.25 |
| 7.2)501 | 52.1)758 | 3.9)3,821 | 20.1)5,290 | 72)9,234 |

## Language Arts

### 2F Writing: Internal Punctuation

Read the following punctuation rules. Key the Learn lines, noting the punctuation used. Key the Apply lines, making the necessary corrections. Save as *U8L2Writing*.

**Rule 5:** Use a comma to set off words of direct address (the name of a person spoken to).

Learn 1  Please let me know, Samantha, if you are going to be absent.

Learn 2  Please let me know, Dr. White, when the exam is ready to duplicate.

Apply 3  Please take the car Jack to get the oil changed.

Apply 4  If you will be patient Mary things will work out.

**Rule 6:** Use a comma to separate the day from the year and the city from the state.

Learn 5  The last conference was held on July 24, 2007.

Learn 6  Sheila moved to Arlington, Texas, in July.

Apply 7  Babe Ruth was born in Baltimore Maryland.

Apply 8  Babe Ruth died on August 16 1948.

## Language Arts

### 2G Writing: Composition

Compose and key a paragraph explaining the steps for inserting a right-aligned header with a name and page number in a document.

Compose and key a second paragraph explaining the different ways you can select text in a document.

Save the document as *U8L2Composition*.

## 6C | Math Calculations

Use the numeric keypad to solve the math problems shown below.

1. Elizabeth and Nancy had an apartment. They each agreed to pay 50 percent of all expenses relating to the cost of the apartment. How much will each of them have to pay if they had the following costs for February: rent, $525.00; electricity, $79.89; natural gas, $169.38; and water, $42.79?

2. Four friends went out for dinner and a movie. The cost of the movie tickets was $36.00 and the dinner came to $68.00. They decided to leave a 15 percent tip and to split the cost of the movie, dinner, and tip equally among them. How much did each person have to pay?

3. Juan filled his car up with gas. The odometer reading was 65,253 miles. Juan drove to Los Angeles to see a Dodgers game. When he arrived, he filled the car up again, using 15.2 gallons. The odometer now read 65,684. How many miles per gallon did Juan get on the trip to Los Angeles? (Round to two decimal places.)

4. Kimberly bowled six games this week. Her scores were 178, 146, 167, 142, 203, and 142. What was her average for those six games?

5. Rachael's team scored 74, 58, 80, and 68 points in their last four games. Rachael scored 40 percent of her team's points. How many points did she score during the last four games? What was her average per game?

## Language Arts

## 6D Writing: Word Choice

Study the spelling and definitions of the words below. Key the Learn lines, noting the word choices. Key the Apply lines, selecting the correct words. Save as *U7L6WordChoice*.

**your** (adjective) of or relating to you as the owner or possessor of something

**you're** (contraction) you are

Learn 1    When is **your** car payment due?

Learn 2    If **you're** planning on going to school this fall, apply now!

Apply 3    Let them know (your, you're) planning on going with them.

Apply 4    When (your, you're) test scores come, let me know.

### Report 1

1. Key the following report using MLA format.

2. Insert a header with your last name and page number. Use 16-point font for the title.

3. Spell-check and proofread the report carefully. Correct all errors. Save the report as *U8L2Recycle*.

indent/double space    *(Header)*
MLA

(Student's name)
Mr. Lonnie Repack
General Science
15 April 20--

Tires, Tires, and More Tires

Have you ever stopped to think about all the tires that are sold each year? The United States has more than 140,000,000 passenger vehicles. Just think of the number of tires needed if these vehicles have tires replaced every other year. About 280,000,000 tires would be sold each year. Add to this figure the number of tires used by large trucks. Some trucks have 16 to 18 tires each. They drive hundreds of thousands of miles each year delivering products to our plants, distribution centers, and stores. What about tires for busses and bicycles? The number of tires that are no longer needed by drivers must also be considered. Have you ever thought about what happens to all these tires? Are they recycled? Are they abandoned?

Unfortunately, far too many tires are abandoned rather than recycled. Abandoned tires often litter the sides of our rivers and creeks or the lands in our forests. Too often, worn-out tires are abandoned in tire piles that are ugly and provide breeding grounds for mosquitoes. These tire piles are fire hazards. If they catch fire, they can burn for weeks, polluting the air. The heat of the fire can cause the rubber to decompose into oil. This oil is likely to seep into and pollute nearby ground and surface water, causing damage to the environment.

The next time you change tires, even on your bicycle, make sure you dispose of them appropriately. If you can, leave them with the retailer that sold you the replacement tires. The old tires can be recycled into useful products such as buckets, shoes, mouse pads for your computer, and dustpans.

### Report 2

1. Open the file *CD-U8L2IDTheft*.

2. Format the report using MLA style. Insert a header with your last name and page number. Use 18-point font for the title.

3. Spell-check and proofread the report carefully. You should find ten word choice errors. Correct all errors. Save the report as *U8L2IDTheft*.

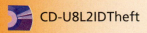

## 6E | Timed Writings

1. Key one 1' unguided and two 1' guided timed writings on each paragraph.

2. Key two 2' unguided writings on paragraphs 1–2 combined; determine *gwam*.

**MicroType**

*Timed Writing*

**A**

**All letters used**

### Quarter-Minute Checkpoints

| gwam | 1/4' | 1/2' | 3/4' | Time |
|------|------|------|------|------|
| 16 | 4 | 8 | 12 | 16 |
| 20 | 5 | 10 | 15 | 20 |
| 24 | 6 | 12 | 18 | 24 |
| 28 | 7 | 14 | 21 | 28 |
| 32 | 8 | 16 | 24 | 32 |
| 36 | 9 | 18 | 27 | 36 |
| 40 | 10 | 20 | 30 | 40 |

**GWAM 2'**

"I left my heart in San Francisco." This expression   5
becomes much easier to understand after an individual has   11
visited the city near the bay. San Francisco is one of the   17
most interesting areas to visit throughout the entire   22
world. The history of this city is unique. Even though   28
people inhabited the area prior to the gold rush, it was   33
the prospect of getting rich that brought about the fast   39
growth of the city.   41

It is difficult to write about just one thing that   46
this exquisite city is known for. Spectacular views, cable   52
cars, the Golden Gate Bridge and Fisherman's Wharf are   58
only a few of the many things that are associated with this   64
amazing city. The city is also known for the diversity of   70
its people. In fact, there are three separate cities   75
within the city, Chinatown being the best known.   80

**GWAM 2'** |   1   |   2   |   3   |   4   |   5   |   6   |

## 2C | Learn to Select Text

The mouse and various key combinations are used to select (highlight) text. Once selected, the text can be changed. For example, the font, color, and size can be changed. Selected text can also be copied, deleted, or formatted.

To select text, use one of these methods:

- To select any amount of text, click at the start of the text and drag the mouse over the text.
- To select one word, double-click on the word.
- To select a large block of text, click at the start of the selection. Scroll to the end of the selection, hold down the SHIFT key, and click the mouse.
- To select an entire document, choose Select All from the Edit menu. (Text in a header or footer will not be selected.)

### Practice What You Have Learned

CD-U8L2Select

1. Open the file *CD-U8L2Select*.
2. Use Select All and change all text in the body of the report to Arial 14-point font.
3. Select the title and change to 18-point font.
4. Select and delete the last sentence.
5. Change all text in red font to black font.
6. Change *Garrett University* to *Paine University*.
7. Save the document as *U8L2Select*.

## 2D | Undo and Redo

The Undo command reverses the last change you made to a document. Undo will restore deleted text to its original place, even if you have moved the insertion point. The Redo command reverses the last Undo action.

To use the Undo and Redo commands:

1. From the Edit menu, select Undo (action). (The action shown will vary depending on what you have keyed or what command you have given. For example, the command may be Undo Typing or Undo Style Change.) Confirm that the desired change was made.

2. If you want to reverse the change, select Redo (action) from the Edit menu.

### Practice What You Have Learned

1. Key the following paragraph.

   The Drama Club from Reed Middle School will perform Cinderella by Charles Perrault Thursday, Friday, and Saturday, November 5-7, at 7:30 p.m.

2. Change *Cinderella* to red 18-point font.
3. Use Undo to reverse the color and size change. Confirm that *Cinderella* is not in red 18-point font.
4. Use Redo to reverse the Undo command. Confirm that *Cinderella* is in red 18-point font.
5. Change *November 5-7*, to red 16-point font. Use Undo to reverse the command. Use Redo to reverse the Undo command.
6. Save the document as *U8L2Undo*.

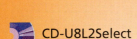

**MicroType**
**TIP**

Click the Undo button on the toolbar to undo an action quickly.

Click the Redo button on the toolbar to reverse a change.

## Math Activities

**6F** ▪ **Math Challenge 7**

### FIND THE WHOLE OF A NUMBER

1. Key a sentence to explain how you find the whole of a number in problems like this: *Ten is 20% of what number?*

2. Solve the following problems and key your answer in sentence form. Round answers to thousandths if needed. For example, an appropriate sentence for the answer to the problem stated above is: *Ten is 20% of 50.*

    2a. 28 is 80% of what number?

    2b. 132 is 75% of what number?

    2c. 3.3 is 300% of what number?

    2d. 240 is 180% of what number?

    2e. If Larry's payment of $60 represents 12% of the loan, how much is the loan?

3. Save your answers as *U7L6Math*.

## Careers ·····················

**6G** ▪ **Career Exploration Portfolio – Activity 7**

▪ You must complete Career Activities 1–3 before completing this activity.

1. Retrieve your Career folder and the information in it that relates to the career cluster that is your first choice.

2. Reflect on the skills and knowledge you have gained in the courses you have taken and the extracurricular activities in which you are involved that will be beneficial in the career you selected as your first choice. Then compose a paragraph or two describing the connection between what you have learned and/or your activities and this career. Print your file, save it as *U7L6Career7*, and keep it open.

3. Exchange papers with a classmate and have the classmate offer suggestions for improving the content and correcting any errors he or she finds in your paragraph(s). Make the changes that you agree with and print a copy to turn in to your instructor. Save your file as *U7L6Career7* and close the file.

4. Return your folder to the storage area. When your instructor returns your paper, file it in your Career folder.

**For additional practice** ▸**MicroType**✦ **Numeric Keypad** ✦ **Lesson 6**

### OBJECTIVES

1. *To learn and practice these word processing features: Font, Font Size, Font Colors, Select Text, Clear, and Undo.*

2. *To format a report using MLA format.*

## MicroType

### Word Processing

**Font Effects**

To change font type and size quickly, make your selection from the drop-down lists on the toolbar.

**Font type**

**Font size**

Other font effects such as strikethrough (~~font effect~~), superscript ($1234^{56}$), and subscript ($1234_{56}$) can be applied in the dialog box by selecting Font from the Format menu.

### 2A | Conditioning Practice

Key each line twice SS; then key a 1' writing on line 3. Determine *gwam*.

| Alphabet | 1 | The judges will quickly pay Zelma for the excellent book reviews. |
| Figures/Symbols | 2 | He needs to pay $3,798 by May 8 to get 15% off on Model #460-12. |
| Speed | 3 | The man in the wheelchair may go with the girls to the town hall. |

**GWAM** 1' | 1 | 2 | 3 | 4 | 5 | 6 | 7 | 8 | 9 | 10 |

### 2B | Font, Size, and Color

The font is the type, or style of letters, in which text is displayed.

You can select the font (for example: Times New Roman, Courier New, Arial, Comic Sans MS) and size you want to use. Size is measured in points. An 11-point font is appropriate for most reports and letters. You can also select the font color.

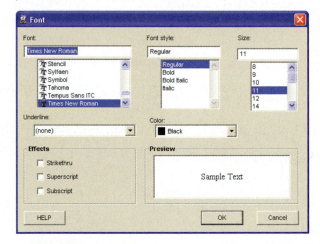

To change font, size, or color before text is keyed:

1. On the menu bar, click Format. Click Font. The Font dialog box appears.

2. Click the font and the size you wish to use. (Use the scroll bars to access more fonts and sizes.)

3. Click the down arrow for the Color drop-down list and click a font color. Click OK.

**Practice What You Have Learned**

1. Key each of the following lines using the font, size, and color indicated.

Key this line using a Times New Roman, blue, 12-point font.

Key this line using a Comic Sans MS, red, 14-point font.

Key this line using an Arial, green, 10-point font.

Key this line using a Courier New, gray, 12-point font.

Key this line using a Verdana, black, 16-point font.

2. Save the document as *U8L2Font*.

# PART 2

Certification

Certified
Management
Accoun...

tarting
es

## Apply and Improve Keyboarding Skills

The computer is used a great deal in school, at home, and at work. People who can key by touch are best able to use the computer keyboard and develop other computer skills. In this part, you will build on the keyboarding skills you learned in Part 1 as you create documents and complete activities.

By completing the lessons in Part 2, you will:
- Learn useful ways to apply your touch keying skills.
- Prepare reports, memos, e-mail messages, letters, tables, and other documents.

- Use popular features of word processing and e-mail software to prepare documents.

In addition to learning useful word processing features and document formats, you will apply your keyboarding skill in several types of activities. You will complete interesting reading, writing, listening, speaking, and math activities to extend your communication and math skills. Grammar, number expression, and word usage skills will be learned and applied. You will take exciting trips through cyberspace while completing the Internet activities. You

will explore various career clusters to help you think about and plan for your future. Our World activities will enable you to explore the world around you, both far and near. You can immediately use what you learn in Part 2 in your school, personal, and family activities and then later in your work.

Part 2 contains three projects. Each project provides a realistic situation in which you can apply your computer keyboarding skills. You will solve problems, be creative, and apply language skills as you finish the projects.

**1" TM**

**Writer's name and page number**

**Report Identification**

Marci N. Beck

Mrs. Sabina

English

17 September 20--

**Title**

Formatting School Reports

**Report Body**

School reports are often formatted using a simple form of the MLA (Modern Language Association) style guidelines.

The top, bottom, left, and right margins on all pages of the report are 1".  A header containing a right-aligned page number appears on every page, including the first page.  The writer's name may precede the page number.

**1" LM**

**1" RM**

The entire report is double spaced.  The report identification information begins 1" from the top or at the default top margin.  The report identification lines begin at the left margin and are double spaced.  They include the writer's name, teacher's name, subject name, and date (day/month/year style) on separate lines.

The report title is keyed a double space below the date.  The title is center aligned and is keyed following the rules for capitalizing and punctuating titles.  The report title may be keyed using a slightly larger font size to make it stand out, but it should not be underlined or placed within quotation marks.  You will learn to change font size in the next lesson.

The body of the report begins a double space below the title.  All lines of the body are double spaced including long quotations, bulleted and numbered items, and tables.

If the report contains references, a works cited page is keyed on a separate page.  You will learn to format a works cited page in an upcoming lesson.

**At Least 1" BM**

# Unit 8
## Prepare MLA Reports

### Lessons 1–7

## LESSON

# 1

### OBJECTIVES

1. *To learn and practice these word processing features: Paragraph Alignment, Header with Page Number, Spell Check.*

2. *To format a report using MLA format.*

### MicroType
**TIP**

*To change paragraph alignment quickly, click the appropriate toolbar button.*

 **Align Left**

 **Align Center**

 **Align Right**

 **Justify**

## MLA REPORTS

### 1A | Conditioning Practice

Key each line twice SS; then key a 1' writing on line 3.  Determine *gwam*.

| Alphabet 1 | New Zealand rugby hits jackpot for qualifying the very next time. |
| Figures 2 | The combinations on the two locks I have are 20-46-7 and 19-35-8. |
| Speed 3 | The big autos did shake when the giant quake hit the busy island. |

**GWAM** 1' | 1 | 2 | 3 | 4 | 5 | 6 | 7 | 8 | 9 | 10 |

### 1B | Paragraph Alignment

Paragraph alignment refers to the horizontal position of a paragraph of text.  Alignment options are Left, Center, Right, and Justified.  The default paragraph alignment is left.

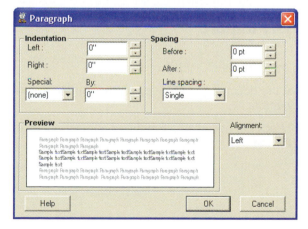

To change paragraph alignment before the text is keyed:

1. On the menu bar, click Format.  Click Paragraph.  The Paragraph dialog box appears.

2. Click the down arrow for the Alignment drop-down list box.  Click on the desired alignment.  Click OK.

To change alignment for existing paragraphs:

1. Click in a single paragraph or select two or more paragraphs.

2. Follow steps 1 and 2 above.

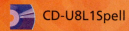
CD-U8L1Spell

**Practice What You Have Learned**

1. Open the data file *CD-U8L1Spell*.

2. Use Spell Check to check the text. Make a handwritten list of the words Spell Check found that were misspelled.

3. When Spell Check is finished, carefully proofread the text. Make a handwritten list of the errors you find that Spell Check did not. Make these corrections to the document.

4. Save the corrected document as *U8L1Spell*.

## 1F | Short Report in MLA Style

1. Study the formatting guides in the report on the following page.

2. Key the report using the format guides.

3. Spell-check the report and proofread carefully. Correct all errors. Save the report as *U8L1Report*.

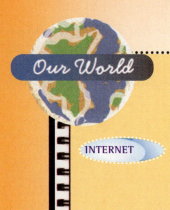

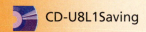
INTERNET

### 1G ▪ Research a Business

Use the Internet to find information about a local or U.S. company that does business in another country. (Examples of large companies you might research include General Electric, Coca-Cola, General Motors, McDonald's, and Exxon.) What products does the company sell in other countries? In what major countries or cities does it have offices? How many people does the company employ? Write a short summary of your findings, using MLA format, your name, your teacher's name, and the current date. Save as *U8L1World*.

*Social Studies*

## 1H | Short Report

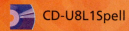
CD-U8L1Saving

1. Open the data file *CD-U8L1Saving*.

2. Format the document in MLA report style. Insert a header for your name and the page number.

3. Spell-check the document. Proofread and correct all errors. Save the document as *U8L1Saving*.

### Practice What You Have Learned

1. Open a new document. Using right alignment, key your name on one line and the current date on the next line.

2. Using left alignment, key the name of your teacher on one line and the name of your keyboarding course on the next line.

3. Using center alignment, key the following text on a new line.

   My Favorite Vacation

4. Beginning on a new line, key the following text using justified alignment.

   My favorite vacation was a trip to the beach. My brother, sister, and I played in the sand and walked on the beach to collect hundreds of shells. My brother found a starfish the first morning. On our last day, we built a giant sand castle.

5. Save as *U8L1Alignment*.

## 1C │ Header with Page Numbers

Headers contain information that appears at the top of pages in a document. A header is used in reports to display page numbers.

**Format Header**

**Insert Page Number**

To create a header with page numbers:

1. On the menu bar, click Format. Click Header.

2. Click an alignment button on the toolbar to choose the position (left, center, or right) for the page number. (For reports, choose Align Right.)

3. Key your last name.

4. On the menu bar, click Insert. Click Page Number. As pages are keyed, the word processor will automatically insert the correct page number.

### Practice What You Have Learned

1. Open a new document. Create a right-aligned header containing your name and a page number.

2. Key the following text on line 1.

   This text is the first line of page 1. It appears below the header.

3. Print the document. Verify that your name and the page number are right-aligned in the header that precedes the text you keyed.

4. Save the document as *U8L1Header*.

## 1D Writing:  Word Choice

Study the spelling and definitions of the following words.  Key the Learn line, noting the word choices.  Key the Apply lines, selecting the correct words.  Save as *U8L1WordChoice*.

**to** (preposition)  in the direction of; at, on, or near

**too** (adverb)  in addition, also, beyond

**two** (noun)  one more than one

Learn 1  I, **too**, hope **to** view the **two** new movies this weekend.

Apply 2  Are the (to, too, two) winners going (to, too, two) go with me?

Apply 3  It's (to, too, two) much to hope for (to, too, two) victories.

## MicroType
**TIP**

Click the Spell Check button on the toolbar to start Spell Check quickly.

Spell Check will not find words that are spelled correctly but used incorrectly.

Also, the software dictionary may not contain numbers, many proper nouns, or scientific terms; therefore, always proofread carefully after using Spell Check.

## 1E | Spell Check

Spell Check is used to check text for misspelled words.  Spell Check compares the keyed words to words in the software's dictionary.  If a word in the text does not match a word in the dictionary, the word is displayed in the dialog box.  Suggestions (what the software believes to be the correct word) and options (Skip Once, Skip Always, Replace, etc.) are given.

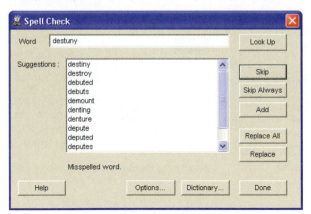

To use the Spell Check feature:

1. Save the document so you can use the unchanged version later if needed.

2. On the menu bar, click Edit.  Click Spell Check.

3. When the Spell Check dialog box appears, click Start.  Spell Check starts at the beginning of the document.  As soon as Spell Check identifies a word not found in its dictionary, that word appears in the Word box and suggestions may appear in the Suggestions list.

4. When a word appears in the Word box, do one of the following actions to continue:

   • If the correct spelling appears in the Suggestions list, click the correct word to select it and then click the Replace button (or the Replace All button to correct all occurrences of the misspelled word).  Spell Check will correct the text.

   • If the correct spelling does not appear in the Suggestions list but the spelling in the Word box is incorrect, key the correct spelling in the Word box.  Then click either the Replace or Replace All button, whichever is appropriate.

   • If the spelling in the Word box is correct, click the Skip Once button (or the Skip Always button to skip all occurrences of the word).  Spell Check will not change the text.

5. Click Done if you want to stop Spell Check before it checks the entire document.  Otherwise, click OK when Spell Check finishes checking the entire document.  Then click Done.

## Memo

**2" (or center vertically on the page)**

**Align headings**

TO:     All Information Technology Students ↓2

FROM:   Ms. Gerry Palko ↓2

DATE:   November 5, 20-- ↓2

SUBJECT:   INTEROFFICE MEMORANDUMS ↓2

Interoffice memorandums (memos) are written messages used by people within an organization to communicate with one another. ↓2

**1" or default** The top margin of the first page of a memo is 2". If the memo is more than one page, use the default top margin or a 1" top margin on the following pages. Use the default or 1" margins for the left and right margins. The bottom margin should be at least 1". ↓2 **1" or default**

Memos have a heading that includes who the memo is being sent to (TO:). Who the memo is from (FROM:) is listed next. The date the memo is being sent (DATE:) and what the memo is about (SUBJECT:) follow. All lines of the heading begin at the left margin. The heading lines are double spaced. Tab once or twice as needed to align the information following the heading words about 1" from the left margin. ↓2

The paragraphs of the memo all begin at the left margin. The paragraphs are singled spaced with a double space between paragraphs. Paragraph headings are optional. When used, paragraph headings are indented from the left margin. Capitalize the first letter of the first word, underline or bold the heading, and follow the heading with a period. ↓2

br

**At least 1"**

## Personal-Business Letter (Block Format with Open Punctuation)

**2" (or center vertically on the page)**

9180 Wayzata Blvd.
Minneapolis, MN 55440-9180
October 15, 20-- ↓4

Mr. Harry Dobish
10916 N. Garnett Rd.
Tulsa, OK 74116-1016 ↓2

Dear Mr. Dobish ↓2

**1" or default** A personal-business letters has several parts. The letter begins with the return address and the date. The letter address comes next. The salutation and the body of the letter follow the address. The complimentary closing and the name of the writer complete the letter. ↓2 **1" or default**

The return address contains the street address on one line and the city, state, and ZIP code on the next line. The date (month day, year) is keyed on the line below the return address. The letter address is keyed a quadruple space below the date. Use a personal title (Miss, Mr., Ms., Mrs.) or a professional title (Dr. Lt., Senator) before the receiver's name. ↓2

A salutation (greeting) is keyed a double space below the letter address. Begin the body (message) of the letter a double space below the salutation. Single space the body with double spacing between the paragraphs. A complimentary closing (farewell) is keyed a double space below the last line of the body. Quadruple space after the complimentary closing and key the name of the writer. ↓2

When all lines of the letter begin at the left margin, the letter is arranged in block format. When there is no punctuation after the salutation or complimentary close, open punctuation style has been used. Use a top margin of 2" or center a one-page letter vertically on the page. Use the default or 1" margins for the side and bottom margins. ↓2

Sincerely ↓4

*Gwen Rubino*

Gwen Rubino

**At least 1"**

## Business Letter (Block Format with Mixed Punctuation)

★
**Star Bank**
1800 Riverside Ave.
Minneapolis, MN 55454-1000

**2" (or center vertically on the page)**

August 12, 20-- ↓4

Mr. Pablo J. Lobos
733 Marquette Ave.
Minneapolis, MN 55402-2736 ↓2

Dear Mr. Lobos: ↓2

Congratulations! You are now the sole owner of the car you financed through our bank. Thank you for choosing us to serve your credit needs. ↓2

**1" or default** The original Certificate of Title and your Installment Loan Contract marked "Paid in Full" are enclosed. File the papers in a safe place with your other important records. ↓2 **1" or default**

You have a preferred credit rating with us. Please let us know when we may serve you again. ↓2

Sincerely yours, ↓4

*Ilya Lindgren*

Ms. Ilya Lindgren
Loan Manager ↓2

ct ↓2

Enclosure ↓2

c Ms. Carla Perez, Records Manager

**At least 1"**

## Small Envelope

Mr. Ralph McNash
5270 Center Drive
Charlotte, NC 28226-0705

← 0.25" TM

0.25" LM

Approximately 2"

Approximately 2.5"

Mr. Karl Fernandez
Tudor Publishers
9812 Rockwood Road
Charlotte, NC 28215-8555

## Large Envelope

Douglas H. Ruckert
8503 Kirby Drive
Houston, TX 77054-8220

← 0.25" TM

0.25" LM

Approximately 2"

Approximately 4"

Ms. Jenna St. John
Personnel Director
Regency Company
219 West Greene Road
Houston, TX 77067-4219

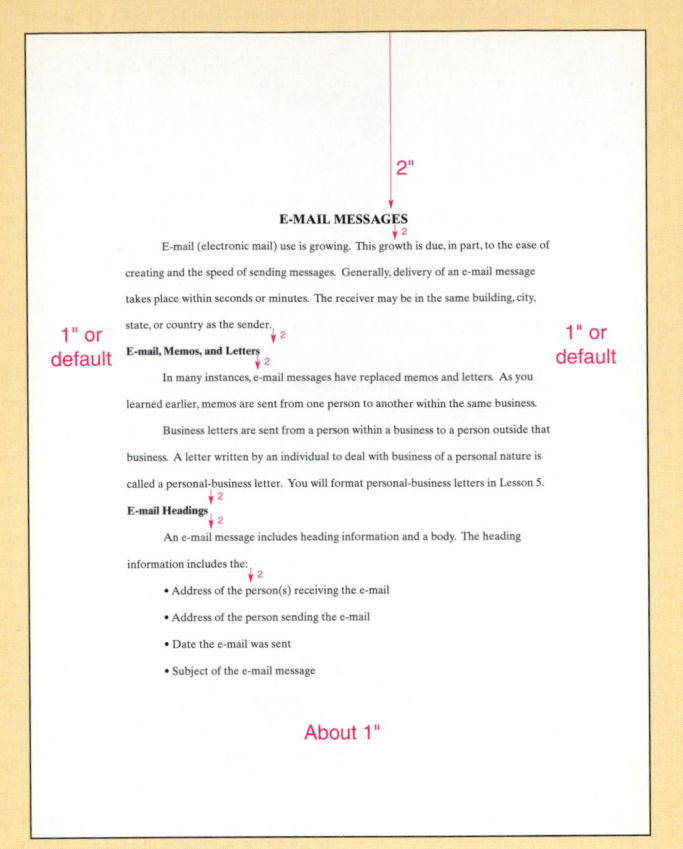

**Standard Unbound Report**

2"

**E-MAIL MESSAGES**

E-mail (electronic mail) use is growing. This growth is due, in part, to the ease of creating and the speed of sending messages. Generally, delivery of an e-mail message takes place within seconds or minutes. The receiver may be in the same building, city, state, or country as the sender.

**E-mail, Memos, and Letters**

In many instances, e-mail messages have replaced memos and letters. As you learned earlier, memos are sent from one person to another within the same business.

Business letters are sent from a person within a business to a person outside that business. A letter written by an individual to deal with business of a personal nature is called a personal-business letter. You will format personal-business letters in Lesson 5.

**E-mail Headings**

An e-mail message includes heading information and a body. The heading information includes the:

- Address of the person(s) receiving the e-mail
- Address of the person sending the e-mail
- Date the e-mail was sent
- Subject of the e-mail message

1" or default

1" or default

About 1"

---

**Standard Unbound Report, Page 2**

1"

Most e-mail programs insert the sender's name and the date automatically. The e-mail address of the person receiving the message should be keyed using uppercase and lowercase letters as given to you.

Sometimes more than one person is sent the same message. A comma or semicolon and a space are usually used to separate the addresses in the To: box. A subject should be included in the Subject: box. Many people delete e-mail messages that do not have a subject line without reading them. Subjects are sometimes keyed in ALL CAPS.

**E-mail Body**

The paragraphs in the body of an e-mail message are usually keyed using single spacing and a 12-point font. Double space between paragraphs. Begin all lines at the left margin.

The body may contain special formats such as varying font sizes and colors. Special formatting features should be used sparingly. All e-mail programs do not support format features in the same way.

1" or default

1" or default

---

**Table Without Grid Lines**

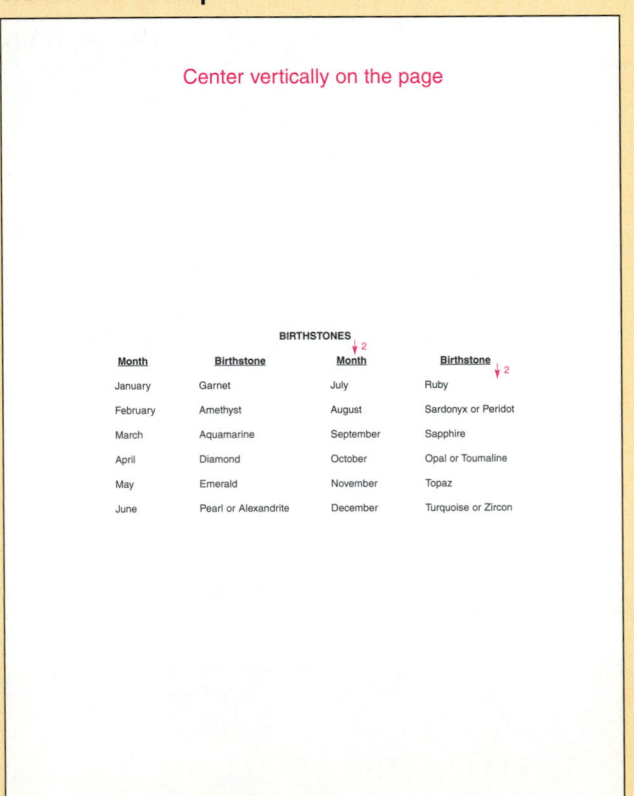

Center vertically on the page

**BIRTHSTONES**

| Month | Birthstone | Month | Birthstone |
|-------|-----------|-------|-----------|
| January | Garnet | July | Ruby |
| February | Amethyst | August | Sardonyx or Peridot |
| March | Aquamarine | September | Sapphire |
| April | Diamond | October | Opal or Tourmaline |
| May | Emerald | November | Topaz |
| June | Pearl or Alexandrite | December | Turquoise or Zircon |

---

**Table with Grid Lines**

Center vertically on the page

| FRACTIONS, DECIMALS, AND PERCENTS | | |
|-------|-------|-------|
| **Fraction** | **Decimal** | **Percent** |
| 1/8 | .125 | 12.5% |
| 1/4 | .25 | 25% |
| 3/8 | .375 | 37.5% |
| 1/2 | .5 | 50% |
| 5/8 | .625 | 62.5% |
| 3/4 | .75 | 75% |
| 7/8 | .875 | 87.5% |
| 1 | 1.0 | 100% |

To find the equivalent of a fraction in decimal form, divide the numerator by the denominator. To change from a decimal to a percent, multiple by 100 and add the % sign. To change from a percent to a decimal, divide by 100 and drop the % sign.

**APPENDIX: FORMAT GUIDES**

## Report Title Page

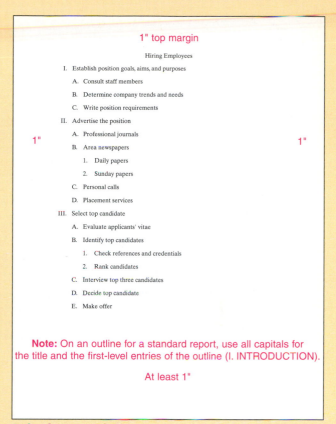

The Way to Happiness — About 1/3 down page

by
Harold McKibben — About 1/2 down page

Ms. Sandy Forde — About 8 1/2" down page
Unified Arts
15 September 20--

About 1"

## Outline for MLA Style Report

1" top margin

Hiring Employees

I.   Establish position goals, aims, and purposes
   A.   Consult staff members
   B.   Determine company trends and needs
   C.   Write position requirements
II.  Advertise the position
   A.   Professional journals
   B.   Area newspapers
      1.   Daily papers
      2.   Sunday papers
   C.   Personal calls
   D.   Placement services
III. Select top candidate
   A.   Evaluate applicants' vitae
   B.   Identify top candidates
      1.   Check references and credentials
      2.   Rank candidates
   C.   Interview top three candidates
   D.   Decide top candidate
   E.   Make offer

1"   1"

**Note:** On an outline for a standard report, use all capitals for the title and the first-level entries of the outline (I. INTRODUCTION).

At least 1"

## MLA Style Report, Page 1

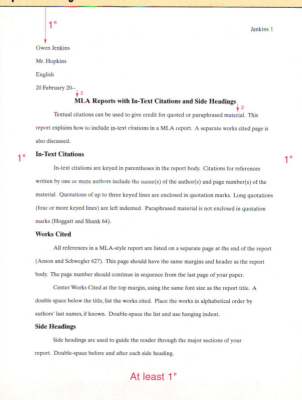

1"

Jenkins 1

Gwen Jenkins
Mr. Hopkins
English
20 February 20--

**MLA Reports with In-Text Citations and Side Headings**

Textual citations can be used to give credit for quoted or paraphrased material. This report explains how to include in-text citations in a MLA report. A separate works cited page is also discussed.

**In-Text Citations**

1"   1"

In-text citations are keyed in parentheses in the report body. Citations for references written by one or more authors include the name(s) of the author(s) and page number(s) of the material. Quotations of up to three keyed lines are enclosed in quotation marks. Long quotations (four or more keyed lines) are left indented. Paraphrased material is not enclosed in quotation marks (Hoggatt and Shank 64).

**Works Cited**

All references in a MLA-style report are listed on a separate page at the end of the report (Anson and Schwegler 627). This page should have the same margins and header as the report body. The page number should continue in sequence from the last page of your paper.

Center Works Cited at the top margin, using the same font size as the report title. A double space below the title, list the works cited. Place the works in alphabetical order by authors' last names, if known. Double-space the list and use hanging indent.

**Side Headings**

Side headings are used to guide the reader through the major sections of your report. Double-space before and after each side heading.

At least 1"

## MLA Style Report, Works Cited Page

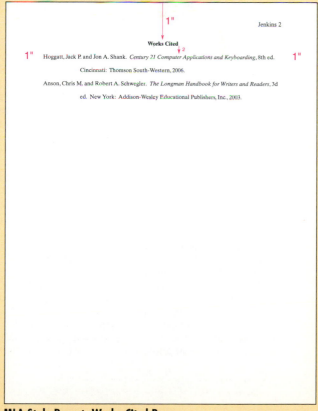

1"

Jenkins 2

**Works Cited**

1"   1"

Hoggatt, Jack P. and Jon A. Shank. *Century 21 Computer Applications and Keyboarding*, 8th ed. Cincinnati: Thomson South-Western, 2006.

Anson, Chris M. and Robert A. Schwegler. *The Longman Handbook for Writers and Readers*, 3d ed. New York: Addison-Wesley Educational Publishers, Inc., 2003.

# INDEX